ROBERT

A Portrait by his Friends

ROBERT RUNCIE

A Portrait by his Friends

Edited by
DAVID L. EDWARDS
with Peter Smith

HarperCollins
FOUNT PAPERBACKS

William Collins Sons & Co. Ltd
London · Glasgow · Sydney · Auckland
Toronto · Johannesburg

First published in Great Britain in 1990 by Fount Paperbacks

Fount Paperbacks is an imprint of
Collins Religious Division,
part of the HarperCollins Publishing Group
8 Grafton Street, London W1X 3LA

Copyright © 1990 by David L. Edwards

Typeset by Medcalf Type Ltd, Bicester
Printed and bound in Great Britain by William Collins
Sons & Co. Ltd, Glasgow

CONTENTS

Preface   vii

1 HIS GRACE
My Friend NADIR DINSHAW   3
A Soldier in the Pulpit VISCOUNT WHITELAW   6
At Sea and in Oxford PETER FRASER   8
Cambridge and After HUGH MONTEFIORE   11
Light in Touch, Large in Vision PETER WALKER   15
A Developing Style RICHARD HARRIES   18
A Man of Power W. H. VANSTONE   20
A Man of Prayer SISTER JANE   22
What I Have Been Praying For
     SISTER FRANCES DOMINICA   24
A Biographer Reflects MARGARET DUGGAN   29
Bonds of Affection ALASTAIR HAGGART   39
The Communicator SIR BRIAN YOUNG   42
A Journey to the Inner City ERIC JAMES   44
In Canterbury JOHN SIMPSON   50
In Lambeth Palace MARY CRYER   53
With Terry Waite EVE KEATLEY   56
Canterbury and York JOHN HABGOOD   59
An Impossible Job? JOHN WITHERIDGE   62
Among the Archbishops PAUL A. WELSBY   66

2 AMID CONTROVERSIES
In a Secular Society GRAHAM HOWES   73
In Mrs Thatcher's Britain HUGH MONTEFIORE   77
Amid Ethical Uncertainties HELEN OPPENHEIMER   85
Amid Many Faiths DAN COHN-SHERBOK   90

3 THE UNITY OF ANGLICANS

The Anglican Anguish RICHARD HOLLOWAY 97
Holding the Church of England Together
  COLIN CRASTON 104
An Evangelical Perspective MICHAEL BAUGHEN 110
An Anglican Catholic View ERIC KEMP 116
A Listening Archbishop Speaks
  DIANA McCLATCHEY 121
First among Equals DAVID SAY 134
A View from the USA EDMOND LEE BROWNING 139
A View from South Africa DESMOND TUTU 144
A View from Central Africa
  WALTER PAUL KHOTSO MAKHULU 148
A View from Australia JOHN DENTON 153
Gathering Local Churches SAMUEL VAN CULIN 156
Authority for Anglicans MARK SANTER 160
Anglican Theology Emerges KEITH RAYNER 164
Anglican Evangelism Emerges MICHAEL NAZIR-ALI 168

4 THAT ALL MAY BE ONE

Ecumenical Progress MARY TANNER 175
Ecumenical Pilgrims PETER CORNWELL 180
In the British Council of Churches PHILIP MORGAN 186
In Europe BARNEY MILLIGAN 193
In China K. H. TING 196
Canterbury and Rome CHRISTOPHER HILL 200
Canterbury and the Orthodox A. M. ALLCHIN 207
Canterbury in the Third Millennium
  DAVID L. EDWARDS 214

5 THE BEST IS YET TO BE

In Retirement (1) LORD COGGAN 225
In Retirement (2) LORD BLANCH 227
Whether Pigs Have Wings JOHN V. TAYLOR 229

PREFACE

When it was announced that Robert (now Lord) Runcie was to retire as Archbishop of Canterbury it seemed natural that a few of his friends should offer a preliminary assessment of his contribution to the Church of England, to the international Anglican Communion and to the problem-filled world around these tension-filled Christian families, 1980–91. Not only is any man who has done so well entitled to the congratulations of his friends, but in this case his friends are quietly angry because some others have been grossly unfair. It has proved easy for critics to concentrate on one part of his large responsibility from a point of view provided by their own convictions which are strong but perhaps not always reflective. In this book some people with some knowledge of his tasks have combined to offer a portrait of a man who, with an almost impossibly heavy workload, and in an exposed position, has done so well because of his character. Not all of his problems, achievements or journeys could be discussed in this space or at this time, and few indeed of his worldwide circle of friends could be included; despite some inescapable and illuminating repetitions, this book does not claim to be comprehensive. Most of those who have served on his staff have felt it proper that their thoughts, however devoted, should remain private for the present. But these fragments may combine to form a mosaic. They may supplement Margaret Duggan's *Runcie* (revised as a Hodder paperback in 1985) and assist other studies, including the official biography (in, we hope, the distant future). They may depict a man who is thoroughly human and thoroughly Christian, and they may increase an understanding of the challenges facing other church leaders, including Archbishops of Canterbury after the one hundred and second. They may also be a help to us ordinary Christians in our discipleship.

The idea of a book of essays or glimpses occurred to two publishers at almost the same time. The two projects have been merged, and the initiatives taken by Peter Smith of Churchman Publishing have been incorporated into the editorial work done by David Edwards on behalf of Collins. All royalties are being given to Christian Aid.

D.L.E.
E.P.S.

Peter Smith died on 13th September 1990, shortly before the proofs of this book reached his home. He will be remembered as a Christian publisher and for his faithful courage confronting cancer.

1
HIS GRACE

My Friend

NADIR DINSHAW

In Gujerati, which is my mother tongue, we have a word *lehnoo*, which is almost impossible to translate into English. It suggests a combination of affinity of spirit and enormous mutual sympathy. It isn't, in itself, a necessary ingredient of love or of friendship, but when it is present in a relationship, then that relationship is immeasurably enriched. And so, although I would not dare to comment on the various other aspects of Robert Runcie's many-faceted life and vocation – and what a brilliant archiepiscopate it has been! – I do feel qualified to stick my neck out and write about him as a friend, full of *lehnoo*, a quality highly valued by my Parsi temperament and, I believe, by his very English one.

Several years ago I was involved, totally unwittingly, in a *cause célèbre*, which resulted in my having to be interviewed by the police. It was my first experience of such a happening, and as rumours and press comments became more fevered, I naturally became increasingly worried. At the height of all this tension Bob (I find it very difficult to think of him in any other way) spontaneously cancelled several appointments in St Albans, motored up to London to have a long and unhurried lunch with me, encouraging and comforting me all the while, and then in an apparently casual tone, but with deep concern underneath it, said to me, "Nadir, why don't you come and stay with us at Abbey Gate House, and see the police there?" As it happened that wasn't practicable, but I shall never forget what a deep impression his generous and sensitive offer of assistance made on me, at a time when I was feeling particularly vulnerable.

Some time later he was telling me of a conversation he'd

3

been having with one of their "helps", a lady who during the course of a somewhat colourful life had had to have recourse on more than one occasion both to the divorce courts and to David Steel's Abortion Act of 1968. The whole conversation was lit with enormous compassion and humour, without a trace of condescension or of being "pi". But at the end of it, his voice changed, and with deep emotion he said, "I hope that when my time comes to be judged, Nadir, Gladys will speak for me". It wasn't the voice of the brilliant, highly cultured Prince of the Church which he is, but of the profoundly penitent and humble servant of God, which is even more his basic *persona*.

I do not think he ever fully realizes how tremendously his company and his presence are valued, but perhaps my final illustration of the quality of his friendship will show how true that is, and might even persuade him to believe it, himself, a little.

Earlier this year I had to undergo major heart surgery at very short notice, and my operation was fixed for a Saturday morning. Immediately the Archbishop heard he arranged to come and see me on the Friday, and I was looking forward to this very much. But on the Thursday afternoon my doctor told me that they had advanced the operation to very early on the Friday morning. Bob was, of course, duly informed, and whilst I regretted very much not being able to see him I accepted it and thought no more about it. (In any case, having to have major heart surgery in eighteen hours' time concentrates the mind wonderfully.) So I was rather surprised when at nine o'clock that night the nurse started tidying up my room, which I thought was a bit excessive under the circumstances. "Must have it looking nice for when the Archbishop comes", she said. I pointed out that she was making a mistake, since the time for my operation had been advanced. "Not at all," she replied somewhat testily, "there's a message to say he's coming at ten o'clock tonight." And indeed, to my great surprise – and delight – that is exactly what happened. The night before a major operation isn't normally a very pleasant time, but I can, unhesitatingly, say that Bob's sympathetic loving-kindness

– and all the laughs we had – greatly warmed my heart; and I will never forget the calm peace which his prayers and blessing brought me.

The Archbishop will, I fear, feel very embarrassed at the whole concept of this book, for he finds it very hard to believe in his own enormous ability, or in the grace of his very lovable personality, but perhaps he might pay some credence to the words of a non-believing journalist. After an interview with him some years ago, John Mortimer had this to say: "Dr Runcie is a man without an arrogant belief, humble before what he regards as a great mystery, tolerant in the way he believes God to be tolerant, an excellent priest who would, no doubt, make an admirable friend."

A Soldier in the Pulpit

VISCOUNT WHITELAW

When I first joined the Scots Guards just before the 1939–45 war, we had an outstanding character as a Regimental Sergeant Major training us. He had a phrase which he used constantly: "Once a Scots Guardsman, always a Scots Guardsman." That is a feeling which I know Bob Runcie and I share after our service during the war in the Third Battalion Scots Guards. What is more, we share that bond of friendship to this day with our brother officers whose careers embrace many different aspects of our national life. Before he retires as Archbishop of Canterbury, Bob Runcie is hosting a reunion for us all at Lambeth Palace, an occasion which I suspect will give him as much pleasure as it will the rest of us.

It will seem a long time since we first met this diffident young figure nearly fifty years ago. I remember that he soon blossomed into a very efficient soldier, popular with everyone and always a most amusing companion. He also soon proved himself a brave leader of men in battle, and so it was no surprise when, as the second in command of the battalion, I heard of his outstanding courage in the battle of Winnekendonk early in 1945. His award of the Military Cross in this action was most popular with us all as we knew how richly deserved it was.

I remember that there were those amongst us who said they were sure that he would join the Church after the war. But I suspect that there was a measure of hindsight in some of these subsequent accounts. What I certainly know is that during his days as a soldier no one was more selfless and more genuinely sympathetic to the feelings and problems of other people than was Bob Runcie.

After the war we saw little of each other until our careers

brought us closely in contact, particularly when he became Archbishop of Canterbury and I Home Secretary. I suppose my close friendship and deep admiration for him made me too uncritical a supporter, but I admit to feeling completely at odds with his critics, especially those in my own Conservative Party. In particular, I was most incensed by the criticism of his address at the St Paul's service after the Falklands War. Contrary to some of the views as expressed in the newspapers, I felt that he spoke exactly for me. His words were those of a soldier who understood war, and he expressed his admiration for those who fought, and in some cases gave their lives, for their country. But surely rightly there was no feeling of triumphal revenge in what he said, for he knew that one's opponents in war are fighting for their country too, and have their wives and families. All his words reminded me that feelings of bitterness and revenge are not only bad grounds for future action, but also strongly against basic religious beliefs.

Frankly, the simple fact that Bob Runcie is essentially a kind and compassionate man has not only enabled him to dominate the Church of England at home, but has also given him respect and affection throughout the world. When I was in Russia with a Parliamentary Delegation in 1986, I happened to mention that I was a friend of the Archbishop of Canterbury, which immediately gave me wholly unwarranted attention from the leaders in the Russian Orthodox Church.

These feelings, however, will not surprise his friends who are aware of his understanding of human nature and reactions, and at the same time his genuine sense of humour. I believe that his critics will soon find that as an Archbishop of Canterbury he will be a very hard act to follow.

At Sea and in Oxford

PETER FRASER

I do not intend to suggest that Dr Robert Runcie is – or indeed, for all I can imagine, ever was – in the sort of quandary which we describe as "being at sea". Instead, I recall under one title two very different aspects of his activities, one as a Cruise-Lecturer for Swan's Hellenic Cruises, and the other as Visitor of All Souls College, Oxford.

We met in 1970 on the deck of a Turkish steamboat which Kenneth Swan used for many years to transport his passengers to then still remote Greek and Turkish sites. The presence of the newly appointed Bishop of St Albans and the Director of the British School of Archaeology at Athens on the *Ankara* at the same time was due to the praiseworthy practice of Kenneth Swan, combined with the persuasive power of "Rik" Wheeler, of inviting academics to accompany his Hellenic tours. The invitations were rarely refused, and it was proper that such cruises, in which several hundred passengers would be thrown together, perhaps on stormy seas, should be accompanied by a chaplain as well as by a medical staff. One such chaplain was Robert, who was able to draw on his own classical studies in Oxford.

It was, and still is, one of the difficulties of a Lecturer on a Swan's cruise that he frequently finds himself required to lecture on a subject of which he has only a slight knowledge. However, Kenneth Swan saw fit to provide a good library, very frequently used by lecturers late at night. This atmosphere of slightly uneasy improvization leading to private confession has formed one of many links between lecturers. Indeed, one might say that it led to a form of academic barter, by which I might help the Bishop out with an awkward date in the Peloponnesian War or the explanation of a curiosity on a site, in exchange for the date of the Second Council of Constantinople or the history of a previously unvisited Orthodox monastery. If I could resolve the question of whether it was the island of Syros or Tenos that lay ahead in the early, hazy light of an April day in the Cyclades, Robert could repay such help by swiftly identifying one or more of the Athonite monasteries as we sailed round the Holy Mountain. Such situations create mutual trust and friendship, and I very soon found that this scholarly bishop was also an admirable travelling companion, sympathetic to all human dilemmas, and possessed of a fund of rich and amusing anecdotes. That he was loved and remembered by the passengers is attested by all who had the good fortune to travel with him.

By his elevation to the Primacy Robert became Visitor to several colleges at Oxford, and it was in his capacity as Visitor of All Souls that I saw him most frequently. The Visitor of a college has no statutory duties, though he has certain "lawful powers" which permit him, notably, to compose quarrels between contumacious Fellows that the Head of the House cannot manage himself, or in which indeed he is himself involved. It will be appreciated that the occasions on which a Visitor is required to exercise these lawful powers are now so rare as never to occur, and Visitors are not under an obligation to visit their colleges (the All Souls statute says, "it is lawful for them to do so once in every ten years, without any request or application by the College"). It was therefore a great pleasure to learn that this Visitor, who had already stayed with me in All Souls while he was Bishop of St Albans, was anxious to strengthen his links with the college. He pleased us by expressing the wish to stay for an extended spell of study and reflection while preparing for the Lambeth Conference of 1988. He came and lived among us (though the ties of public business called him away more often than we could have wished), enduring stoically the difficult silences, and hardly less difficult conversations, of communal breakfast at All Souls, and when he left, as quietly as he had come, I think there was a feeling that we had lost a little warmth. From his private visit the college profited far more than it would have done from a solemn Visitation, and, for his part, I hope that he felt that the college was still fulfilling one of the chief purposes for which his remote and venerable predecessor, Chichele, had founded it, namely to form a bridge between the university and public service.

Now I hope to see him more often, by land as by sea, and in the meantime as I sit in the Hall of Brasenose College, of which we both have the privilege of being Honorary Fellows, I look at that tall portrait of him that hangs over the fireplace, and think how truly he represents that combination of liberal understanding and moral courage which is necessary for the survival of the best in an age of intolerance.

Cambridge and After

HUGH MONTEFIORE
Bishop of Birmingham 1978–87

I knew Bob Runcie best in the fifties and the sixties, although we were in fairly close touch in the eighties when he was Archbishop and I was at Birmingham.

In 1949, after finishing his degree at Oxford after the war, Runcie arrived at Westcott House, Cambridge, for two years' residence at his theological college. I had arrived a year earlier, also after finishing my post-war degree at Oxford; so we overlapped for a year in that fairly closed society of forty-five ordinands. At that time there seemed a lot of us who had got First Class degrees, and Runcie was among them. But he was not a theologian, having distinguished himself in history. Harry Williams was on the staff, who later became a well-known Christian radical; but at that time he was an orthodox and highly amusing Anglo-Catholic straight from All Saints', Margaret Street. We were all fond of him; but Runcie, who came from a more Catholic background than most of us, seemed especially to admire him. In those days Runcie was a friendly, clubbable and kindly person – characteristics he has of course always retained – with a certain fondness for cricket and for amateur theatricals. He was already a good mimic, and I can remember him, at a concert, wiping his nose on his surplice as he brilliantly took off Professor Norman Sykes. Seven of us there were eventually to become bishops. Fortunately none of us was ambitious for high office; and I don't think that it then ever entered anyone's head that Bob would become Archbishop of Canterbury, although it was clear that he had a fine ministry ahead of him.

In those days it was the done thing to "go north" for one's first curacy. I suppose life was easy in the university cities

of Oxford and Cambridge, and perhaps we felt we ought
to make a clean break. I went to a parish in Newcastle-on-
Tyne. Due to my vicar being consecrated a bishop, after a
few weeks I found myself on my own in the parish, having
to rely greatly on the neighbouring clergy; and the Vicar of
Gosforth seemed exceptional. He told me how badly he
needed a colleague, and it seemed to me a marvellous parish
in which to start. I suggested that he got in touch with Bob
Runcie, and to my surprise and delight Bob decided to come.
I know he was very happy there, and I found it good to have
a friend next door. Once again we didn't overlap for long,
because within two years I had gone south to join the staff
at Westcott House; but I realized that Bob was making his
mark in Gosforth. Of course the girls in the parish idolized
him; but he managed to withstand their blandishments.

Shortly after I joined the staff of Westcott House, Alan
Webster (later Dean of St Paul's) decided to leave in order
to go to a parish, and once again Bob followed me after a
year. Bob became the Chaplain, I was Vice-Principal, and
Ken Carey the Principal of Westcott House. Bob and I had
an exceptionally heavy work load, for between us we had
to do all the teaching, not to mention looking after what was
dubbed "the common life" in that rather closed society. I
found it rather isolated me from my family, but Bob was
still single. He had a very easy style, and was a brilliant
conversationalist – he always has been – while I was
comparatively tongue-tied and unforthcoming. I greatly
admired him both as a priest and as a colleague; and he was
friendly too to my family. He taught history, the Old
Testament and liturgy, while I had to try to cope with the
New Testament and doctrine. He would not, at this stage,
I think, have thought of himself as a theologian. At that time
he tended to sit on the fence over theological issues. A great
agitation was taking place about the formation of the Church
of South India, and a symposium in favour of it, called *The
Historic Episcopate*, was being produced from Westcott
House. Bob preferred not to contribute. He would not
declare himself as either pro or anti.

After a couple of years I went off to be Dean of Caius

College nearby. Yet again Bob shortly followed me. He became Dean of the college next to mine, Trinity Hall, where he was clearly very popular among the undergraduates. He did not try to take part in the work of the Divinity Faculty, but he did supervise in ancient history in his college. I will always remember him taking me out to tea because "I have something to tell you" – it was his engagement to Rosalind Turner; and he was so very happy.

I kept in touch with Bob and Lindy when they moved to train ordinands at Cuddesdon. Our Visitors' Book shows their signatures quite often, and no doubt it was the same at Cuddesdon. I was impressed particularly by the care he took to provide pastoral training outside the college, as well as by the time-consuming nature of the job. It was here that he became a "workaholic". He was an outstanding Principal, and as a liberal Catholic he was right in the Cuddesdon tradition. I was not surprised when he was made Bishop of St Albans. I rather lost touch with him, being engaged in the hurly burly of life at Great St Mary's, Cambridge; but as St Albans was my wife's family home, I was aware that he was a very good and much loved pastoral bishop. At that point he was put in charge of the Anglican-Orthodox Commission. To cope with the Orthodox you really have to be theologically minded, and I think that from this period stemmed his serious engagement with theological issues.

I remember when he was appointed Archbishop. I was lecturing at Stockholm Cathedral as the news came through, and I was simply delighted. He was the best of the candidates, and the Commission chose well. None the less, some queries naturally surfaced in my mind. Two years, apart from Cuddesdon, as a parish priest – was it long enough experience? Clearly it was. His ordained ministry so far had lain in fair pastures – would he be able to cope with the Church in the inner city? As everyone knows, he has made it a major concern, and he was happy to make the Commission on Urban Priority Areas "the Archbishop's Commission". Above all, would he be able to come off the theological fence? Well, in the end he did. With regard to

South India, it was he who proposed that we should be in full communion. With regard to remarriage in church after divorce, it was he who brought the matter up again in General Synod after it had been set aside. And he has even approved – eventually – the ordination of women to the priesthood. I know there are some who think none the less that he has been too indecisive. They should remind themselves that he did not choose himself to be Archbishop of Canterbury – he was chosen by others. He even took some time to accept. He is by temperament a man who seeks reconciliation rather than confrontation, and he is naturally cautious about taking a line which is not traditionally Catholic. I think that he has developed into being far more decisive than he once was. He has been a far better Archbishop than it was reasonable to expect!

By temperament I am always in favour of a strong lead, although like others I prefer that the lead should be in the direction that I myself would like. I think that in fact Runcie has served us very well, simply by keeping a comprehensive church united and reasonably good tempered during a difficult period. The Church of England is still one, as well as being encouraged to become more holy and catholic and apostolic. For that alone we should all be most grateful. It has been done by his pastoral touch – for example, he knew just what to say when three thousand Brummies arrived on pilgrimage at Canterbury.

Light in Touch, Large in Vision

PETER WALKER
Bishop of Ely 1977–89

His lightness of touch is what I have chiefly remembered from meeting Robert Runcie for the first time. That was in 1953. He was Chaplain of Westcott House, and I was feeling my way as a schoolmaster towards ordination. But behind that lightness of touch, one knew, was the impressive combination of an Oxford First in Greats and a Military Cross with the Brigade of Guards (and one noticed later that he never seemed to need to parade that decoration). You realized that he never took you, or the Church of England, with anything less than total seriousness. And finally you understood that the buoyancy came from an unlaboured faith in God and was part of the quiet assurance of a man who had known himself proved early in life.

To have written so about a friend comes near to impertinence. But magnanimity about what has been said about him will one day be seen as a mark of Robert Runcie's greatness, the lack of a need to make a point defensively. Only, in the present climate of the Church as well as the world, such quietness seems to be often misunderstood.

We were in the same work, in similar places, in the 1950s and 1960s. What, in those years, might I see as illuminating, or illuminated by, what I have just said? When after the years as Dean of Trinity Hall, he went to be Principal of Cuddesdon and (equally important to him) incumbent of the parish, he handed over to me (then Dean of Chapel of Corpus) the Hon. Secretaryship of the Cambridge Mission to Delhi. I was often, later, to reflect with admiration and a touch of envy on his easy mastering of that substantial portfolio – the shrewd assessment of place and people, the personal *auctoritas*, that commitment and affection had

15

gained for him. Cuddesdon would soon be finding – and I was conscious of this when, as Principal of Westcott, I was competing with him soon afterwards for good ordinands – a leadership all the more searching for a touch of the laconic in its style and with no narrowness in its horizons. "I believe in Cuddesdon", he had said. He was never a man – this was a facile misunderstanding of him – to "make it up as he went along".

At each crucial change in his ministry, I reflect, he moved into situations that were on the threshold of radical change (foreseen or not): the ferment in the universities in the 1960s; the play-off from that, and from all that was focused in *Honest to God*, into the theological colleges, to make them frontier places in the Church of England – these things for a start. Trinity Hall was, I suppose, an ideal fit. He was probably appreciated best – and flowered in response – by the layman and the outsider, who sensed his ability, appreciated the lightness of step and the deep seriousness, not for ever placarded, out of which it came, and held him in affectionate regard. Nor is it always recognized how valuable a preparation for the presidency of a diocese, or province, or Communion, it is that a man should have been a member of so mixed and able a body as the Fellowship of such a place, which a Master must somehow hold together and help to find its common mind.

And Cuddesdon? The danger in the theological colleges in those years – as has duly emerged subsequently in the Church of England on the ground – was not the "rebels" themselves, but the defensive reaction which looked backwards rather than to the future that God was calling the churches into, and made for a taut introversion in the Church. Robert Runcie kept his head, his lightness of step, his *integrity*, asking always which way God was calling us, refusing to be hustled. He was a Prince of Principals. And in the Canterbury years – into which, in a true continuity, he was to bring also the experience of presiding over a frontline diocese that was beginning, like the others, to come to terms with massive impending changes in resources and deployment, and in danger of the introversion and sectarianism that all such preoccupations can bring – he was surely the same Runcie; seen most clearly for the man he is, and always has been, at the Lambeth Conference of 1988, among the bishops who could smile at themselves and with him, and whose horizons were those where the real future lay.

Was all this Westcott tradition or Cuddesdon tradition? The Church of England has a dimension greater than that implied by asking final questions in such terms: and who has known that better than Robert Runcie?

A Developing Style

RICHARD HARRIES
Bishop of Oxford

To a student at Cuddesdon preparing for ordination in the early 1960s, one of the minor masterpieces was the Principal's introduction of visiting speakers. In two minutes Robert Runcie managed to convey the essence of the person and whet our appetite for a theme of great significance to us, whether or not two minutes before we had thought the person at all interesting or their subject of the slightest importance. These introductions revealed all the qualities that were to be characteristic of the Archbishop at every stage of his career and in almost every situation – warmth, naturalness, self-deprecating humour and a highly developed sense of the way the world is. It all seemed so easy, part of the person. But it wasn't easy. People who happened to go behind the scenes, down some back corridor or into some obscure lecture room, would find, five minutes before the lecture, the Principal pacing up and down, carefully arranging these words on the mantlepiece of his mind. This was the art that conceals art.

At every theological college the Principal's lectures on prayer and pastoralia are a high point. Cuddesdon at that time was no exception – professional, in the best sense, practical and polished. Perhaps more revealing were the annual newsletters. In those days the earth had not begun to shake but tremors were being felt. Under Edward Knapp-Fisher Cuddesdon had been a good but somewhat austere place. Women were allowed into the college for half an hour after the Sunday Eucharist, when it was assumed that the grace of the sacrament would keep the lusts of the young men down. (The lusts of the young women were not considered.) Bob Runcie wanted to open up the college, ever so gradually, to change on various fronts. But he was conscious of the great weight of the Cuddesdon tradition; clergy up and down the country read his newsletters. So his style was designed above all to keep a changing institution together, the present in sympathy with the past and always hopeful. It was a style that came into its own during the last years of his Archbishopric, as he struggled to keep the Church of England and the Anglican Communion together over the issue of the ordination of women; a style designed to give every faction a feeling that it was understood and had a part in the process. More fun were the stories he told at end of term revues. A superb mimic, his ecclesiastical jokes are still the best ones I know.

As Archbishop, sometimes called upon to pronounce several times a day, he has for much of the time been dependent on drafts offered by others. More characteristic of the man we knew at Cuddesdon have been the innumerable "few words" at more informal gatherings, and the after dinner speeches. Quite superb have been his short appreciations of General Synod members who were retiring. His ability both to enter into the mind and character of someone else and to convey this to a sympathetic audience with warmth and wit win people to him, whether or not they share his viewpoint. Television does him a disservice because he is cut off from the physical rapport between him and the audience.

Le style est l'homme même. This man has a wonderful capacity for entering into the feelings of others. He also has a finely tuned sense of institutional life, what is and what is not possible. If he had wanted an easier life he would have chosen to be an ancient historian. Perhaps even now he might write a biography of one of the Palaeologi in fourteenth-century Byzantium, when a brief artistic flowering occurred in the tiny part of the empire that remained, even though it was in a state of terminal decline. His feel for people and institutions, together with the painful turmoil of his own period of office, could contribute towards a classic of historical understanding.

A Man of Power

W. H. VANSTONE
Canon of Chester

When in 1949 the students of Westcott House decided to perform Shaw's *Androcles and the Lion* in the college garden, our unanimous choice for the part of the Roman Emperor was Robert Runcie. By his bearing, his personality, his intellect and his distinguished record in the war Robert was already an impressive and powerful figure: he was already *omnium consensu capax imperii* – "in everyone's opinion fit for high office". When in due time he was appointed to the highest office in our Church none of his friends was surprised; and we were all delighted not only for Robert's own sake but also because a man who is used to possessing power is less likely to flaunt or abuse it than one to whom power comes as a novelty and the wearing of the purple as an unfamiliar and heady experience.

In the last five years or so Robert has, I think, had more power at his disposal than any of his recent predecessors at Canterbury. The heavy television coverage of public events in which he has been involved has made him a well-known "personality" to taxi-drivers, stallholders on the market, and people whom one meets on trains: and – to judge from what I have heard such people say about him – he is a very popular personality. If he were inclined to do so he could win a large and vocal popular following for his own views on controversial matters of theology, morals or politics.

Sometimes, when his views on such matters coincided with my own, I have wished that he would use his popular influence to defeat the opposition and lead his cause – and mine – to victory. But to do so would not accord with his style or his principles. Even in private conversation he does

20

not "talk for victory". He does not "cut one down" by his intellectual powers or, by his personality, shame one into professing what one does not believe, or embarrass one into deferring to a view to which one does not assent. Never, in public or in private, have I heard him exploit his personal feelings and sensitivities in order to defuse criticism, silence opposition or win support.

As Archbishop Robert has used his powers, both personal and official, for one purpose only – to sustain the well-being of "the body" of the Anglican Communion in general and of the Church of England in particular. For a body divided and rent asunder there can be no well-being: and so the unity of our Church and Communion has been Robert's primary and paramount concern. For the sake of unity he has left many personal views and feelings unexpressed in public: and to his worldwide travels and addresses in the service of unity he has given all the time and energy which might otherwise have been used to distinguish his own name as a scholar and writer.

I have sometimes heard Robert described as, and criticized for being, "a liberal archbishop". If "liberal" means "woolly-minded" the description is absurdly inept: for his mind, in comparison with that of his typical critic, is razor-sharp. But if "liberal" means, as it used to mean, "generous", the description is apt. He has expended his exceptional powers not in acquiring wealth (as he could have done in business) or personal reputation (as he could have done in the political or academic world) but in serving the well-being of the Church to which, at his Ordination more than forty years ago, he gave his allegiance. This has been his graciousness: and it is for this reason that I find it easy to think of my oldest friend as "His Grace".

A Man of Prayer

SISTER JANE

Our Archbishop has presided over the Anglican
Communion at a time of steady growth, and a system that
is developing can never be comfortable, whether it is a
human being or a civilization. There will inevitably arise
many conflicts and anybody in a position of leadership has
to suffer the impact of these conflicts personally. Our Lord
shows us God's way of doing this, and I believe that our
Christian commitment is tested and proven by the degree
to which we follow his example. Do we respond to what
happens to us, particularly to criticism and opposition, with
self-protective aggression, fighting back in the manner of
our attackers, or do we try like Jesus to receive, suffer and
absorb, so allowing God to transfigure the situation,
drawing the sting and halting the spread of evil?

The belief that differences, even contradictions, are
somehow to be contained rather than confronted and
eliminated is one aspect in which humanity as a whole is
advancing; and to have applied this principle in the
leadership of our Church must have been costly indeed.
Here, surely, Bob Runcie has taught us more by his example
than could have been done by any amount of wise and holy
words written and spoken − though of course these too
have not been lacking.

Our Community, the Sisters of the Love of God, has
known Bob as a good friend who has become very dear to
us since the early sixties, when he used to bring Cuddesdon
ordinands to be shown round. I'm sure I was more in awe
of him then than I ever have been since! Our Hemel
Hempstead House is in St Albans diocese, and when he was
its bishop he used to come for quiet days, which usually
ended with a chat. Since he has been Archbishop he has

come to Fairacres a number of times, and for some years has made a habit of spending Good Friday at our Bede House in Kent. Obviously as a member of an enclosed community I have not had much experience of his public life: but I know him as a priest who prays and genuinely relies on the prayer support of others, also as someone who certainly does not take himself too seriously and is great fun to be with.

What I Have Been Praying For

SISTER FRANCES DOMINICA

I had a dream of a maze. There were some people very close to the centre; only a single hedge separated them from the very heart of the maze, but they could not find a way through. They had taken a wrong turn right at the very beginning and would have to return to the gate if they were to make any further progress.But just outside the gate others were standing. They were further away from the heart of the maze, but they would be there sooner than the party that fretted and fumed inside.

I long to be able to speak while archbishop with men and women who stand outside the Christian Church. I would like to say to them, ''You can teach us so much if together we could look for the secret of the maze-like muddle in which the world finds itself.'' I ask for your prayers that I may be given the grace to speak like that and to listen . . .

So the new Archbishop of Canterbury, on the occasion of his enthronement, set the tone for his leadership of the Anglican Communion. He would not be limited by the confines of the institutional Church. Rather, all the energy of his living and his loving was to be spent in discovering the Kingdom of God with – and in the very midst of – the people he would serve, women, men and children of all sorts and conditions, churched and unchurched.

Robert's period at Canterbury has come at a time when many people claim that it is the duty of the hierarchy of the Church to make definite pronouncements on moral issues; there is a demand that we should be told whether an issue is black or white, good or evil, of God or the devil. The fact that the vast majority of those who clamour for this type of leadership will choose to ignore it if it causes disturbance in their personal lifestyle is not so often aired. The vote goes to the person who promises to restore a real or imagined past, full of certainties and security. This has never been, nor ever can be, Robert's way. Believing in the dignity of each person and the God-given right and ability of individuals to wrestle with the discernment of good and evil as it affects their own lives, along with the gift of free will which is our heritage, Robert does not make judgements of the nature many demand of him. To do so would be to adopt a style of leadership which would inevitably militate against the underdog, the unloved, the marginalized – the very people for whom the Church, following the example of her Lord, claims to exist. ''Those who are well have no need of a physician, but those who are sick. I came not to call the righteous but sinners'' (Mark 2:17). This is an archbishop who has been heard to say, ''I'm all right with sinners. It's the righteous I'm not so good with''. It could be said that his greatest fault, humanly speaking, is his tendency to believe in the integrity and innate goodness of each individual. This can be seen as weakness or as a Christ-like gift. If it is a gift it is one which risks disappointment and denial. But it can also be the life-giving catalyst essential in enabling a person to be true to him- or herself and so to resemble more closely the God who created us in his own image and likeness.

My prayer has been that he will have the courage of his convictions, the courage to be true to the leading of his innermost self, at that place where he comes face to face with his God. This is a man who walks with God and who prays to have the mind of Christ. Buffeted about by dissension within the Church, political wrangling, inhuman pressure of demands made on him, the expectation that he should be able to pronounce on any subject at any time – all this and more, is enough to crush a man whose natural tendency it is to question both his ability and his self-worth. I have prayed that God will give him the emotional and physical stamina to survive.

With the help of an itinerary, praying the Archbishop through an overseas visit has left me, for one, breathless and exhausted. It seems impossible to fit so much into each day, and to do justice to each encounter and event. Whether at home or overseas Robert has been painstaking in his preparation for each occasion in which he has a part. Others might justifiably consider that the various functions at which he has been required to preside or to speak have varying degrees of importance and of significance to the Church and the world, and therefore demand a greater or lesser amount of his time and energy for prayer, thought and preparation. He himself has, however, always been conscious of the fact that for those on the receiving end, even when they comprise the smallest group in the seemingly dimmest of parishes, the occasion has been the cause not only of careful planning but of considerable anticipation and expectation. What his listeners often have not realized, nor would he wish them to do so, is that, while for them this may have been an historic event, for him it has been one of several functions on that same day. The result of his labours has almost invariably been to leave his listeners with the impression that not only have they heard the Word of God, but that the words which may well have enthralled, amused or inspired them have been produced effortlessly. Robert's fluency has led people to believe that he has a natural gift, that this has been an occasion where he has felt at home and relaxed and that the cost to himself has not been very great. Nothing could be further from the truth. Over the years he has worked until the small hours night after night, wrestling with sentences and means of expression, in order that the Word of God be spoken and his Kingdom furthered. I have prayed for God to strengthen and support him, to encourage him when he has despaired of adequate time for preparation of each event.

I have prayed, too, for peace of mind and of heart for him, recognizing at the same time that, for him, God's will has often been wrought out of agonizing and considerable anguish and that perhaps it has to be so. While a highly complex nature can be a source of enrichment and enlightenment to others, the person concerned may well suffer torment and self-doubt. Quick, decisive judgements do not come easily to a man who is conservative by temperament but radical by conviction. Every statement has its opposite, every certainty its shadow. The shadow may lie closer to the truth than the certainty. It must at least be heeded. Therefore at times when Robert has been the subject of uninformed gossip or cruel criticism, it has been my prayer that Jesus Christ, who knew hatred, contempt and denial, would comfort him.

Small boys are not impressed by persons of rank or position: football enthusiasts are a more interesting proposition. So it was that Lee decided it was worth offering to take this Liverpool supporter on a guided tour of Helen House, the Oxford children's hospice where Lee was a frequent guest. His explanations about admissions policies and the like quickly gave way to discussions about the relative merits of Tottenham and Liverpool. Later that year, the two clubs met for the Cup Final. Lee received a message of condolence from the Archbishop, who was visiting Japan on the fateful day. Liverpool had been the victors.

He is, supremely, a compassionate pastor whose call to high office has carried with it the pain of being removed from what he describes as the ''sharp end of things''. In his address at a Service of Remembrance and Thanksgiving for children who were friends of Helen House and who had died in the past five years, Robert said to the families: ''Thank you for the privilege of sharing here for a little the atmosphere which your children have created and the blessing which they have given to the world . . . These children have left their mark on my life . . . There's always a future for our deepest loves, for our God is not a God of the dead but of the living.'' As well as thanking God for the lives of their beloved children, the families thanked God for so sensitive and loving an Archbishop.

The demands and expectations focused on an Archbishop of Canterbury have probably always been unrealistically great, but never more so than during this last decade. There is work enough to keep a good handful of hard-working

Christians fully occupied, yet one man is expected to carry the burden and be answerable. "The thing I miss most," he said recently, "is having enough time to pray." Anyone who is close to him knows that he sees prayer as the very ground in which the relationship between a Christian and his Creator is nurtured and grows. Without prayer we perish. He is himself utterly faithful to the living out of his conviction, through the offering of the Eucharist, the daily recitation of the Office, and time spent alone with God. Yet the constraints of his particular office are very great and they have not allowed him the stretches of time he longs for. I have prayed that he would be upheld by the prayers of the countless women, children and men he serves, and that he would find consolation in the fact that God does not necessarily ask that we spend long hours kneeling in prayer, but rather that we walk with him all our days. I have asked God that in all the loneliness, the longing and the loving Robert may know that God is his constant companion – and that the Kingdom is in our midst.

A Biographer Reflects

MARGARET DUGGAN

In April 1983, when Robert Runcie had been Archbishop
of Canterbury for just three years, I rashly concluded his
interim biography, *Runcie: The Making of an Archbishop*, with
the opinion that he "is a very remarkable man, and is well
on the way to becoming a great archbishop". Since then
I have often been asked whether I still held to that opinion.
To the first half of the sentence I have said an unhesitating
yes, and yes again. Dr Runcie has shown himself, through
eleven difficult and stressful years of our national history,
to be a very remarkable man indeed. But it is only now, as
he nears the end of his time at Lambeth Palace and
Canterbury, that I can attempt to justify my use of the word
"great" – a judgement that properly belongs to history.

In these last decades of the twentieth century, when scant
respect is shown for any public figure, and the media's joy
– or so it often seems – is to denigrate, debunk, or dig out
the dirt on anyone who dares make the headlines, the idea
of greatness is a thoroughly unfashionable concept. Even
the word itself has been devalued to the point where
"great" is no more than a vague noise of agreement. Yet
the dictionary still defines it, when applied to persons, as
indicating someone of outstanding character, ability, and
historical importance. A Christian looking for greatness
would go further, and require moral and spiritual qualities
as well as those of intellect and practical achievement; while
those who come into personal contact with the great man
or woman would also look for human warmth, compassion,
and the gifts of friendship.

On all these counts, Robert Runcie has scored highly.
There is no doubt about his historical importance in the short
term, in having held the Anglican Communion together.

The record of his successors will show whether he did more than postpone the inevitable. But his greatest personal triumph came during the Lambeth Conference, where we watched him walk with his tall athletic grace (quite remarkable in a man of sixty-seven) among Anglican bishops from all over the world, and could see how clearly he was the outstanding and most-loved personality of them all. The many rumours of the imminent break-up of the Anglican Communion came to nothing as the bishops united round their focus of unity. Dr Runcie's assiduous foreign travel, to virtually every Anglican province on six continents, and his gifts of intelligent sympathy and friendship unstintingly offered, had paid off.

At home in England he has had a tougher time, partly through his own inadvertent making. It has been very noticeable how, in the eleven years he has been Archbishop, the mass media have suddenly discovered the news value of the Church to an extent far beyond anything known by his predecessors. There have been a number of contributory causes, such as the Church's own growing expertise in communications, and the advent of the General Synod as the sort of confrontational institution the media can understand. But, in the forefront, has been Robert Runcie himself.

From the first, the professional sceptics of press and broadcasting recognized that here was a new sort of archbishop: a grammar-school boy who had commanded a tank and won the Military Cross, kept pigs as a hobby, and talked in a language they could understand. On his side, he was the first of his line to recognize that the media were a tiger he must be prepared to ride if the Church was to play its part in national life. This was part of his realism; for without media interest in the late twentieth century, in a world where reality is validated by appearing on television, the Church (while undoubtedly remaining the Body of Christ) would soon be invisible outside its own membership.

It was with this same realism that he allowed me to write his biography at such an early stage of his Primacy. Like it or not, if he was to be an effective archbishop, he must accept the fact of public interest. So it was with only decent reluctance that he agreed to co-operate, and then did it with great charm. But conceit is very far from being one of his characteristics. An unexpected difficulty I kept running into was the way he genuinely seemed to be more interested in talking about his friends than about himself. His habit of self-deprecation died hard, and precious time would slip by while I tried every way to bring the conversation back to the events of his own life. When I could get him on that subject, virtually every story he told was against himself.

That happened on the good days. Occasionally I would arrive at Lambeth Palace to find him very, very tired indeed, and then he needed to talk therapeutically about what he had been doing in the previous few hours. I began to see just how hard he drove himself: a gruelling schedule from early morning to midnight, and very rare days off. I also learned, from seeing him at it, and travelling with him to major events, that all those apparently spontaneous speeches, the wit and the charm and the funny stories which so endeared him to those he met, were the result of meticulous homework as he read the briefs prepared for him, annotated them again and again, and made them his own.

During his first three years as Archbishop – the years covered by my biography as first published – events conspired to keep him in the headlines. He had a leading role on the two great royal occasions of the Queen Mother's eightieth birthday and the wedding of the Prince and Princess of Wales. He met the Pope in Africa and invited him to England. His "special envoy", Terry Waite, had his first success at bringing hostages out of Iran. And then there was the momentous visit of the Pope to Canterbury: with all the controversy beforehand when Dr Runcie had to face ugly anti-papist demonstrations in Liverpool; with the Pope himself nearly cancelling the visit because of the complications of the war with Argentina; and the final glory of the service in Canterbury Cathedral when Archbishop and Pope greeted each other as brothers. These formed a succession of "highs" against a steady background of official visits in Britain and overseas, of incessant meetings, festival services, preaching, speaking, pastoral counselling of all sorts of people (some in the highest reaches of national life), and immense amounts of correspondence and administration. There were always the sour comments of those few journalists and others who compulsively sneer at bishops, but during this period Dr Runcie knew his greatest popularity and could hardly put a foot wrong.

An ominous change came when he preached at the service commemorating the Falklands War, deploring war as a sign of human failure, and remembering the Argentinian as well as the British dead. It was said at the time that the Prime Minister was angry, though she was seen to greet him warmly at the end of the service, and both she and Dr Runcie have denied any coolness between them at that point. There is no doubt that a number of right-wing members of Parliament and the right-wing popular press never forgave the Archbishop for preaching such an uncomfortable Christian message, rather than providing the jingoistic triumphalism they wanted to hear.

From then on Dr Runcie was viewed with suspicion by certain members of the Government, particularly when he supported causes and social issues that implied criticism of government policies. In particular, the launch of the *Faith in the City* report brought wild accusations of Marxism. For a considerable while there appeared to be an orchestrated campaign by a number of politicians and certain newspapers to discredit him, and even force him to resign. In 1986 they reached an absurd peak of innuendo when at least one tabloid newspaper tried to imply that the Queen and Prime Minister were in earnest consultation about how to get rid of him and appoint the Bishop of London in his stead. Even when he was deliberately misrepresented, Dr Runcie managed to weather these attacks with remarkable patience, not allowing them to shake his nerve. But the most unpleasant manifestations of this campaign were reports that his marriage was breaking up. There were malicious attacks on his wife, Lindy, and one newspaper got hold of some old photographs of a sort that would be no more than ordinary in any family album, but, when labelled "archbishop's wife" and blazoned across a centre-spread, could be made to appear scandalous. This was very hard for both of them to bear.

It was also hurtful for him to withstand the attacks from those within the Church, and from those fellow-travellers of the Church, who were forever demanding "a lead" just so long as the lead was in the direction they wanted to go. Controversies over doctrine, particularly those raised by the Bishop of Durham, were very difficult for someone who was himself well versed in current academic theology, and yet understood how speculations that were commonplace in university circles could readily serve to undermine the "simple faith" of many Christians who had not been exposed to such exploratory thinking.

Robert Runcie, as I suggested in my biography, is temperamentally a Catholic traditionalist, and intellectually a liberal. It is part of his character to be generously perceptive of both sides of any argument in which Christians differ, and to put reconciliation before dogma. It is this reluctance to commit himself to hard-line views which has often drawn the accusation of fence-sitting and indecisiveness. But his critics would never understand that it was not only his instincts for fair play and generosity which made him look at all sides of every question, and give his opponents the benefit of the doubt; his deep feeling of responsibility for the whole worldwide Anglican Communion also made him hesitate to make any decision that might alienate some part of it, or, indeed, alienate some other part of the Universal Catholic Church. Thus, for a long time it was hard for him to vote in favour of women priests – even though he had no personal problems with the theology of ordaining women – because of the way the issue was not only threatening to split the Church of England, but was also likely to prove an insurmountable barrier to reunion in any sense of the word with both the Roman Catholic and the Orthodox Churches. It was only when he became convinced that it was truly for the good of the Anglican Church as a whole that he finally voted positively for the women.

Cautiously liberal probably best defines his stance, which makes it all the harder that he had to endure the unhappiness which surrounded the now notorious Crockford's Preface which accused him of liberal élitism and lack of firm principles. This anonymous and bitter attack on him by one whom he had always treated as a friend, the outcry which surrounded its publication, and the subsequent suicide of Canon Gareth Bennett who had written it, constituted one of the most painful episodes of Dr Runcie's Primacy. The other great ache has been the continued absence of Terry Waite for which, even though Waite went to Beirut against his advice, Dr Runcie inevitably feels a responsibility. Yet, through it all, he has kept his integrity. He has as much vulnerability and sensitivity as – perhaps more than – most men, yet he has suffered all these attacks with visible courage and patience. Though at times he has spoken to his intimates with exasperation about the amount of extra work and stress he and his hard-pressed staff have been caused (not least by some of his fellow bishops going off on their own tack without regard for the repercussions at Lambeth Palace), in public he has remained unruffled, generous, and intent on his life of service as pastor and primate to both Church and nation.

He has never ceased to drive himself hard, and has expected and received the same high standards from his staff at Lambeth Palace. This will be one of his most valuable legacies to his successor, for no other modern Archbishop of Canterbury has been so well served. From the first he realized that he could not do the job of Primate as he believed it should be done unless he had an adequate team to help him; and this he has built up through the years. He has always had a rare gift for picking the right (if sometimes unexpected) people, and Terry Waite, Richard Chartres, Christopher Hill, Eve Keatley and John Lyttle are only some of those who have served him with distinction. By Vatican standards it is still a ridiculously small staff to support the Primate of a worldwide church but, under the leadership of Bishop Ronald Gordon, the dozen or so who make up the team, together with their secretarial help, keep the

Archbishop in touch with every aspect of his immense task, in church and secular affairs, both at home and overseas.

Ability, energy, self-discipline and charm: it is this last quality which has made the greatest impact on those who have met Robert Runcie. He has an exceptional talent for making everyone he meets feel special. He listens closely to what they have to say, and has the knack of appearing to take them into his confidence. Indeed, with those he trusts, even among the members of the press, he will talk with a relaxed freedom which is very attractive, and has won him a host of loyal friends in all areas of life. For all the public criticism and carping he has had to endure, few men in his position can have inspired so much affection.

Part of the secret has been his very humanity. He is not afraid of admitting he is as other men are. Pomposity is not in his nature, nor could it be with the sort of family he has. With an independently-minded and outspoken wife, and two lively modern children (James now a BBC producer, and Rebecca now working for a campaigning organization) he has little chance in his private life to play the pontiff, even if he wished to. A bishop, who has been his friend for many years, once suggested to me that: ''Bob's saving grace has been his slightly prickly marriage; the only thing in his life where success has not come smoothly. It has kept him human and in touch with real life.'' That might have been overstating the case, but there is no doubt about it that the Archbishop has not had the cosy support from a model clergy wife that some of his predecessors have had to their dubious advantage; and perhaps for this very reason he has had a better understanding of human relationships and modern marriage in the late twentieth century.

Rosalind Runcie, ''Lindy'' to her friends, is her own woman. From the start she made it known that she did not want her husband to become Archbishop, because she did not want to leave their home in St Albans. She also said memorably that ''too much religion makes me go pop''; and it was known that she openly objected to accompanying the Archbishop on many formal occasions. Though she reluctantly moved into Lambeth Palace, she has always spent a minimum of time at their other home in Canterbury, and has regularly returned to a house she bought in St Albans to give piano lessons to her regular pupils there.

But it is part of her nature to put down, wherever she lives, roots that grow slowly at first, and then take a tenacious hold. Every time the Runcies have had to move because of his job, she has been dragged metaphorically kicking and screaming to the new address. She did not want to leave their first home in Cambridge, any more than she wanted to leave St Albans. And one can guess that she will feel equally heartbroken to leave Lambeth Palace – and with good reason. For during the past eleven years she has master-minded the transformation of both the house and its garden. She has not only had a talent for finding the right experts to help her, but also for raising the considerable sums of money that have been needed.

Lambeth Palace is a formidable building, part mediaeval, part nineteenth-century, now mostly given over to offices and public use. Its grand rooms and corridors are dauntingly hung with portraits of many of the Archbishop's a hundred and one predecessors. Yet, with skilful colouring, new upholstery, rearrangement of furniture, and plenty of flowers, Mrs Runcie has made it a warm and welcoming place. Her greatest work has been the garden. Eight hundred years old, and with nine acres, it is the largest private garden in London after that of Buckingham Palace. It was run down and overgrown when the Runcies moved in, and little evidence existed of its former layout. Mrs Runcie set about raising the £25,000 needed to restore it. Some of the money came from private individuals; some from fund-raising events, including Mrs Runcie's own piano concerts; and donations, labour and materials were given by trade and industry, particularly those connected with horticulture. London Zoo contributed rhino dung. Well-known professional landscapers and gardeners laid the acres out, and planted them with two hundred trees and six hundred rose bushes, as well as many hundred other plants. The result is a garden full of beauty and interest which is frequently open to the public.

At one point while this work was going on in the garden, Lindy Runcie showed what a determined and courageous lady she can be. It was during the worst episode of beastliness on the part of several tabloid newspapers, claiming the Runcie marriage was on the rocks, and insinuating scandal about Mrs Runcie herself which hurt her deeply.

It so happened that a group of nature conservation volunteers had just finished planting a "wild" area, with boggy pond, at the far end of the garden, and had called a press conference about it in Lambeth Palace. It was not the sort of event that would normally attract more than a few gardening or wild life correspondents. But when it was known that Mrs Runcie would be there the press turn-out was enormous, with all the gossip columnists and those from the tabloids who hoped that Mrs Runcie could be trapped into indiscretion. It was a pouring wet day, and the Archbishop's press secretary, the experienced Eve Keatley, expressed pleasant, if sardonic, surprise that they were all so interested in wild gardens. Mrs Runcie, she said, would be delighted to answer questions about the garden, but about nothing else.

At that point Lindy Runcie appeared in mackintosh and wellingtons, with a large umbrella, and invited them all to go with her to see the garden. In the hope of a story, they could not refuse; and the journalists, all in their suits and polished shoes, slipped and slithered through the ankle-deep mud, desperately trying to keep up with an insouciant lady who laughed and turned aside all their impertinent questions to chat learnedly about gardening. It is to the credit of the press that most of them reported next day their own discomfiture at being so well and truly led up the garden path.

Her fund-raising has not only been for the garden. During her time at Lambeth Palace she has raised over £400,000 for charities by her piano concerts. She has never believed herself a great pianist, but has talent and dedication, and, with the additional cachet as Archbishop's wife, has given pleasure to many audiences. She is also considered by her pupils to be a marvellous teacher with infectious enthusiasm. For all her outspoken lack of interest in much of her husband's work, she seems to have found real satisfaction in her role in recent years, and much to enjoy. Both the Runcies like good company, and mixing with lively, intelligent, people of affairs. There is no doubt that, when they retire to St Albans, both of them will be in demand for many years to come.

Has he been a great Archbishop? I believe so, in so far as our present world with its cynical values allows. For eleven years he has been steadfast under intense scrutiny. He has given himself utterly to his role as he saw it, and as he has recreated it. He has fought a good fight with all the blunted weapons available to him, and has been faithful to the Lord who, as he said confidently when he was appointed, "would see him through". What more could we have asked?

Bonds of Affection

ALASTAIR HAGGART
Primus of the Episcopal Church in Scotland
1977–85

I first met Robert Runcie at the first Anglican Primates' Meeting, at Ely in November 1979, when he was Archbishop Designate. Most of the Primates hadn't met him before, since his engagement in Anglican-Orthodox relations had meant that he had been present at the recent Lambeth Conference for only part of the time. So we were very curious – what sort of person was this new Primate? My memory is of one who smiled much and easily, who listened a lot, who was at ease with himself, and so enabled us to be at ease with him. In the years that followed we got to know him well. Here was someone who took his office seriously but not solemnly (he never "inhaled" the grandeur): who knew that all that any of us has through which to exercise our ministry, however exalted, is our own humanity. And this is what came over, too, in his Presidency of the British Council of Churches. He was courteous, genial, but competent too, because he did his homework and trusted others to brief him beforehand. Consulting others, sharing in their concerns, listening, but making up his own mind, sometimes, for some, a little slow in speaking his mind (as in the question of the ordination of women). Not that, at least in the BCC, he succeeded in commending episcopacy to the non-episcopalian churches! Shortly after his last assembly of the BCC, a Church of Scotland representative, reflecting on the ecumenical achievements of that body and speculating about the new ecumenical bodies emerging, saw no future for any suggestion that the Free Churches in England or the Church of Scotland should "take episcopacy into their system"; nor could he see any

acceptable compromise emerging. Indeed, the proposals for
the new bodies had as easy a passage as they had through
the various church assemblies, not least his own General
Assembly, precisely because they carried no commitment
to any proposals for reunion. We mustn't, he thought,
abandon faith nor, indeed, hope, far less charity, but we
had better eschew illusion. Perhaps the same realism applies
to our relations with Rome and Orthodoxy.

But within the Anglican Communion Robert Runcie
certainly commended not only himself but his
understanding of his office. Here again his humanity came
through. It was well expressed in *Bonds of Affection*, the title
given to the report of the sixth (1984) Meeting of the
Anglican Consultative Council. It is a phrase he has
frequently returned to, yet always aware not only of its
strength but also of its dangers, of an easy lapse into
romantic, candy-floss relationships, where no hard
questions are asked about truth, authority, and the proper
relationships between the Universal and the Provincial.
"Conflict", he said in his keynote address at Lambeth '88,
"is particularly painful because the glue that binds us
together is not so much juridical but personal, informal and
expressed in worship. . . . So we tend to shy away from
a conflict which has such disastrous potential. This is, of
course, a very serious mistake. . . . The creative use of
conflict is part of the process of discerning the truth. . . .
At the heart of our faith is a cross and not, as in some
religions, an eternal calm."

Theologically Robert Runcie has a strong ecclesial sense,
yet he could never, I think, be described as "a great
ecclesiastic" – and thank God for that! He was always
aware of the world out there, of humanity outside of, or on
the fringes of, the institutional church. There were "bonds
of affection" there, too. Sir Peter Medawar, in his
marvellous *Memoir of a Thinking Radish*, reflects on the
common habit of obituarists concluding their article with the
terse "He is survived by his wife and two children". Thus
a lifelong intimacy, influence and support is written off. But
Lindy Runcie is not to be so easily dismissed. A professional

in her own right, she has continued working as a performer and teacher of the piano, remaining very much her own woman, and not at all an appendage to the Archbishop. This is not the place for further comment, yet no piece on Robert Runcie's ministry can ignore the influence of his wife and family, which has helped to make *humanity* the mainspring of a great and generous Primacy. He once said in a debate in the General Synod: ''I would not want to belong to a Church which could not carry in its ranks those who have no taste for ecclesiastical debate, those who are not very religious, those who half believe and half don't believe. For many of these, the poetry and the music of the traditional liturgy can express for them the inexpressible since it does not have to pack its message into capsules of ideas. How could I deny such people a place, since I am very happily married to one of them?''

The Communicator

SIR BRIAN YOUNG
Director General, Independent Broadcasting Authority
1970–82

Headmasters have good jungle drums to tell them which preachers will command the attention of boys; and my first contact with Bob Runcie was when he came to Charterhouse to preach in 1958. He introduced us to Adoni-Bezek, a character whom none of us knew and who seemed to have stepped straight out of the pages of *Tamburlaine the Great*; he then carried us brilliantly from the vicious spiral of the Old Testament to the virtuous circle of the New. It was unforgettable.

When in the mid-seventies a new chairman of the Central Religious Advisory Council was needed, the IBA and BBC were percipient enough to ask for Runcie. There were slight hesitations in church circles (''The man isn't even in the Lords yet''), but we got our way. He chaired CRAC with great distinction, winning the regard of those around the table and the respect of those whom CRAC advised. One quibble only: seeing which way the wind of the Annan Committee was blowing, CRAC recommended that the seventy minutes of Closed Period, when both BBC and ITV showed religious programmes, should be no more. This I regretted; no doubt he was right as a reconciler, but (like others later who wanted one answer and received a middle way solution) I should have preferred him here to stand against the tide.

Of his time at Lambeth I have never had the same feeling. For me, what he said struck just the right note: his tone was always thoughtful and balanced, compassionate and (in season) funny. As a preacher, or after-dinner speaker, or teacher, he has been outstanding. I have never listened to him without pleasure and admiration – and it was easy to sense that others present had the same response.

Why has this not been more fully recognized by the man and woman in the pew? Some who do not know him tell me that his voice is unimpressive. Are they perhaps thinking of the caricature in *Spitting Image*, which reduces all victims to absurdity? Some have wanted him to take their own line on difficult issues (at whatever cost in alienation of others) and have been impatient with his moderation and sweet reason. The most unscrupulous of these have run monstrous campaigns in the press to belittle his quality and influence. He has preserved a most Christian silence in the face of these, helped (I trust) by awareness of how contemptible they appeared to any who knew him. His efficiency, his talents and his personality have given us over the past decade a communicator at Lambeth in a mode that lay unfulfilled for a generation when William Temple had died. He has truly been someone we could relate to, learn from, and love.

A Journey to the Inner City

ERIC JAMES
Director of Christian Action

I first met Robert Runcie more than thirty-five years ago. His personal gifts drew me to make my sacramental confessions to him while he was Dean of Trinity Hall, Cambridge, and I was Chaplain of Trinity College. That meant he came to know a good deal about me; but it also meant I knew much about him: his kindness, care and compassion, and his wisdom and judgement. In Cambridge Robert wisely married Lindy. She also became a close friend of mine. She was always the most vivacious companion. Her conversation invariably set the table alight, and no one ever looked more lovely on Ladies' Night in Trinity. I was particularly proud of her, I remember, in the Indian silk which Robert had brought back for her from his visit to the Cambridge Mission to Delhi. Robert seemed to like me to look after Lindy – and let him have an evening by himself, getting on with his work.

In February 1970 he was consecrated Bishop of St Albans and asked me whether I would like to join his staff as Canon Missioner. He wanted a personal pastor for the clergy. He underlined that what the clergy told me I would often not be able to tell him, and that he would respect that. He wanted particular attention paid to urban areas which, because they were in Hertfordshire and Bedfordshire, were apt to be underestimated. He wanted a "theological college without walls" to be pioneered, building on the experience of the Southwark Ordination Course. Preaching, not least in the Abbey and Cathedral Church, would be important. And the first things he wanted done were the reshaping of the leaflet for the annual diocesan week of prayer and an immediate report on the Diocesan Retreat House. These priorities indicated his own personality.

Robert was head and shoulders above all his staff. We held him in high regard and even reverence; but at the same time he was a close friend. To me, unmarried, Lindy and Robert and the children provided what seemed like a second home. There was hardly a day when I didn't pop into Abbey Gate House. It was a busy, happy home. Lindy's super-efficient running of the house – everyone piling into the washing up – was legendary. I loved her music-making and admired the way she maintained her own identity as a music teacher. On Christmas Day, after lunch, we would all go for a walk together. Often Robert would walk a little ahead of us, lost in his own thoughts.

My years as a kind of staff officer to Robert were entirely satisfying. We had relatively few disagreements, but the way he handled one of them remains powerfully in my memory. We had lunched together in London with a third party. On the way back in the train to St Albans, we battled over an area of disagreement. Uncharacteristically, he tried to win the argument with a clever, wounding, personal remark. I returned to my house hurt and dejected. An hour later, a letter fell through the letter box on to the mat. It was a hand-written apology. Not all bishops are capable of that.

When in 1979 Donald Coggan announced his resignation as Archbishop, I had no doubt who should succeed him; but the appointment of Robert Runcie looked unlikely. His contemporaries who had better academic qualifications were apt to make superior remarks about him, not recognizing the range of his gifts, his political skill, and the quality of leadership he had evinced in his diocese. One afternoon that July we were driving down the M1 back to St Albans, when he suddenly pulled into the side and stopped. With his hands still on the wheel, he said: "*If* I were asked to be Archbishop – I'm not saying I *have* been – how d'you think I should answer?" I said, immediately and unhesitatingly: "I've no doubt you should accept." He replied – clearly in some distress: "I can't. I can't. I'm a child." After a long silence, I said: "I could never respect you if you refused – how could you face other clergy and tell them they should go and serve in a particularly difficult post or do a difficult job?" He did not answer. Then we talked about Lindy. She would undoubtedly be distressed at leaving St Albans. "Of course," Robert said, "Lindy would be marvellous. I've no doubts about her." He eventually started the car again and told me he was going next day to see John Turnbull, Canon of Ripon, who had been his vicar when he was a curate, but who was then dying of cancer. When I saw Robert on his return from that visit I knew in a moment he had virtually made his decision. His inner uncertainty had been exorcised by the counsel of his erstwhile vicar; and he had "steadfastly set his face to go to Jerusalem". I am clear that this story should now at length be made public and set within the context of the history of discipleship. Jeremiah was told: "Say not, 'I am a child' " (1:7).

After the Brixton Riots of 1981 the Religious Affairs Correspondent of *The Times*, Clifford Longley, looked back at the 1960s and quoted from that period "incontrovertible statistics showing the progressive decline of Anglicanism as a pillar of national life: falling baptisms, falling confirmations, falling Easter communicants, falling marriages. And, judging from the quotes from the clergy, morale was falling too." But Longley went on to say: "Those same graphs and curves, asked in 1981 for their verdict on the Church of England, would have to reply that all manner of things are well." I was frankly amazed at such an analysis and wrote to the Editor of *The Times* saying: "There is one central and crucial area in which the prophets were tragically right, and which, astonishingly, Clifford Longley ignores: the relation of the Church of England to the vast inner-city areas of land. . . . I should myself like to see the immediate appointment of an Archbishop's Commission." I spelt out what its brief should be. That letter was published on 27th May 1981. I sent a copy to Robert Runcie and eventually, in April 1982, the Bishop of Stepney invited me, at the Archbishop's request, to meet with the informal group of urban bishops. But he warned me: "A preliminary sounding out suggests that quite a few of us do *not* think a Commission is the way forward. . . ." On 22nd June I argued my case and, to my surprise, the bishops agreed that proposals for a Commission should be drawn up. The draft which I had sent the Archbishop was revised and it was agreed that as Director of Christian Action I should be one of the people working full-time for the Commission. But the important thing was that the Commission should be, and be seen to be, broad-based: a representative cross-section, truly an Archbishop's Commission.

Before the end of June 1983, when the Commission was announced, much had to be done to secure a man of sufficient stature and experience to chair the Commission (Sir Richard O'Brien), to secure funding and a secretariat, to engage the membership, and to gain the approval of the Standing Committee of the General Synod and the support of the Roman Catholic and Free Churches. These were the terms of reference: "To examine the strengths, insights, problems and needs of the Church's life and mission in Urban Priority Areas and, as a result, to reflect on the challenge which God may be making to Church and Nation: and to make recommendations to appropriate bodies."

As a Commission we visited thirty-two towns and cities outside London and nine areas of London. After two years' work, our Report *Faith in the City* made thirty-eight recommendations to the Church and twenty-three to the Nation. Perhaps the most significant two sentences were: (1) "It is our considered view that the nation is confronted by a grave and fundamental injustice in the UPAs. The facts are officially recognized but the situation continues to deteriorate and requires urgent action. No adequate response is being made by government, nation or church." (2) "Somewhere along the road which we have travelled in the past two years each of us has faced a personal challenge to our lives and lifestyles: a call to change our thinking and action in such a way as to help us to stand more closely alongside the risen Christ with those who are poor and powerless. We have found faith in the city." What was also of huge significance was that the Report was unanimous.

The gifted secretary of the Commission, John Pearson, seconded for two years from the Department of the

Environment, had returned to the Civil Service before the launch of the report at the beginning of October 1985. So I found myself helping newspapers to prepare their articles. the *Sunday Times* phoned me on the Saturday afternoon apologetically to say that they weren't running the article we had prepared because Downing Street had told them that they could say a cabinet minister had commented that our report was a "Marxist" document. The Government's attempt to rubbish *Faith in the City* had begun before it was published. But it back-fired. The *Financial Times* said: "These are not revolutionary proposals from a Church of Militants, but sober suggestions mainly within the Government's own terms of reference. They deserve a thoughtful hearing."

An Archbishop's Officer for Urban Priority Areas was soon appointed, Prebendary Pat Dearnley, and an Advisory Group was set up with link officers in every diocese, to monitor and stimulate action. Christian Action enabled me to work virtually full-time alongside Pat Dearnley in the years that followed, and I have observed that issues of urban deprivation and regeneration are high on the agenda of national and local government. A crop of more local reports has sprung from the original *Faith in the City*. There has been a lively theological debate, and a debate as to whether a basically market-oriented approach can ultimately be sufficient, acceptable, or indeed successful as a means towards the agreed end of removing poverty and dependence. The Church Urban Fund has been set up, and dioceses are well on their way to raising their target of £18 million. Over two hundred projects have already been grant aided. The establishment of the Committee for Black Anglican Concerns and the Simon of Cyrene Theological Institute are not the least significant achievements of our report. But the "grave and fundamental injustice in the UPAs" undoubtedly remains – indeed, the situation continues to deteriorate.

Faith in the City meant far more to Robert Runcie than the setting up of an Archbishop's Commission, receiving its report and listening to debates in Synod and diocese. It has taken him into the inner-city of city upon city, and led him to visit pre-school play groups for Bangladeshi children in church halls; Bible study groups in high rise flats; the NUM area HQ in Barnsley, dockland Liverpool and Tyneside. It has taken him into the board rooms of prestigious companies – indeed, into the Bank of England itself – to meet with urbane executives, and confront and challenge them with the facts of the urban situation. No one can deny that *Faith in the City* is one of the most significant reports an Archbishop of Canterbury has ever provoked, and that he himself has untiringly given it his personal support. But it is important to remember that this has been only one of this Archbishop's initiatives. Because I came to live in Lambeth, I was able to see some of the pressures upon him and occasionally help by being one of his band of script writers. I cannot forget – as the friend and biographer of Bishop John Robinson – how he made time to visit John as he lay dying. John, born in the Precincts at Canterbury, was delighted to see him. He was particularly touched by Robert's idea that his theological library should furnish a small room, Cranmer's Parlour, in Lambeth Palace, close by the chapel, in which the Archbishop and his successors might "study to be quiet".

"God is friendship", said Aelred of Rievaulx. It has been good to have had an Archbishop of Canterbury who so clearly believed that.

In Canterbury

JOHN SIMPSON
Dean of Canterbury

As the work of the Archbishop has increased, so tension has grown between the different tasks, and since Geoffrey Fisher's time the loser has been the diocese of Canterbury. Robert Runcie has been the first Archbishop of modern times to recognize that to run a diocese is just not realistic for either the Archbishop or the diocese. But to admit this creates tensions of another sort. Integral to the Anglican notion of the Archbishop's Primacy has been the fact that he is a diocesan bishop on a par with his fellow bishops. For the Archbishop to divorce himself from Canterbury, and in particular its Cathedral, would be to cease to be Archbishop of Canterbury and become a presiding bishop on the model of the Presiding Bishop of the Episcopal Church of the United States of America, who has no diocese. Robert Runcie's way out of this dilemma may not have satisfied everyone, but it has preserved his contact with the people of Kent, whilst building on the Archbishop's historical relationship with the Cathedral. What is often forgotten is that he is an historian, a fact which has determined his attitude to Canterbury. But he has never succumbed to that antiquarian attitude which characterizes many historians.

From the outset of his archiepiscopate he abandoned most of the administration of the diocese to the Bishop of Dover – a radical solution to a practical problem, but one that in no way was allowed to sever personal links with his diocese. In the early years, he tried to be in Canterbury for half the weekends of the year, and on those occasions visited many parishes. Recently it has not been possible to maintain this record, but diocesan festivals and synods see him presiding, and he has taken his share of ordinations, confirmations, institutions and parish visits. And the nub of his relationship with Canterbury has been the Cathedral. His enthronement in the place of Becket's martyrdom, only a few hours after Oscar Romero, Archbishop of San Salvador, was martyred, made the most profound impression on him and gave rise to what could be called a "devotion" to the place. In the light of this, the most natural thing was for him to bring the Pope to Canterbury, and for them to light candles commemorating modern martyrs, and then together to pray where Thomas died. But also, the Patriarchs of Constantinople, Antioch and Alexandria have publicly accompanied him to Canterbury, and Desmond Tutu, and then all the bishops of the Anglican Communion, at the 1988 Lambeth Conference, which now should be called the Canterbury Conference!

He has amply fulfilled his "Cathedral" role – preaching at the greater festivals, confirming the choristers and the King's School pupils, and on all but one occasion presiding at the special Martyrdom ceremony on 29th December. No other Archbishop this century has asked for his own key to the Cathedral, and on occasions, of an evening, he has been discovered showing groups of his friends around "his" Cathedral. But perhaps most significant of all has been to come across the Archbishop kneeling unobserved at a Sunday 8 o'clock Prayer Book Communion Service, in the church where, every day, he has been prayed for in his ministry to the nation as well as to the Anglican Communion.

Perhaps only in the years to come will the full significance of his dedication of a Compass Rose, symbol of the worldwide Anglican Communion, in the Nave of Canterbury Cathedral, be fully appreciated. Robert Runcie has made Canterbury Cathedral, in fact, the centre of a worldwide Communion. Before his time, it was, in affection, such – now, that affection has been transformed into something tangible.

However, just as remarkable a feature of Robert Runcie's time at Canterbury has been the direct personal relationship which he has had with people, whether they have been church congregations, farmers at the Kent Show, old people for whom he has carved turkeys at Christmas, students at Kent University, the ordinary people of Canterbury, industrialists, businessmen, academics. The fact is that he has set out to mix with a whole cross-section of people, and by the interest he has shown in them and in their concerns. They have felt that he knows them, and, of course, as a result of this, their confidence in him has grown. During his time as Archbishop every Mayor of Canterbury has looked on him as a friend, and the warmth of his relationship with the city of Canterbury knew no bounds when, at the opening of the 1988 Lambeth Conference, he was privileged to announce that Canterbury's Mayor be henceforth "Lord Mayor". Engagements in the city have been a priority: never absent from Cricket Week, only occasionally absent from the Mayor's Ball, always at the people's carol singing in the Longmarket each Christmas Eve.

He has not made Canterbury his home – that has been Lambeth – but Canterbury has been where he has come to be refreshed, to gain different perspectives, and to imbibe tradition, which is, in fact, what is of most importance to him as a man. For there is a sense in which he has all the attitudes and feelings of a bishop in the Eastern Orthodox tradition. Understand that, and you have a clue to understanding Robert Runcie.

In Lambeth Palace

MARY CRYER
Bursar of the Palace 1981–90

When I arrived in Lambeth Palace in early January 1981 change was in the air. The Chief of Staff, Ross Hook, formerly Bishop of Bradford, was already installed in that new post, and Terry Waite had joined the team a month or so before me. The new Archbishop had brought his Domestic Chaplain and Personal Secretary with him from St Albans, and the office moved abruptly from a rather antiquated look to an extremely up-to-date one, with all the latest office furniture, including word processors, dictating machines, photocopiers, Telex and Fax machines and answerphones. The Secretariat was to expand considerably, having a Press Office based at Lambeth itself rather than across the river at Church House; and as Dr Runcie intended to pursue and speak on many subjects, it was necessary to engage researchers and advisers to help him prepare speeches. In 1984 Bishop Ronald Gordon arrived from Portsmouth to head this enlarged staff and to be "Bishop at Lambeth" in succession to Bishop Hook, who retired. It says much about the importance of the developing work, and about Dr Runcie's power of persuasion, that these two diocesan bishops were willing to leave their own independent spheres of work.

The Archbishop had gone on record in the early days as hoping to open the Palace regularly to the public, in much the same way as happens in National Trust properties. I was in on the preliminary discussions, but it was soon realized that his dream would be impracticable. Nowadays the Church Commissioners own the Palace and pay all the maintenance bills – as they do in all the other bishops' houses in the Church of England. The building was not in a good state of decoration, and when it was seen that it was to be used much more a scheme to put this right was begun which was to last for many years. By the time the staterooms and corridors were redecorated, the thought of hordes of people passing through the rooms on a daily basis, wearing out new carpets and disturbing those at work, gave cause for concern. So a compromise was reached: it was agreed that it was possible for church, professional and charitable bodies to use the lovely rooms for fund-raising events, award ceremonies, receptions, book launches and conferences when the diary allowed it, and weekly conducted tours were given to small groups. It helped a great deal that Mrs Runcie was a talented musician and was able to give recitals for charities of her choice. Lambeth Palace was to become much sought after for events of all kinds. Never before had so many people admired the ancient parts of the building which date back to the thirteenth century, or gazed at the portraits of earlier Primates. Bit by bit each part of the building was restored to its former glory, culminating in a major undertaking instigated by Dr Runcie when the chapel was restored so that it looks much as it did after Archbishop Laud's changes in the seventeenth century. This chapel had been badly damaged during air raids on London, and the restoration done shortly after the war reflected the austerities of those difficult days and did not lend itself to present-day worship.

Dr Runcie took an active interest in what was being done in this restoration programme, though his busy diary gave him little time for leisure to enjoy his days at Lambeth properly. He was often seen only on the point of departure or return. We often feared for his health. He was stronger than he looked, but even so he was often at the point of exhaustion with all that was expected of him. Yet he had time to deal with individuals who came into his orbit. A tall, lean man, with a gentle manner and sad eyes, he has immense charm and the ability to speak to people easily at every level. I often took people round on a conducted tour, and would make it clear at the start that they were unlikely to see the Archbishop himself. Sometimes, however, he would appear at the top of the staircase coming out of his study on his way out to an engagement, or he would be returning home with the chauffeur carrying his luggage. Often his heart must have sunk into his boots as he saw us standing there expectantly, when he wanted nothing better than to retreat into his study and be quiet for a moment. But he would smile warmly and approach the party, asking who they were and where they came from, and would immediately launch into a conversation with the nearest people, showing a knowledge and interest in their home town or society. Frequently a group from the States was visiting the Old Country. He would make their tour of Lambeth the high spot of their visit to England. Quite often someone would say afterwards that they thought the Archbishop came over on TV as rather indecisive, and were not at all impressed with him. But after such a chance encounter the same person was charmed by him and walked out of the front door in quite a different frame of mind! He was extremely good with children too, and it was not all that rare for him to stop his car as it drove out of the gate on his way to an afternoon function, so that he could get out and speak to the teachers and children.

Although the stresses of the job often got to him Robert Runcie was tough and coped with them very well. He found little time for exercise, except for walking when he was at the Old Palace at Canterbury or some swimming at a nearby pool in London. The gardens at Lambeth are extensive and Mrs Runcie has raised the money to undertake a massive restoration programme of replanning and replanting. Dr Runcie has watched this going on mainly from his study window, as he has had little time to spare for such pleasures, but it is in the garden that I shall always remember him. I carry a picture of him one wintry afternoon after a session in the General Synod, returning tired and grey faced from the noise and heat of the chamber, walking round the perimeter of the garden, with hunched shoulders under his overcoat, a lonely figure bearing the burden of high office with charm and dignity.

With Terry Waite

EVE KEATLEY

Archbishop's Press Secretary 1983–90

From the time of Terry Waite's capture in Beirut in 1987 myths have grown and multiplied which obscure the real man. Yet the story of his appointment by Archbishop Runcie as his Secretary for Anglican Communion Affairs is perfectly straightforward. In 1979, at the end of Archbishop Coggan's time, the first meeting of the Primates of the Anglican Communion was held in England, at Ely. This meeting produced an explosion of business and a recognition that the needs of the Anglican Communion would make growing demands on any Archbishop of Canterbury. It was an area in which the Archbishop would benefit from a specialist member of staff.

One of Runcie's great strengths has been to search out dedicated staff and to delegate. He heard of Terry Waite from Bishop Oliver Tomkins, retired Bishop of Bristol, who had known Terry both in his Church Army days and when he was working in Africa for the Uganda Lay Training Board. Runcie is bored by plodding bureaucrats, but when he met Terry he saw dynamism, good humour, an easy knowledge of world travel, imagination and even vision. During a prodigious number of overseas visits Terry could always make the Archbishop laugh and they became good friends.

So how did Terry find himself in the tragic circumstances which overtook him in January 1987? The answer lies partly in his own character and also in a series of extraordinary events.

He has a quality of derring-do; it is not for nothing that his favourite remembered childhood reading is the *Boy's Own Paper*. He also has a north-country independence which encourages him to think against conventional wisdom and to follow a personal hunch. His first venture in Iran in 1980–81 showed all his best qualities. Three British Anglican missionaries and four Iranian Anglican clergy had been imprisoned there following the Iranian revolution of 1979. The Foreign Office in London were trying to deal with the Iranian Foreign Ministry on behalf of the British hostages but had come to a dead end. The exiled Bishop of Iran asked for help and the Archbishop thought that Terry Waite might be a suitable emissary. He was absolutely right. Terry was excited by the challenge and his sense of drama and dash came to the fore.

He emerged from the plane in Tehran wearing a borrowed cassock, and went to the church belonging to the small Anglican community. He was leading Evensong from his beloved Book of Common Prayer when shooting was heard outside, and a group of Revolutionary Guards armed with sten guns entered the church. Their leader was an idealistic young revolutionary of twenty-four who, by incredible luck, turned out to be a former private secretary to the prime minister. Terry established a rapport with this young man and, building on this fragile contact, was eventually able to meet and talk with powerful figures. His highly personal diplomacy, and his undoubtedly sincere commitment to the imprisoned missionaries, succeeded where more formal methods had failed. He was able to persuade the authorities that the missionaries were not malevolent conspirators.

Terry's triumphant return to England with the three Anglican missionaries was carried off with bravura. The media were captivated. The general public saw him as a sanctified Scarlet Pimpernel. From then on, his post was full of poignant, usually unanswerable, requests to rescue the lost and the imprisoned. Terry has a warm heart and he found these requests deeply upsetting. Meanwhile, the media continued to suggest that he could do anything, and it was hard to resist this challenge to his courage.

In 1984–85 Terry Waite carried out a second successful mission, this time in Libya, and brought back four British hostages held by Colonel Gaddafi. Terry certainly did a lot of hard work on the case, but in hindsight it is difficult to know how much he was used by Colonel Gaddafi, who undoubtedly wanted publicity.

From then on, an epic inevitability swept Terry Waite into an international game more subtle and devious than he appreciated. The predictable outcome was his own capture. Critics have said, understandably, that Archbishop Runcie should not have allowed Terry Waite to take that last journey back to Beirut in January 1987, or indeed that he should have stopped the whole venture sooner. But Runcie is a man who gives his staff responsibility and then stands by them. Terry had become so passionately and personally involved in the fate of the hostages held in Beirut that he was like a man possessed. He would have suffered agonies of self-reproach if he had not made the final attempt. He also – and this is where the psychology of the *Boy's Own Paper* comes in again – was determined to prove his innocence of any secret deals, by walking unarmed into danger. Runcie would have had to have been absolutely ruthless to stop him. In hindsight, of course Terry Waite should not have made that last journey to Beirut. Living with that knowledge undoubtedly changed the character of the Archbishop's last years in office and made him seem a sadder and an older man.

Canterbury and York

JOHN HABGOOD
Archbishop of York

The advent of Synodical government in 1970, and the steady erosion of the role and significance of the two Convocations of the clergy, has had as one of its consequences the transformation of the official relationship between the two archbishops. As joint Presidents of the General Synod they share responsibilities as national church leaders, as well as in more mundane matters such as ordering Synodical business and making a large number of appointments. Provincial autonomy is now virtually restricted to the overall pastoral care and discipline of the clergy, and the consecration of bishops. These structural changes have provided an impetus for closer personal as well as closer working relationships between the two archbishops, and when these work well, as I believe they have during the Runcie years, they make the task of being an archbishop much less isolated and exposed. And this is of value to the Church as well as to the archbishops themselves.

The Archbishop of Canterbury must inevitably take the limelight. He is rightly perceived as the main national leader of the Church of England. His position in London, his role at the centre of affairs, both ecclesiastical and national, the interest of the media in always going for the top man, make him the major focus of interest and the Church's prime spokesman. The Archbishop of York, as I see it, should not try to ape him in this role, but should use his opportunities to engage in more specialist activities, and to work out in a more detailed way some of those commitments for which no Archbishop of Canterbury could possibly have sufficient time. In the British Council of Churches, for instance, the Archbishop of Canterbury has been *ex officio* President, has led the Assembly on major occasions and, with other church leaders, has been seen and acknowledged as its public face. My own role in the British Council of Churches, as a member of its Executive Committee and, latterly, as Chairman of the Inter-Church Process, has had a much lower profile, but I believe has been of value in generating confidence and in expressing the Church of England's commitment to ecumenism on a day-to-day basis.

A similar division of responsibility has been possible at the international level. The Archbishop of Canterbury's role as the focus of unity for the Anglican Communion is unique to his office. An Archbishop of York could not substitute for him in this role although, like any other bishop, he must sometimes travel overseas as part of that interchange between bishops which communion entails and requires. The fact that I have been a member of the Central Committee of the World Council of Churches, and Chairman of one of its sub-units, has given me a major alternative sphere for international work, and has meant that the two of us, while both travelling widely, have tended to meet different constituencies.

The amount of committee work entailed in leading a national church is enormously heavy. Here again, there are opportunities for the two archbishops to share, not perhaps exploited as fully as they might have been, but nevertheless sufficient to make joint leadership a reality. In the House of Bishops, for example, it has been my task to chair the Standing Committee of the House, which prepares its agenda and makes decisions on matters which are not judged as requiring a decision of the whole House. Chairmanship of the Standing Committee of the General Synod is also sometimes shared, and the two archbishops frequently consult on difficult issues. In the General Synod itself there can also be distinctive roles, and there remains an explicit recognition of the continued existence of two Provinces in the fact that, when the Synod meets in York, the Archbishop of York takes the chair. In Synod debates, Bob Runcie's style has usually been to make a magisterial statement near the beginning of a debate. My own role in debates has more often been to speak fairly late, and to try to pick up some of the points already made. These differences partly reflect differences in speaking style and my own willingness to speak more or less off the cuff, but I think they also reflect the need for two different functions. Some archiepiscopal utterances need to be comprehensive and eirenic; others can afford to be more controversial and direct.

The constructive use of such differences can only be effective if relationships are good. For me, one of the happier features of the past seven years is that this has been so. The relationship between us has been warm, friendly and supportive. Only those who do not know us can describe us as two of a kind, despite the fact that we have Westcott House and Cuddesdon in common. The truth is that we are two very different people who have enjoyed working together, and this has been a source of strength through a time when the leadership of the Church has been under huge pressures and, sometimes, the object of extraordinary attacks. Our staffs also have maintained close contact, and there has been a particularly strong and fruitful liaison between our two Press Officers. A consequence of this co-operation is that we have not felt it necessary to duplicate public statements. Indeed there have been important occasions when one of us has spoken on a particular issue, while the other has deliberately kept silent.

One of Bob Runcie's great strengths has been his readiness to consult with others. That this should have been interpreted by some as evidence of weakness represents an extraordinary failure to understand what leadership actually entails. It has been precisely his willingness to listen, to learn and to share, which has won him such affection among those close to him, and I count myself lucky to have worked with a colleague who made partnership so easy.

An Impossible Job?

JOHN WITHERIDGE
Chaplain to the Archbishop 1984–87

The archiepiscopal vocation which Robert Runcie has followed since 1980, and which he will bequeath to his successor, is (as it stands) an impossible one. It has been so for at least a hundred years. "It is a very remarkable office to which I have been called", confided Edward Benson exactly a century ago; "one which ought to and really does crush one to the earth when one thinks of its responsibilities." Randall Davidson said it was "an impossible job for one man", and Cosmo Lang complained that his workload was "incredible, indefensible and inevitable". William Temple did "the work of a Prime Minister with the staff of a Head Master", and Geoffrey Fisher believed "that the first requisite of an Archbishop is to be as strong as a horse".

One measure of Dr Runcie's achievement as Archbishop of Canterbury has been his constant determination to devote himself to all aspects of his office. To do so he has had to enlarge his staff at Lambeth and Canterbury, and to delegate much more than his predecessors. Until 1980 the essential staff at Lambeth Palace consisted of three principals – a Senior Chaplain, a Lay Assistant and a Domestic Chaplain. In the last ten years this has been expanded into a much more realistic and effective private office. This is headed by a former diocesan bishop who relieves the Archbishop directly of a number of responsibilities. The Domestic Chaplain, who used to carry responsibility especially for the diocese, has been replaced by a Chaplain in Canterbury. The Chaplain at Lambeth acts now as a kind of private secretary, and has inherited a mixture of tasks from the old Senior and Domestic Chaplains. In addition, there are four specialist

Secretaries — for Public Affairs, Ecumenical Affairs, Anglican Communion Affairs, and Broadcasting, Press and Communications. There are also now an Administrative Secretary and a Research Officer.

All these may be sensible, perhaps inevitable, developments, but whether they have generated more work than they have saved is debatable. Certainly, the pressure of work that a man as scrupulously conscientious as Robert Runcie has still felt himself bound to shoulder has been immense and unrelenting. Frankly, another man of his age, but not blessed with his admirable constitution and stamina, might not have survived. The Church really must take a long, hard look at the office. It must ask itself: ''What is it realistic of us to expect of the Archbishop of Canterbury?'' Without such a review of the role, the next Archbishop will, I am afraid, find himself enslaved to the same intolerable burdens, and the same criticisms and vilifications from the disappointed, which Dr Runcie has had to bear.

At present the Archbishop is the bishop of a diocese with the pastoral care of over two hundred and fifty parishes. Of course much of the day-to-day work can be delegated to suffragans, but the Archbishop is the bishop in more than name. He must get to know his parishes and his clergy. He needs to chair his synod and his staff meetings. He must confirm and ordain. He is expected to celebrate and preach in his cathedral, especially at the great Christian festivals. It has been argued that an Archbishop would be better off without this load, but I am not convinced. I certainly think that time spent on diocesan affairs must be strictly limited, but an Archbishop without a diocese would not only be a very un-Anglican figure, but he would soon become isolated from the day-to-day life of the Church. He would be in danger of becoming even more of an ecclesiastical bureaucrat than he is already. Dr Runcie is fond of quoting Chesterton's maxim that ''nothing is real unless it is local''.

Second, despite the independent authority of every diocesan bishop, the Archbishop, as Primate of All England, has prime responsibility for the Church of England. In today's bureaucratic Church this means a month of the

Archbishop's year is taken up with the business of General Synod and its Boards and Committees. I am no enthusiast for the Synod. I am not convinced that such a system is either inevitable or advisable. As the Archbishop's Chaplain I used to have to sit through hours of fruitless debate, and cut a path through reams of superfluous paper. I was often reminded of Bismarck's celebrated conviction that "the great questions of our time will not be settled by resolutions and majority votes". Bismarck, of course, offered "blood and iron" instead, and I am not suggesting either of these as an alternative. But ours is an episcopal Church, and it does seem to me that matters especially of worship, belief and order should be decided by the House of Bishops under the chairmanship of the Archbishop of Canterbury. This would not only be healthier for the Church of England, but it would certainly make the Archbishop's task more manageable and congenial.

Third, the Archbishop of Canterbury presides over the worldwide Anglican Communion which has some sixty-five million members. Robert Runcie has travelled far more than any of his predecessors and (in his early years with considerable assistance from Terry Waite) he has made ministry to the Communion a priority. Visits to various parts of the Communion in turn can take two months of each year. They can be moving and rewarding. But they are often made gruelling and exhausting by constant travel, punishing climates and local conditions, the remorseless round of speeches and sermons, receptions and meetings – and with the support of a staff of just two or three. The Lambeth Conference in 1988 clearly demonstrated that now the Archbishop of Canterbury is really the one element that can hold this diverse federation of Churches together, and give it some sense of identity and shared history. But I wonder whether this is not too much to expect of an Archbishop? If the future of the Communion depends on the efforts of one man, then perhaps it is time to allow complete independence and autonomy to the various provinces.

Fourth, the Archbishop has a strategic ecumenical responsibility as the representative of a significant slice of the Christian community, and one with sympathies towards both Catholics and Protestants. That means more travel abroad, and at home it means more committees, conferences and councils. All this is important work, and it is not for the Church of England to do or not to do anything to impede the Gospel imperative of unity. But I do wonder whether more of the Archbishop's representative role could not be shared, especially with York or London.

Last, but not least important, the Archbishop of Canterbury still has a unique role to play in our national life. This extends far beyond his duties in the House of Lords, and his influence in the country is out of all proportion to the number of churchgoers. He is looked upon, not least by the media, as the voice of Christianity in England. He is expected to pronounce on every moral or social issue, to articulate the nation's grief at times of mourning or disaster, and to officiate at occasions of national unity and celebration, such as a royal wedding, or, supremely, a coronation. At a time when the Church of England is in retreat from its traditional role as a national, established Church, it is perhaps this area of the Archbishop's responsibilities which is least secure. Changes must be made but, in my view, economies here would prove deeply damaging to the Church's mission and ministry to this country. When the opinions of even a diocesan bishop are of little interest to the public (unless they happen to smack of heresy or politics), the Archbishop of Canterbury's is really the only Christian voice which people are willing, and expect, to hear. For that voice to be withdrawn from the national stage could leave us disturbingly short of Christian conscience and confidence.

Twenty years ago Edward Carpenter concluded his history of *Cantuar: the Archbishops in their Office* with these prophetic words: ''It would be tragic indeed if, 'at such a time as this', he were to shrink into a merely local figure presiding over an inward-looking community preoccupied with its own life. *Dei gratia* this need not happen. The present is a call to wisdom, to integrity, and to greatness.''

Among the Archbishops

PAUL A. WELSBY

Canon Welsby, who was Chairman of the House of Clergy in the General Synod 1973–80, wrote *A History of the Church of England 1945–80* (Oxford University Press, 1984)

So often in the history of the Church God raises up the right person to match the time. In spite of the desolation experienced at the death of William Temple in 1944, no one could have led the Church of England through the mighty task of administrative and financial reorganization in the postwar period better than Geoffrey Fisher. Amid the theological upheavals and the spiritual questionings of the sixties, Michael Ramsey possessed the theological equipment and spiritual gifts required for leadership at such a time. Donald Coggan, a man firm in his faith and full of hope, was able to strengthen morale and to enable the Church to recover its nerve and confidence in the seventies. Robert Runcie was called to the Primacy at a time when once again the Church was to be beset with controversy but with a much greater polarization of opinion than was apparent in the sixties. The qualities he possessed were those needed by an archbishop at this time – the absence of a rigid theology or a judgemental temperament, a refusal to oversimplify issues and a determination to consider and attempt to understand a question from every point of view before making a pronouncement. On his appointment he signalled his determination not to become a "platitude machine". In that he has succeeded.

He has clearly seen his main task to be to hold together the various emphases which exist both within the Church of England and within the Anglican Communion. This has given rise to the criticism that he has failed to give the lead which is expected of an archbishop. But the Archbishop of

Canterbury is neither an autocrat nor a pope. He has to represent the Church of which he is Primate, and the Church of England is well known to be a body which tolerates a wide variety of views and interpretations. Since 1970 the General Synod has provided a forum for open and frequent argument and, with that, a challenge which previous archbishops did not have to face and in many cases can scarcely be imagined as facing. Partly through his influence over the Synod Runcie has kept extremists and fundamentalists in check, and has stood firm against all attempts to narrow the basis of the Church of England – or the Anglican Communion.

When the Bishop of Durham aroused the controversy over his views about the Resurrection and the Virgin Birth, Runcie did not descend on him like a ton of bricks as Fisher did on Barnes of Birmingham in 1947, nor did he display the initially unsympathetic over-reaction of Ramsey to Bishop John Robinson's *Honest to God* in 1963. Instead, he affirmed his own belief in the historicity of the Resurrection and led the House of Bishops in a discussion which begat the eirenic report, *The Nature of Christian Belief*. So that the crisis, too, was defused.

The notorious Crockford's Preface recalled the phrase that he "is usually to be found nailing his colours to the fence". This is quite untrue, for he has expressed his strong convictions quite as firmly as his predecessors, whether in his sermon after the Falklands War or on government economic policy, homosexuality, the Bomb or the Resurrection. Unlike Coggan, who tended to see social problems in terms of a failure in personal religion, Runcie sees them as in great part the consequence of the structure of society itself, and he has not been afraid to voice the needs of minorities and the disadvantaged. His whole-hearted support of *Faith in the City* shows that he is not reluctant to express opinions which are unpopular with the government. When he retires he will leave the Church more relevant to society, while the existence of the Church Urban Fund will be one of the lasting achievements of his Primacy.

Another of the highlights of his Primacy was the visit of

the Pope to Canterbury in 1982, the signing of the Common Declaration and the establishment of ARCIC II. His attitude toward the ordination of women illustrates again the nature of his desire for unity for, although he accepts that such ordination will come, he continues to plead for "gradualism" and consensus because of the possibility of schism within the Church and strained relations with Rome and Orthodoxy. On the other hand, he has had less influence than his three predecessors on relations with the Free Churches. He felt unable to give unqualified leadership over the Covenant Proposals, and in the crucial debate in the General Synod in 1982 his speech in favour was somewhat lukewarm.

While Runcie is a man of deep and disciplined spirituality, there is a "holy worldliness" about him which both his two predecessors lacked. He enjoys the good things of life and is interested in a variety of secular matters. It is hard to imagine Michael Ramsey or Donald Coggan keeping pigs! Again, unlike his two predecessors, he has a more realistic outlook on the world, and because of his wide-ranging interests, his innate friendliness, his charm of manner and his conversational gifts, he probably reaches the "ordinary" person more easily than did his immediate predecessors. Because of this we have had in Robert Runcie the most effective communicator of any Archbishop of Canterbury this century, with the possible exception of William Temple.

Ever since the war there had been criticism of the lack of an adequate staff at Lambeth to support the archbishop in his crushing burden of administration. Fisher seemed to cope, but he was exceptional. Owen Chadwick has shown that there were considerable administrative problems at Lambeth in Ramsey's day, and the lack of staff well-nigh overwhelmed Coggan. Early in his Primacy Runcie established an able and realistic secretariat at Lambeth and delegated most of his diocesan functions. Peter Cornwell has written that "as he tries to make Lambeth more efficient, while always appreciating the catholic wisdom of Michael Ramsey and the apostolic simplicity of Donald Coggan, he has come to have a special admiration for the administrative contribution of Geoffrey Fisher." His reliance on his staff is, however, a reminder that Runcie is no one-man band. Indeed he consults far more often and far more widely than any of his predecessors, and has a far greater range of personal contacts, both clerical and lay, than they had. He has used other people's drafts when preparing speeches in a manner which would have been foreign to Lang, Temple, Fisher, Ramsey or Coggan, but which he has made his own and which has enabled him to speak on a variety of subjects, for a variety of audiences, which would otherwise have been impossible.

He has sometimes been compared with Randall Davidson, Archbishop of Canterbury from 1903 to 1928. That comparison holds insofar as, like Davidson, he has been concerned to hold together the Church of England by weighing all points of view, refusing to capitulate to extremists, and being shrewd enough to know when to speak and when not. Like Davidson he has desired to preserve both the unity of the Church of England and the liberty of the theologians, but it is doubtful whether Davidson really understood the theologians, whereas Runcie does. Runcie's concern for the public life of the nation and his desire to reduce tension in Church and nation are also reminiscent of Davidson. So far, so good, but Davidson was non-intellectual, safe, boring, distrustful of drama and – as William Temple said of him – "the essence of kindness and sanity – without a glimmer of inspiration". Robert Runcie is certainly kind and sane but, unlike Davidson, he is intellectual, is colourful rather than boring, does not mind taking risks, is not averse to a bit of drama, and to those who know him, listen to him and work with him, he is a source of considerable inspiration. It will not be surprising if history judges him to be the most "all round" archbishop this century has seen.

2

AMID
CONTROVERSIES

In a Secular Society

GRAHAM HOWES
Fellow of Trinity Hall, Cambridge

Most twentieth-century Primates would identify at least two dimensions to a secular society. One is a "secularizing" process whereby, as the Oxford sociologist Bryan Wilson describes it, "religious thinking, practice and institutions lose social significance". Here, as Christianity becomes more marginal, its beliefs become increasingly personal and private. The Church of England, the State Church, suffers numerical decline, and operates mainly as a licensed sect, giving spiritual tone to national events and sanctifying the *rites de passage* of an increasingly materialistic majority. The second dimension is a society where – to quote Robert Runcie – "the language of secular morality is going through terminal disorder" and there is real uncertainty as to what moral absolutes to affirm in a morally relative world. Sexual, social and economic morals are confused, and the tensions between care and control, individualism and collectivism remain unresolved. Simultaneously, the high-profile issues – poverty, housing, nuclear weapons, AIDS, urban decay, crime – proliferate and demand both Christian presence and Christian prophecy. The Church is expected to respond, by word if not necessarily by deed.

For any Primate, such a dual scenario – of institutional decline and escalating pastoral concerns – is about as tempting as taking over the wheel of the Titanic. For Robert Runcie the task has been exceptionally daunting. All too visibly, tensions within the Church itself, within secular society, and between Church and society (not merely Church and State) have been played out, personalized and projected on to both the man and the office he holds. He leads a church which, in his own phrase, "is clinging on by its fingertips'', where ''a religious leader cannot, nowadays, command; he can only warn. He cannot control; he can only encourage''. It is all too easy to accuse him of failing to turn back the rising the tide of secularism or to lead people back to an ideal – and idealized – world of simple faith and regular practice.

Outside the Church itself the conflicts produced by secularization are even more acute, and perhaps more deepseated. In a society which has become uncertain as to whether the Established Church *ought* to occupy the high moral ground (or at least the middle), an archbishop can enjoy a high public profile (a kind of Chaplain to the Nation) without being able to exert much more influence. He can answer the call for an authoritative Christian voice to address the nation, but this does not guarantee him a national hearing. And this archbishop has been caught up in a massive cultural sea change. It has been difficult to sustain, let alone proclaim, his own inherently liberal values of tolerance, fraternity, interdependence, compassion and consensus in a climate of conviction politics, possessive individualism and a debased version of the Protestant ethic – a world where, as he puts it, ''social justice and social equality are less important than a dynamic market economy''. Above all, in responding to the secular, he is impaled upon a twentieth-century version of Cardinal Morton's fork. If he is outspoken or interventionist on social issues he is being political. If, like William Temple, he affirms ''the Church is concerned with principles and not policy'' he is being vague and unworldly and failing to give firm leadership. (If he cites R.H. Tawney as to how ''spiritual activity is of prime importance'' he can be labelled as unworldly or guilty of spiritual pride.)

When the ecclesiastical history of the 1980s (or his own ''official'' biography) comes to be written I am quite sure that he will bear close comparison with William Temple in his response to the secular world, and in the way he has left his Church stronger and more relevant to that world. The reasons for this are of course complex. Institutionally – especially through the Lords and the General Synod –

he has explicitly identified the Church of England with such overtly secular issues as prison reform, racism, housing, poverty and the health service. *Faith in the City* was but the highest point in a more sustained process of engagement. Individually, he has the enviable capacity to confront a secular issue, strip it first of all jargon or pretension, and then identify its Christian imperatives with clarity, yet without over-simplification. But at the same time he also perceives the secular world primarily in terms of relationships rather than structures. To accompany him to a school or police headquarters or hospice or office block is a very illuminating experience. He has an extraordinary capacity for making those he meets, however humble (indeed, especially the humble), feel unique, cherished, listened to, with their mundane occupation turned temporarily into a sacred vocation, worthy in God's sight. He makes them feel affirmed – as indeed they are – as individuals rather than mere employees.

Yet beneath the sharp mind and the human touch are some powerful theological insights. These too he brings to secular debate. His approach is always – to borrow the language of his own Oxford philosophical background – intuitive rather than formally rational. Four motifs are regularly invoked. He feels both the Gospel imperative and the moral force behind what T.S. Eliot called ''well-being in community''. For him ''community'' is ''an essential part of the Christian vision which sees human beings very much as co-workers or partners with God in the work of Creation''. Hence he remains anxious that this is being gradually weakened by current belief ''in a crude individualism, excessive collectivism – or purely economic objectives''. Secondly, he believes in a Social Gospel, where ''people often find spiritual succour through a church that shows *secular* compassion''. Hence, Christians must speak up for the poor and the powerless both in body and spirit. Sometimes, he has said, ''one might think that in the present climate the demonstration of compassion for the weakest of our society is some dangerous and subversive instinct. It is not. The protection of the weak is the first charge on a government's responsibilities.'' And a Church's too, he would no doubt argue.

Thirdly, he recognizes how the holy and the transcendent can be disclosed in the ostensibly secular, as part of a Christian vision of creation. He can find this in an AIDS hospice, a divided mining community, and the tramps sleeping rough in the cold of a London winter, as well as among the principalities and powers. Here he discloses not so much unworldliness, but clear faith. To bring such theological resources to bear upon the secular are highly necessary in a contemporary Primate, and Robert Runcie has never hesitated to deploy them. They are doubly necessary when the Church – and its leader – is the object of such unprecedented, and unprincipled media flak, when government policies often seem to embody all that is demonic and destructive in a secular culture, and when to speak of common good and the Christian ethic is to invite accusations of ecclesiastical Luddism, Marxist theology or gross sentimentality.

It is also necessary within a Church of England which itself seems tempted to embrace rather than transcend secular culture, to become a kind of ecclesiastical IBM where professionalism counts for more than the priesthood and prophecy, and where the Filofax is mightier than the Gospel. Robert Runcie is impatient, indeed contemptuous, of not only what he calls ''salvation by bureaucracy'' but of such a facile accommodation to the secular. He is right. R.H. Tawney once said that ''a Church will cease to count as soon as it ceases to think''. In a secular world Robert Runcie has greatly helped the Church of England – indeed all Christians – to continue to do both.

In Mrs Thatcher's Britain

HUGH MONTEFIORE

Dr Montefiore was Chairman of the Church of England's Board
for Social Responsibility, 1983–87

When Robert Runcie became Archbishop of Canterbury it
was inevitable that he should comment on national affairs.
Every Primate of All England is bound to be involved in such
matters. Some, such as Becket, Cranmer or Laud, have paid
for this with the forfeit of their lives. Others have
unwaveringly supported the powers that be. Among the
Primates of the last two centuries, most, like Randall
Davidson, have steered a middle course. When challenged
in 1907, he gave an impressive list of matters in which he
had intervened over the previous twelve years. But not
everyone approved. Hard things were said about him, just
as they are said now about Runcie. Since Davidson's time,
national involvement has been able to increase, helped
recently by Runcie's success in establishing a personal staff
at Lambeth and by his talent for enlisting the help of
Christians knowledgeable in various aspects of our national
life. This has enabled him to make informed contributions
on a wider range of subjects than any of his predecessors,
as his published collections show.

Before Runcie came to Canterbury, he had not taken a
public stand over social and national affairs. Certainly he
had spoken out about remarriage after divorce, but only in
the ecclesiastical context of remarriage in church. He had
not sought the centre stage. He was known to be a reconciler
by temperament. He did not always find it easy to take sides.
His interventions could therefore be expected to be careful
and prudent. It is really most remarkable that he is generally
perceived as being more inflammatory in his utterances on
national affairs than any of his more recent predecessors.

I believe that when the record is properly examined he will be seen to be as judicious as any, with the possible exception of Archbishop Davidson. This is not intended as a criticism. I recognize (albeit with some reluctance) that it is prerequisite for an Archbishop of Canterbury, when commenting on national affairs, above all to show prudence, which is after all one of the four cardinal virtues.

With hindsight it seems an augury of things to come that Budget Day was announced for the date already fixed for Runcie's enthronement, thus preventing MPs being present. This clash was avoided when Budget Day was changed, but controversy was already looming over the ethics of homosexuality. In an inconclusive General Synod debate on the subject, Runcie said that he "inclined to the view" that it was neither a sin nor a sickness but a handicap ("inclined to the view" is typical of his caution). Homosexuals soon began to suffer adverse publicity because of AIDS, and some church people started an increasingly virulent campaign against them, which was reflected in some of the mass media (encapsulated by the *Sun* headline "Poofs in the Pulpit"). Runcie was unfairly accused of being soft, because he would not make sweeping condemnatory pronouncements on the matter. It must be remembered, however, that Archbishop Ramsey before him also drew on himself public rebuke for his views in this area. He supported the Wolfenden Report which proposed that homosexual practice between consenting adults in private should cease to be a criminal offence. He was savaged in the House of Lords, and even accused of contributing to pornography through the pages of Hansard! Runcie was more prudent here than Ramsey.

Already too in 1981 Runcie was expressing his concern for the homeless, who increased in number throughout his archiepiscopate, partly as a result of government measures and changes in DSS allowances. He also showed concern about the provision of low-cost housing, and the standard of accommodation available for the poor. In this he was not alone. Housing has been a continuing preoccupation of Church Assembly and Synod; and the problem was to be spotlighted in the *Faith in the City* report. Garbett had published in 1933 a "historic document", *The Challenge of Our Slums*, which was applauded by Sir Austen Chamberlain. Temple had regarded it as axiomatic that "every child should find itself a member of a family housed with decency and dignity". Such views were acceptable in their day but were hardly welcomed by a Thatcherite government which was trying to make people stand on their own feet, and which by so doing was reducing the amount of rented accommodation (by selling off council houses), and forcing families into bed and breakfast lodgings.

Over matters of foreign policy previous Archbishops had involved themselves. Fisher had disapproved of military action over Suez. Ramsey had said that the Government would be justified in using force in the event of UDI in Rhodesia. Runcie, however, did not disapprove when in 1982 we went to war with Argentina after its invasion of the Falkland Islands. This successful campaign rekindled British patriotic sentiment, and the "Falklands factor" restored to Mrs Thatcher her waning popularity. At the Thanksgiving Service in St Paul's Cathedral, the Archbishop naturally gave the address and having won distinction for gallantry during the 1939–45 war he knew what he was talking about. He did not give thanks directly for victory, but rather that the attempt to settle the future of the Islands by force had been thwarted. He spoke of pride in achievement and courage, and grief at loss and waste "as we pour into prayer our mourning, our pride, our shame and our convictions". He asked for compassion to be extended to Argentinian parents who had lost their sons. "War", he said, "is a sign of human failure and everything we say and do in this service must be in that context." These Christian sentiments ran directly counter to the mood of the jingoistic press, and they were unwelcome to the ears of many who were elated by a British victory. Yet Archbishop Temple during the last Great War had publicly stated that he did not think it right to pray directly for victory; and Runcie's words sound restrained when compared with those of Archbishop Davidson when he addressed the King and Queen and both

Houses of Parliament in August 1918: "There is also a form of wrath which may denigrate into a poisonous hatred. . . . It may corrupt and defile us with a horrid miasma. . . . That peril is no mere possibility. It exists."

At home alarm was beginning to be felt at the virtual supersession of the 1662 Prayer Book by the Alternative Service Book, and there was a threat of parliamentary legislation. Like Ramsey, Runcie successfully restrained this parliamentary threat of liturgical veto. Meanwhile the drama of the Miners' Strike was unfolding. David Jenkins in his Enthronement Sermon at Durham had called Magregor, chairman of the Coal Board, an "elderly imported American", and invited him to go home. Some ignorant people thought Runcie could and should have disciplined him for this. Actually, in a far-ranging interview published in *The Times* in October 1984 the Archbishop praised the exchanges of correspondence which resulted from this sermon.

This interview gained wide publicity, not least because *The Times* chose to publish it two days before the annual Conservative Conference. Runcie prudently refused to recommend policies. "Archbishops should stick to principles, deal with attitudes, encourage questions, stimulate thought." What gained most publicity, however, were his remarks about the shift from consensus to confrontation, feelings of anxiety about the well-being of long established institutions, a sense of puzzlement and frustration in society leading to increasing violence, and the belief that, with growing poverty in the midst of growing prosperity, this was not a decent society in which to live. While he explicitly said that he sought the middle ground, the interview was perceived as extreme and inflammatory. But Runcie was speaking here in line with the questioning of his predecessors. Coggan had asked what sort of society we wanted to live in; during the General Strike the BBC had refused to broadcast, and the *British Gazette* to publish, Davidson's attempt at national mediation; while even Cosmo Gordon Lang had said in 1911: "I cannot but see the picture of the monotony of toil which they are called upon to bear, of the uncertainty of unemployment which haunts them day to day, of the comforts that are common to us which are shut out. . . . Our best self in the contemplation of this inequality says that these things ought not to be.''

In 1986 the report of the Archbishop's Commission on Urban Priority Areas was published. *Faith in the City* receives attention elsewhere in this book. In a General Synod debate the Archbishop warmly endorsed the report; but I notice that he said nothing about the twenty-three detailed recommendations to the Government contained within it, which had caused some annoyance in government circles (I am sure that he would have had them costed had he been a member of the Commission). On its publication in 1985 the immediate response of a government minister (believed to be Mr Tebbit) was that the report was "Marxist" in orientation. This ridiculous comment focused national (and government) attention on a vital subject. Runcie was in line here with his predecessors, Archbishop Davidson's commission in 1918 on *Christianity and Industrial Problems* and Archbishop Temple's in 1938 on *Men without Work*.

During this period government policy on immigration and on South Africa was much in the news. General Synod resolutions on both subjects were in conflict with government policy, asking for sanctions against South Africa, and an end to unfairnesses in immigration policy, especially those which caused the disruption of family life. Runcie spoke in debate in favour of the Church's viewpoint on South Africa, and gave much needed support to Archbishop Tutu. As for immigration, I remember a difficult occasion when a deputation led by Runcie went to see Sir Leon Brittan (then Home Secretary) at the Home Office. But Runcie was only expressing the mind of the Church, and following his predecessor. Ramsey had strongly upheld the black cause in South Africa and had accused the government in so many words of breaking faith with Ugandan Asians; and for this he had even received threats of assassination!

In 1988 the Lambeth Conference took place, with the divisive issue of women priests and bishops chief on its

agenda. The media were hostile: gloomy prophecies about
the future of the Anglican Communion abounded, the
Religious Affairs Correspondent of *The Times* even writing
about (and perhaps hoping for) its future disintegration. In
fact the conference reinforced the bishops' desire to stay
together. The following year (1989) Runcie, like his three
predecessors, officially visited the Pope, repaying the Pope's
visit to Canterbury in 1981. Some years earlier, the Anglican/
Roman Catholic International Commission had reported
theological agreement about the need for a universal
primacy in a united church, an office which would naturally
fall to the Bishop of Rome; but no one had taken much notice
of this astonishing suggestion. Before Runcie left for Rome,
it was reported in an Italian periodical that he would be
willing to accept such a Universal Primate. The media blew
the matter up during the Archbishop's visit, raising British
constitutional issues and accusing Runcie of selling out the
Queen in favour of the Pope! They did not – or would not
– realize that Runcie was alluding to a reformed Primacy
of an utterly different character to the present Roman
Catholic Papacy. It was, I suspect, the media's way of
expressing hostility to Runcie.

During the very same weekend as Runcie's visit to Rome,
the Institute of Directors published a hyped-up press release
on an interview which Runcie had given to its journal *The
Director*. The Archbishop agreed that wealth needed to be
created for a healthy society but he insisted that there is no
automatic connection between wealth creation and a happy
society. He resisted the idea, constantly repeated in the
media, that the Church and the Government are at odds;
but he said that the Church had better contacts among
poorer people who live in those areas where the
Conservative Party has little support. He agreed that
differences do exist between Church and Government
because the Church not only believes in the unique value
of the individual but also in the importance of the society
to which individuals belong. ''It is when we put our
competitive demands before the needs of others that the
structures of community life break down.'' He expressed

fears about current individualistic ethics which bordered on Pharisaism, tending to equate success with God's reward for righteousness. "This can lead to judgements being made about the unsuccessful, the unemployed, the poor and the unintelligent which are both uncharitable and untrue." The media chose to see this interview as an attack on Thatcherism as such. But in fact the Archbishop was right within the mainstream of archiepiscopal tradition, in commenting in this way on the moral tone of the nation. Archbishop Davidson way back in 1894 had urged the penetration of economics by religion. On becoming Archbishop of York, Lang made his maiden speech in the Lords on the People's Budget! Archbishop Garbett had called unemployment "the factory of the unemployable", while Archbishop Temple had urged the importance of society as well as that of individuals, claiming that economics is not a sovereign domain.

1990 was the last year of Runcie's time at Canterbury. During the year the terrible disturbance at Strangeways Prison in Manchester took place. It so happened that just at this time, Runcie published a pamphlet about prisons, commenting on their old-fashioned nature and the urgent need for reform. He pointed out on TV that an inmate was only allowed one change of underpants a week. He made it clear that he was not blaming the present Government, which was merely continuing the policies of previous administrations. Blame rests upon us all. Here too Runcie was following in the steps of his predecessors. Temple, for example, gave the first annual lecture instituted by the Clark Hall Fellowship on *The Ethics of Penal Action* and he also spoke on behalf of the Howard League.

From this cursory survey it is clear that he has spoken with wisdom and prudence, that his contributions have been within the broad stream of archiepiscopal utterances, and that he has pressed for Christian principles rather than for particular policies. Why then has he had such an appalling press? The reasons are complex. Firstly, the immediacy of the media has vastly increased. Remarks which used to be tucked away in places like Hansard are now instantly headlined and flashed round the world. Secondly, few journalists today have much sense of history, particularly church history. In this secular age, most of them are ecclesiastically illiterate. Again, the mass media are now far more competitive, so that the tabloids are more irresponsible and the "qualities" more sensational. Mrs Thatcher's administrations have ended the postwar political consensus. New policies require fresh moral scrutiny. This has angered the predominantly Tory press and many Tory MPs because they can no longer rely automatically on church support. The absence of a strong political opposition during much of this period has given greater prominence to the views of an independent Archbishop (just as this has happened to members of the House of Lords). To these we have to add the passive support of certain highly placed ecclesiastics (who must be nameless) who disapproved of Runcie. This informal triple alliance accounts for this gross misrepresentation. The verdict of history will show, however, that the Church of England can look back with real gratitude to the national pronouncements of Robert Runcie.

Amid Ethical Uncertainties

HELEN OPPENHEIMER

Lady Oppenheimer has written extensively on moral questions.

People talk easily about a twentieth-century "revolution" in ethics. Revolution is a strong word: its connotations of total upheaval are surely stronger than we need. The revolving of roundabouts and the returning of swings, whether delight or nausea are induced thereby, are a less drastic image for the uncertainties of our times. It is true that the accumulated inventiveness of human beings has changed our lives. Anaesthetics, contraception, aeroplanes, refrigeration, telephones, antibiotics, television, computers have transformed the way we think about many questions. Yet still love and hate, suffering and celebration, birth and death, are the raw material of the human condition under God: the continuing terms of reference for anyone entrusted with the responsibility of leading a Christian church. It is a matter of prudence and charity to keep looking out for the recurrences among the alterations, and indeed for the improvements among the deteriorations.

It remains true, however, that our times, like most times, are full of uncertainties, and an Archbishop of Canterbury is expected to steer his way through them with supernatural confidence. Robert Runcie has had to understand and reckon with old and new controversies in social, political, sexual and medical ethics difficult enough to daunt full-time experts in any of these areas. He has needed to appraise liberations, achieved and demanded, of women, young people, theologians, ethnic minorities, homosexual people, and people of all kinds with special circumstances, handicaps and disadvantages, whether inflicted by fate or fault. He has been obliged to enter into matters of politics but forbidden to become a politician; he is expected to understand technical questions, new since his own education, without being given enough time to study them; he needs to draw on deep spiritual resources while going from one duty to another all round the world.

What are the possible ways of approach for a church leader? He can take sides from the outset, for or against the promised or threatened changes; he can sit on the fence; he can invite opinions and then choose judicially between them; or he can strike out a line of his own. Whichever of these he does, he is likely to be blamed, whether for accommodating to the world or for being out of touch. It needs to be said that the saddest accommodation of the Church to the world in our time is Christian permissiveness towards petty and ill-informed blame for people with high responsibilities.

Robert Runcie's characteristic style has been to listen and then adjudicate between the contenders. It is because he has resolutely refused to rush into taking sides that he has been assumed to be open to criticism for sitting on the fence. Taking sides is what people are demanding when they ask for a strong lead. They are apt to suppose it to be obvious which way such a lead would go if it were given. The Archbishop's refusal to allow his influence to be pre-empted in this way, far from being a failure to exercise authority, has been precisely a manifestation of Christian authority. Of course when he came to Canterbury his mind was not a *tabula rasa*. On the matter of remarriage after divorce, for example, he had already taken up a position. Having followed the arguments for years, he put the weight of his episcopal and then his archiepiscopal authority on the liberal side: not, it must be emphasized, as part of a permissive revolution but as a better way of understanding the teaching of Christ.

In some ways it is extraordinary that "sitting on the fence" should be a favourite accusation brought against him by hostile critics. He has indeed refused to be cast in a party mould but has made individual decisions, often courageous, to back one side or another. It may be fair to say that he has a reluctance to let contrary arguments go by default: but this reluctance has nothing to do with indecisiveness, still less with time-serving, and everything to do with fair-mindedness. People who do not like his measured and thoughtful style of responding to the problems are quick to cry "Fudge!" Sometimes that is the cry of the partisan who cannot bear that the arguments on the other side should have a good run for their money. But unless one is to be partisan oneself, one must also attend, as he has to do, to the reason for the indignant cries, which are generally not only partisan but principled. It is a built-in feature of moral problems that any decision is likely to hurt someone. Fairness to all sides is an ideal which can hardly be fully achieved when everyone is sincerely appealing to eternal verities but some practical decision has to be made at once. Moral arguments are serious and difficult, and wherever one stops one is breaking off in the middle. The harsh dilemma in which the twentieth century, perhaps any century, places its leaders is to force them to break off in the middle. If a Christian leader lets the argument run for as long as he can before revealing his own stance, he tends to be blamed for not pronouncing sooner; and then because he has shown a reluctance to hurt he is blamed even more for the hurt he has to inflict in the end.

This defence against charges of "sitting on the fence" or "fudging the issues" is, indeed, defensive. Appreciation can be more positive than that. It is too soon to say where Robert Runcie's lasting achievements lie and which of his policies will be approved by the hindsight of history: but this can be said, that his characteristic procedure of taking advice, weighing the arguments and then coming to a decision, is much more than a justifiable attempt to cope with an impossible task. It is a thoroughly hopeful way of seeking to "have the mind of Christ". There are plenty of moral questions today, questions of medical ethics in particular, where it is simply not possible to read off answers from Holy Scripture. This is not a matter of believing or not believing in inspiration: the biblical authors, however inspired, were often not addressing our problems. What more can one ask of an Archbishop of whom decisions are required than that he should do what this Archbishop has constantly done: listen, think, and weigh up what he has heard in the light of the whole Gospel, while meantime setting an example of what Christian charity looks like in the midst of controversies old and new?

It is often said of a good pastor that he is able to make each person feel like the one who matters, and Robert Runcie has that encouraging gift; but his listening as Archbishop is of a different and more authoritative kind. He is able, in giving his full attention, to allow each person to remember that there are others to be listened to. One's pet answer will be given full weight, but one can be confident that this will not be at the expense of other Christians' pet answers. He can look behind bigotry and narrowness to see what is the principle at stake. If he feels it is time to pronounce, he will take advice yet put his own stamp upon it. If a colleague has studied a subject he will back that colleague, not compulsively put in his own word about everything. He is required to think fast but declines to think in slogans. He does not consider it unimportant that some human beings, wrong headed and prejudiced or indeed sinful as they may seem, are being written off by other people's ethical certainties. Are the Muslims profoundly shocked at Western freedom? Is divorce being treated as a more unforgivable offence than any other? Do Argentinians suffer in war as well as British? Need we abandon the renewal of friendship with the Roman Church because we have to deplore its intransigent authoritarianism? There is no inconsistency, though a good deal of courage, in keeping these questions alive, in continuing to pay heed to people who are easily thought of simply as adversaries. The variety of people to whom he is prepared to listen ought to refute anxious talk about a "liberal establishment". The variety of the answers at which he arrives, the way he is willing to combine the traditional with the radical, his very unpopularity in some quarters, ought to refute accusations of "wetness".

Sometimes a Christian thinker can enter into a question and explore it with a fresh mind so as to show it newly

illuminated to the contemporary Church. Surely Robert
Runcie could do this better than most; but the nature of his
office is such that he is never given the chance to pause long
enough on one problem. It must be as tantalizing to him
as it is impoverishing to his fellow Christians that his
wisdom and experience have had to be deployed in breadth
rather than in depth. Unjust attacks and even unpopularity,
hurtful as these can be, may not after all be diminishing:
the constant pressure for instant understanding of
multifarious dilemmas is a more threatening aspect of what
the Church at present asks of its leaders. Perhaps retirement
will give him the opportunity to pursue questions and follow
lines of thought for their own sake and not because they
are on the agenda; to speak when he has something
particular to say; to be heeded as himself and not because
he is the Archbishop of Canterbury.

Is that after all to project one's own notions upon him,
assuming that scholarship must always be the most
authentic pursuit for a Christian leader, and so to underrate
his primacy after all? It is a higher and more difficult moral
calling to draw out the gifts of others, to hearten and
encourage both by individual words and public utterances,
and by his informed and sensitive interest to make
difficulties, worries and troubles less heavy.

For forth he goes and visits all his host,
Bids them good morrow with a modest smile,
And calls them brothers, friends, and countrymen. . .
That every wretch, pining and pale before,
Beholding him, plucks comfort from his looks.

Amid Many Faiths

DAN COHN-SHERBOK
Lecturer in the University of Kent

I first met the Archbishop at a party. As a rabbi I had been recruited to teach the "Theology, Morality and Law" slot to a group of men and women who had come forward to be trained for the Anglican ministry, and as a reward for my services I was included in a very delightful party in the village of Harbledown, a couple of miles outside Canterbury. There I was introduced to Robert Runcie and we had a nice chat. When the party came to an end, I put on my coat and began the slow trudge back to my house. It was extremely cold and as I lumbered along, a large black car shot past me and stopped abruptly fifty yards ahead. The door opened and a purple arm extended. I was beckoned into the lighted warmth within. It was a model pattern for Jewish/Christian harmony.

We met on several occasions after this at the University of Kent at Canterbury. He is marvellous at social occasions, remembering everyone's names, asking after their families, finding friends and interests in common. I particularly remember a Christmas dinner at Darwin College. He already had had a busy day. In the late afternoon he had given a paper to the Centre for the Study of Religion and Society on "Religious Broadcasting Today", and he had responded to questions with patience, courtesy and considerable wit. Then he was expected to attend a banquet with a hundred complete strangers. He never flagged. Round the room he went, speaking to everyone, exchanging jokes, showing interest and giving every appearance of enjoying himself. He sat through the long meal, chatting to his neighbours and being appreciative about the food. It was a masterly performance.

Most frequently I met the Archbishop at inter-faith gatherings. In 1986, he gave the Sir Francis Younghusband Memorial Lecture at Lambeth Palace to mark the fiftieth anniversary of the World Congress of Faiths, and he spoke on *Christianity and World Religions*. He had recently visited India and, in his own words, he "went with a genuine, but somewhat notional, commitment to the need for dialogue between the great faiths." He "returned with a deep sense of the urgency of our need to listen, revere and reflect. . . . Before there were the certainties of an encapsulated Western Christianity. After, there are new ways of thinking about God, Christ and the world." It was a remarkable lecture for an Archbishop of Canterbury to give. No longer was the Church perceiving the non-Christian world as a mission field to be conquered. There was a genuine recognition of the work of the Holy Spirit in the other religions of the world. Religious diversity was to be seen as a rich spiritual resource from which all could learn. As the Archbishop put it, "it takes humility and sincerity to concede that there is a certain incompleteness in each of our traditions. . . . We must recognize that ultimately all religions possess a provisional, interim character as ways and signs to help us in our pilgrimage to Ultimate Truth and Perfection." The Archbishop was rejecting the traditional Christian triumphalism which claims that there is no salvation outside the Church. He was advocating mutual reconciliation and a move towards creating conditions for greater community and fellowship. He ended his talk by saying: "A rich diversity of religious experiences and forms is one of God's greatest gifts to his world. But it requires from us the virtues of understanding and sympathy, humility and readiness to listen and to learn. Only then can we build a greater global unity in the spirit of faith, hope and love."

The Archbishop has always been a friend of the Jewish community, and has shown his good will in so very many ways. The Appeal for the Council of Christians and Jews was launched from Lambeth Palace. He awarded a Lambeth Doctorate of Divinity to the Chief Rabbi, and there have been many visits to Jewish events, meetings with Jewish leaders, and discussions behind the scenes. He has also made some important speeches. In all these addresses his intelligence and sensitivity shone through. To the congregation of the West London Synagogue he said: "Of course at the centre of the corporate Jewish memory in this generation stands the appalling horror of the Holocaust. I comprehend the magnitude of that horror. You *feel* it. " And he went on to ask: "Can I say *anything* to your corporate memory – a memory which includes not only the Holocaust, but a multitude of other wrongs which Jews have suffered at the hands of Christians? To ask for your forgiveness might be proper, but too easy a gesture. The wrongs done are too great and too many for such simple and facile atonement."

I was privileged to help the Archbishop with some of his talks to the Jewish community. There was a wonderful sense of harmony in hearing the Archbishop, as a Christian leader, addressing a Jewish audience while knowing that he had hammered out his ideas with a rabbi previously. I think his knowledge of Judaism rather surprised his audience. At his speech to the World Conference of Progressive Judaism, he used a story about a Hasidic rabbi. Poor Rabbi Julia Neuberger who spoke immediately afterwards was going to use the same story! Yet despite his wide grasp of the Jewish tradition, there was nothing milk-and-watery about his point of view. He never tried to minimize the distance between the two faiths. His Christian convictions shone out. Even as he acknowledged Christian guilt for the Holocaust, he affirmed the true Christian duty of following the example of Jesus of Nazareth. As he put it in his sermon marking the fiftieth anniversary of the Kristallnacht, when the Nazi persecution of the Jews intensified: "Our task as Christians is to hold sincerely to our faith in Christ and to speak of our desire to be conformed in his life, death and resurrection. . . . As we remember the streets of Germany littered with broken glass, we must not simply despair of the past. . . . What lies before us is the task of creating a world in which such tragedies do not take place again. The planned destruction of the Jewish people did not succeed. Out of suffering God brought a new-found liberty. As we

Christians would say, out of death he brought resurrection.''

In the summer of 1989, the traditional mediaeval miracle plays were staged in Canterbury Cathedral. My wife and I saw them as guests of the Archbishop. After a very jolly dinner at the Old Palace, we went into the great nave where we all sat on the floor. Before us was enacted the expulsion of Lucifer from Heaven and the creation of Adam and Eve. Then the whole audience moved around the Cathedral for the other scenes. As story after story unrolled in front of us, the Archbishop of Canterbury and the Canterbury Rabbi laughed at the jokes, shared in the poignancy, were stirred by the excitement, enjoyed the familiarity of a shared cultural tradition and prayed together at the end. It was a marvellous evening. If all churchmen had had the imagination of Robert Runcie in dealing with their Jewish neighbours, the history of Jewish/Christian relations would have been far happier.

3
THE UNITY
OF ANGLICANS

The Anglican Anguish

RICHARD HOLLOWAY
Bishop of Edinburgh

Why has Robert Runcie's time as Archbishop of Canterbury
been so full of controversies? I go back to Jesus, who told
us that he came to bring not peace but a sword, and that
we would be guided into all the truth. I think there is a
connection between these two sayings, since truth-seeking
involves us inescapably in conflict. As human beings search
for truth, they come up against the phenomenon of truths
that are in opposition to each other. Most of the conflicts
that characterize human history are not about the battle
between right and wrong, truth and error, but the battle
between opposing rights or opposing truths. But some hope
lies in what philosophers call the "dialectical" model. A
truth is stated, a thesis, and this is immediately opposed
by a contradictory truth, an antithesis, and these two
struggle or wrestle together; and from that struggle emerges
some kind of synthesis that is not just an artificial unity of
the two opposing truths, but is itself something that
transcends them both.

If we turn to theology, we discover that religious people
and institutions have no route to truth which miraculously
avoids the need for clash and conflict. Of course, many
religious institutions believe that they have this infallibility,
but their claim is passionately contested. The one thing that
we can say with confidence about all religious claims is that
they are contestable, and have been and will go on being
contested. The model I like is the model of the *continuum*,
the rope that stretches from A to Z, divided up into sections
along which people position themselves. And it seems to
me that the particular piece of string we call Anglicanism
is best described as a struggle between what Paul Tillich

called the "Catholic substance" and the "Protestant principle".

Two realities or approaches to the experience of truth seem permanently in contention within the Christian, indeed within the human, community. They are the principles of revelation and reason. By revelation we mean that knowledge or truth that seems to come from above, comes directly from God and has a givenness and objectivity about it. Of course, people will debate both the nature and the content of revelation and the means whereby it was given. Nevertheless, at the heart of the Christian tradition there lies a claim that something came from God that is simply given, self-evident, has its own authority within itself and has to be submitted to. But there is another great reality in history: reason, with its critical, probing, questioning dynamic. Reason often seems to be in necessary conflict with revelation: it is always seeking to discover more about revelation, indeed may often contradict the apparent claims or the alleged claims of revelation. And if the focus of the supernatural revelation is scripture, then the location of the principle of reason is clearly the turbulent mind of humanity.

In Anglican experience this conflict, this "endless war twixt truth and truth" (Boethius), is expressed in three strands of spiritual reality. These three strands or cords are woven together, in theory, into a rope that is not easily broken; but, in fact, the strands often seem to unravel from each other and jerk and wriggle away from each other, rather than binding together. The strands are scripture, tradition and reason. Scripture has to be interpreted, and interpretation is best done over a long period by as many people as possible, giving rise to a broad and deep river of experience that we call tradition; and always there is the individual reason, the private thinker tackling, questioning the authority of scripture and its extension, tradition. In a mysterious way, these three elements that are strongest when wound together tend to separate in actual Christian experience. This is an inescapable human reality: the need for companionship and support, even in truth-seeking, leads to the grouping of the like-minded, those congenial with one another. Roughly speaking, we could say that those who emphasize scripture to the exclusion, or at the expense, of tradition, group themselves into the evangelical Protestant Churches, while Catholics emphasize the continuity of tradition, with scripture being seen as part of tradition rather than the fount of it. Those who exclusively emphasize reason tend to end up in Liberal Protestantism, Unitarianism or atheism, because if you emphasize human reason to the exclusion of revelation, you can end up excluding the supernatural altogether. The fascinating thing about Anglicanism, however, was that it did not separate in this way. Rather than becoming a party committed to a single idea, it became more like a parliament in which rival parties jockeyed for power. The Reformation of the Church of England was a conservative revolution. It retained much from the past though it absorbed many of the new ideas that were in ferment on the continent, and the Anglican Reformation went on evolving for several hundred years; indeed, could be said to be evolving still. We are an inclusive Church so we lack the cutting edge of sectarianism. The price we pay for our inclusiveness is a permanent tension between ourselves and a frequent inability to decide issues, because there is a stand-off among the rival parties. This is what I call the *anguish* of Anglicanism, the discomfort that is intrinsic to its nature.

Let me give a specific example of how this discomfort expresses itself over a very current issue – the issue of homosexuality. It is often wrongly said by people that there is a simple or single attitude to this question, but that is far from being the case. There are, in fact, at least four positions being held by Anglicans and they all tend to emphasize particular aspects of the three-fold cord of scripture, tradition and reason.

The first attitude is what moral philosophers call "punitive non-acceptance". This is often held to be the biblical position, though it is extremely doubtful if the Bible has any knowledge or understanding at all of homosexuality as we know it. Nevertheless, there are a few texts in scripture that talk not so much about homosexuality as about certain same-sex activities, and they are all disapproving. Punitive non-accepters certainly believe that homosexuality should be morally rejected, but they also believe it should be punished. Indeed, if they are true to the scriptures they cite so frequently, they should treat it as a capital offence.

The second attitude is described by moral philosophers as "non-punitive non-acceptance". This attitude believes that homosexuality should never be approved of or consented to. It is always a sin, though not necessarily a crime, so they would not call for the punishment of homosexuals. However, the attitude they adopt to them results in the subtle but cruel punishment of social opprobrium and marginalization.

The third attitude is called "qualified acceptance", and an ascending level of acceptance is offered. This attitude is held by fair-minded, moderate traditionalists who remember Goethe's warning to "distrust all those in whom the urge to punish is strong". Partial accepters would have an interrogatory routine something like this: "Change your sexual orientation, if you can. If you can't change your orientation, abstain from sexual acts, if you can. If you can neither change your orientation, nor abstain, then behave responsibly. Remember the ideals of fidelity. Stick to one lover. Do not play the field. Do not get lured into promiscuity. It is better for you to have one lover than to be tormented with loneliness and lust. After all, there have been times when the Christian Church has treated marriage as a reluctant concession to human carnality; it has even been defined as 'a remedy for fornication for those that have not the gift of continence'."

Finally, there is the doctrine of "full acceptance". For many people, sexual relations are evaluated, not by the position or gender of the bodies involved, but by the intentions of the heart and by interior qualities such as love, trust and gentleness.

Behind all these attitudes to human sexuality there lie serious moral issues that are constantly and hotly debated: can human sexual activity be validated or understood simply by an examination of what happens between the bodies?

Are there sexual acts that are always intrinsically wrong, without reference to the intention or consent of those committing the acts? Or does all bodily action derive its value only from the intention of the agent? The important thing to remember in all this is that, though the issues are far from straightforward, we ought to go on informing our minds and consciences and to know at least where we stand on the issues, so that we are not the prey of unconscious forces, attitudes or revulsions.

The Anglican Church is a family or fellowship, in Greek *koinonia*, in Latin *communio*, of autonomous provinces, and each province has a Primate or Chief Bishop. Each province is self-governing but only within certain limits. For instance, each province is free to decide its own attitude to marriage discipline or the way it organizes the selection and ordination of candidates for the ministry; it is not free to decide, for instance, to abandon the doctrine of the Holy Trinity or the divine nature of Christ. In other words, it has the freedom to control its own attitude to secondary or tertiary theological matters, but not matters of primary importance. The difficulty is in deciding what is primary and what is secondary.

The Lambeth Conference of 1988 met amidst a series of dire predictions about the end or breakup of Anglicanism, and one or two bishops have continued the doomsday scenario into their post-Lambeth posturing; but that is not what happened and is not going to happen. There *are* strains and tensions and we acknowledged them; but we also recognized that these tensions and disagreements are part of the very nature of Anglicanism, and we affirmed that they help to define our very distinctiveness and that we must go on living with them, no matter how painful it is. Two perceptions started to emerge at Lambeth, two insights that will be useful to the whole Christian community. The first was the idea of Reception. When a new idea is mooted or some apparently radical departure from tradition is proposed, it takes time, sometimes a long time, for such an idea or proposal to be ''received'' by everyone, but in time the new thing is either abandoned or finally received by all

– and the body moves on. Linked to the idea of Reception is the idea of Contextuality. Each part of the Church is set in a particular context and that context affects the Church's social and theological agenda. An issue that is hot in America may be absolutely cold in Africa, and *vice versa*. Polygamy, for instance, is a topic of intense interest and importance in Africa, but it is not an issue in Scotland. And, by the same token, women's ordination is a hot issue in Europe and America, though it is hardly even on the agenda of the Church in Melanesia; and so on.

I found the mature wisdom that underlay the recognition of the importance of Reception and Contextuality something to admire and celebrate at Lambeth, because it is real and makes sense. This is actually how people are and how the Church is! Isn't it good to belong to a Church that recognizes that amazing variety and does not insist that everyone should walk in step to the same tune?

Anglicanism loves freedom and space. As the Coverdale Psalter reminds us, ''Thou has set my feet in a large room''. Anglicans believe that this allows the many-sidedness of truth to be expressed. But this freedom, this spaciousness, brings with it an acute sense of discomfort, because no position, no point of view, goes for long unchallenged, so Anglicans tend to be in a permanent state of discomfort and disagreement with one another. This makes us slow to judge, both because we believe that people should not rush to judgement, and also because we find it difficult to get our act sufficiently together to make judgements that stick. However, we do not endure this discomfort simply out of weakness, but because we have fundamentally accepted the necessity and purifying value of conflict as being an inescapable part of the theological and spiritual enterprise. To the outsider this can appear baffling; it can look as though anything goes, that we can believe anything we like. That, of course, is far from the case. Nevertheless, we have always preferred to express our beliefs in worship and in liturgy rather than in ironclad, bolted and padlocked, confessional statements and credal formularies. As we worship, so we believe. We would rather be together on our knees than marching in step to the beat of a single drummer. Anglicanism is a religion for the mature, and the mature know how to live with pain. John Donne wrote our epigraph:

> On a high hill truth stands
> and he that would reach her
> about must, and about must go.

Holding the Church of England Together

COLIN CRASTON
Vicar of St Paul's, Boulton,
and Chairman of the Anglican Consultative Council

"You cannot have Christianity and not have differences!" This assertion of John Henry Newman was borrowed by Robert Runcie in introducing a report in 1987 on the divisive issue of the ordination of women to the priesthood. He was quick to add a balancing judgement of his own. "In spite of and in the midst of our deep differences on this question, we can still claim to be the Body of Christ." Unity in diversity has been a major concern in his leadership. Assessment of this role requires some description of the Church he has had to deal with. I begin with the tradition to which I belong. As his Primacy, and the 1980s, dawned, Evangelicals in England were continuing to grow in numbers, confidence and influence. The contrast with forty years earlier was remarkable, at any rate in respect of the more conservative of them at that time. Liberal Evangelicals of those days had lived at greater ease in the Church of England, but conservatives had kept some distance from them and had felt more marginalized than any group in this century. In 1941 I was told by a senior Evangelical that the movement was finished in the Church of England.

A sense of marginalization can be both self-inflicted and the consequence of unfair treatment by more powerful forces. Conservative Evangelicals had failed to react creatively to new scientific knowledge, to modern biblical studies and to emphases of the Anglo-Catholic movement. In reaction to the latter they defined doctrines of the Church, the ministry and the sacraments in terms of what they were not, rather than what they were. And interdenominational links with fellow Evangelicals mattered more than Anglican

The new Archbishop greets the crowds as he leaves Canterbury Cathedral

The Enthronement in Canterbury Cathedral, 25th March 1980

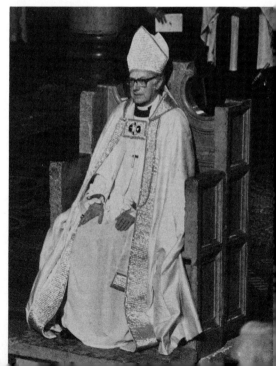

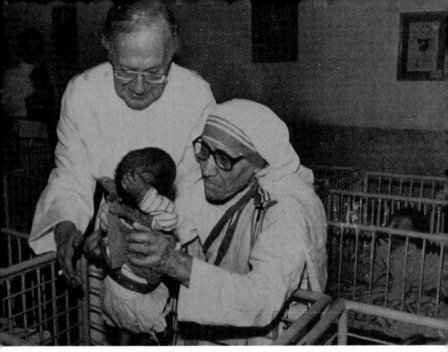

With Mother Teresa in India, 1986

With Mother Francis Dominica at Helen House, Oxford 1987

Exchanging a yellow scarf with the Dalai Lama at Lambeth Palace, January 1984

With Pope John Paul II, Rome, 1989

the Temple of Heaven, king, January 1982

Left: With Alexander Solzhenitsyn at Lambeth Palace, May 1983

Middle: With Dr Billy Graham at Lambeth Palace, January 1984

Below: With Sir Harry Secombe filming "Highway", Easter, 1988

Above: With the Ecumenical Patriarch at Leeds Castle, 1987

Middle: On a visit to the Home Office with ministers from Brixton, June 1981

Left: With Archbishop Desmond Tutu during the Lambeth Conference of 1988

The Archbishop operating a mechanical
digger at an assisted building project

Umpires at the Lambeth Conference
Cricket Match, Canterbury 1988 - with
Bishop David Sheppard

At Oxford House Community Centre,
London, October 1984

With Mrs Runcie in the garden of Lambeth Palace

Receiving the Freedom of the City of London, January 1981. With the family - Rebecca, the Archbishop, James and Rosalind - are Mr Anthony Howitt and Lady Gardener Thorpe

At St Martin-in-the-Fields High School, Tulse Hill, October 1984

membership. But then, their stance, even though including positive aspects – stress on conversion, assurance of salvation, atonement objectively provided at the cross (sometimes presented in crude terms, it must be said), the supremacy of Scripture – did not find much sympathy with other traditions or those in authority, some of whom had reacted strongly against fundamentalist expressions of Evangelicalism. The more conservative of their colleagues were frowned upon by the bishops and preferment to higher office in the dioceses denied them.

The recovery and growth of the movement since 1945 began mainly with two factors, a steady increase in ordinands owing much to the Billy Graham Crusade in 1954, and a revival of biblical scholarship first evident in the Tyndale series of commentaries. With emergence from a siege mentality came a willingness to review attitudes and to revise agenda. A turning point came at Keele 1967, a National Evangelical Anglican Congress. It marked a "conversion" to the Church of England, with a commitment to work wholeheartedly within its comprehensiveness, even if many Evangelicals would still regard themselves as guardians of the Reformation and thus the true Anglicans. Together with a fresh attempt to articulate basic Evangelical theology there was openness to the renewal of the local church in liturgy and shared ministry. And so with expanding horizons they found the spectrum of their movement broadening. This led to a reaction from the more conservative, surfacing at and continuing after a second congress in 1977 at Nottingham. It focused on the approach to "hermeneutics" (the interpretation of the Bible) adopted by a majority of Evangelical scholars, but it also touched developments in the theology of the sacraments and the ministry, ecumenical dialogue with Rome and the social and political implications of the Gospel.

So the movement as the 1980s began was a broad-based, numerically stronger but more loosely-bound association than hitherto, struggling with inner differences (not least on the ordination of women) and also with the impact of the Charismatic emphases. Serious suspicions of others, particularly bishops, who appeared to be undermining orthodoxy in doctrine and morals, especially in sexuality, continued; and there was still discontent with the Evangelicals' under-representation in the hierarchy of the Church, despite their full involvement in synodical structures.

Treading more warily, one must attempt an assessment of the Catholic tradition. After reaching its zenith in the 1920s and '30s and having shaped the Church's development in the twentieth century to a considerable degree, the movement found itself increasingly fighting a rearguard action from the postwar years. The prospect of full communion with the Church of South India stimulated a threat of large scale defections by Catholic clergy. Similarly, on grounds of failure to safeguard a Catholic interpretation of episcopacy and ministry, proposals for union with the Methodists and subsequently for a Covenant with several Free Churches, met with strong opposition. In the search for church unity rapprochement with churches maintaining the threefold order, and especially Rome, was clearly preferred.

Divorce and remarriage in church is another move which Catholics have resisted. Convocation regulations framed when a Catholic interpretation of indissolubility prevailed came under increasing criticism from others. Successive attempts to make marriage discipline more flexible in pastoral application have met Catholic opposition. The ordination of women saga has proved the most emotionally charged divide for Catholics with, again, possibilities of secessions. Women in the priesthood and episcopacy appears to them, however, as but one part of a package of betrayal of Catholic faith and order. A liberal approach to revelation, credal statements and Tradition is seen as the root cause of the Church's ills. But there are liberal Catholics as there are "open" Evangelicals (they prefer that adjective to "liberal"). Firm adherents to the Catholic position have felt marginalized, as Evangelicals once did, though their numbers remain substantial. When fighting rearguard actions consumes time and energy, and anxieties and disappointments build up, little room is left for creative thinking, new expressions of theology, and that has been a lack in recent decades.

The Liberal tradition is harder to assess. For one thing, many given the label by others are not sure they want it, if it implies rejection of cardinal orthodox beliefs. They hesitate to line up with the theologians of a radical approach to Scripture and Tradition, but try to keep an open mind (again, "open" seems preferable to "liberal") on ways of interpreting faith in the light of new knowledge, particularly in what they consider secondary matters. When the General Synod began in 1970 a New Synod Group, later renamed Open Synod Group, was formed, intended not to exclude anyone but to draw together all open to development where seen to be needed. Some of is programme for reform was practical, for instance, change in the appointment, deployment and terms of service of clergy. There was firm commitment to ecumenism, unity schemes with Free Churches being the first objective. Reform in the discipline affecting divorcees wishing to remarry in church, and support for the ordination of women also figured prominently in its programme. The early years of the Synod saw some encouragement for those seeking reforms, but meeting frustration on several fronts they have had to settle for a slower pace of change. And as for those more radical in theology and its implications for life, the force of conservative opposition must have induced in them a sense of marginalization.

Bearing in mind the anxieties and frustrations of the different traditions in the 1980s, and not forgetting those who belonging to no grouping were just "Church of England" and caught in the crossfire, one might wonder who did not feel marginalized! But that would present too gloomy a picture. There was no lack of positive gains and prospects as Robert Runcie moved to Canterbury. A new Alternative Service Book was imminent, the fruit of strenuous yet amicable efforts to devise liturgy acceptable to all traditions. A new style of appointing diocesan bishops had been negotiated. There was progress in international ecumenical dialogues. Among other practical reforms a new Pastoral Measure was on its way, and a new system of paying and pensioning the clergy was in force. And despite continuing divisions there had been some meeting of minds across party lines.

Against this background, what sort of leadership has been expected of the Archbishop? No doubt each grouping in the Church has had its own specification, shaped by its own priorities. To have offered "strong leadership" suiting one lot could have meant marginalization of others. The proper question is, What sort of leadership have the turbulent 1980s needed? Certainly not one of direction by edict. Rather, the more difficult way of exercising skill and patience in holding divided groups together while a common mind can be sought. *That* leadership has been offered so effectively by Robert Runcie that the whole Anglican Communion has cause for deep gratitude to him. His role as one "not to command but to gather" was never more evident or appreciated than at Lambeth 1988. But the reaction to him then was not just for his leadership in the conference, his warmth of personality and his vision of a family of autonomous churches interdependent and holding together for the sake of the Church Catholic, but for the sense of purpose he had stimulated through his five years' preparation for it and the encouragement to all parts of the Communion in his travels.

In his speeches he has consistently urged "hard theological endeavour" as a basis for unity, and acknowledged the dangers of a bland plea of comprehensiveness by Anglicans. Early on he advised the English Doctrine Commission of the need to articulate Anglican teaching more clearly, and he warned more than once against doctrinal indifference, though he approved the T.S. Eliot maxim of "continence in affirmation". He has been firm in his advocacy of the role of bishops, individually and collectively, in serving the unity of the Church and in preserving and renewing its faith. He maintained in 1985 that as a bridge-builder, true to the ancient title of *pontifex*, the bishop "attempts to bestride the narrow worlds of mindless dogmatism on the one hand and rootless individualism on the other''. At the same time in the government of the Church the Archbishop balances the authority inherent in the episcopal office and that of the bishop in council with laity and clergy. His influence in the choice of bishops was criticized in Bennett's Crockford's Preface. Having shared in over three-quarters of the appointments in his time (as a member of the Crown Appointments Commission), I can testify to his fairness to all traditions.

An Evangelical Perspective

MICHAEL BAUGHEN
Bishop of Chester

Archbishop Robert Runcie leaned back in his chair and said, "This is an answer to prayer". There was a strong murmur of agreement springing from a general feeling of relief. The House of Bishops had been called together exceptionally in the week after Easter 1986 for a final attempt to agree the text of the report on *The Nature of Belief*. A group of bishops representing all theological perspectives had worked for many long hours over several months, under the godly chairmanship of John Baker, Bishop of Salisbury. By respect for one another and careful listening they had produced a report on which they all fully agreed. It was a remarkable achievement, bathed in prayer. Regrettably, when the report came to the whole House of Bishops there were potshots and, from one or two bishops, broadsides fired. Without the advantage of a small group taking time together there was a major problem in this large group. Robert Runcie was determined that the bishops should be united. He could not live with the idea of a disunited doctrinal statement by the House of Bishops of the Church of England. The tension between orthodoxy or credal statement and radical liberalism erupted. John Baker was deeply pained (and had a heart attack shortly afterwards). After various suggested wordings had been considered in two meetings, and a degree of give and take had happened, we met that Easter week. Most of us travelled to London and entered the room with dragging feet and an aching heart. But the atmosphere was not what we expected. It was, indeed, one of peace and of God being with us. The final wording of the chapters in question was accepted. "This is an answer to prayer" was Robert Runcie's heartfelt and accurate response.

It is this grounding of life and ministry in prayer which has permeated the archiepiscopate of Robert Runcie. He has meant business with God. He has given himself to an incredible work-load in the strength which comes from that relationship. Nowhere was this more clear than at the Lambeth Conference in 1988. He began it looking drawn and aged. He ended it looking ten years younger. It went well. More than that, he drew the love and admiration of the whole conference – and this affection reached its climax in the final days of that great assembly. Here, indeed, was no pompous prelate but a *primus inter pares*, a humble man of God, resisting the pressure to make him a Super-Primate, rejoicing in the acceptance of the meeting of Primates as its alternative, and yet still quietly and clearly our leader in the Anglican Communion. This is only possible in a man of grace, humility and prayer who wants to put his Lord first.

It was this recognition of Robert Runcie's godliness that made Anglican Evangelicals warm to him as our Chief Pastor. When he graciously came to the great gathering of Anglican Evangelicals at Caister in May 1988 he was given a warm and loving standing ovation. It was a genuine response to him as a man of God, and criticisms or theological differences were secondary in such a direct person-to-person meeting. His address, lasting almost an hour, had been well researched and prepared, with his usual gathering of input beforehand from people in the group he was to address – yet, as always, with his personal touch and genuine opening of the heart to the vast crowd. He offered a positive request for more ecclesiology from Evangelicals (causing the totally unjust newspaper headline ''Archbishop slams Evangelicals''!) This request was met both by a feeling that he was not up to date on what had been produced by Evangelicals on ecclesiology, but also by a readiness to take the matter up more strongly, as happened in the next Anglican Evangelical Assembly. The response was possible because of the context of love and godliness in the total address.

Similarly, in autumn 1989 he spoke to the Senior Evangelical Anglican Conference at Swanwick in

Derbyshire. An enormous warmth manifested itself there, with deep appreciation of his major address on the New Age Movement and of his whole personal style and approach. He must have felt the positive and loving atmosphere of that conference. Indeed, he was clearly much at ease within those gatherings because of the warmth expressed to him.

Evangelicals have had to put up with the word "fundamentalism" being thrown at them often in recent years (but not by Robert Runcie). Yet, titles like "liberal", "evangelical", "fundamentalist", "radical", "catholic" all have such a variety of shades and meanings that it might be better to ban their use for the next five years! Robert Runcie would call himself a liberal but he is the sort of liberal who seems to respect the doctrines of the Church, its credal statements and its biblical authority. This was seen in the homosexuality debate in General Synod as well as in *The Nature of Belief* and many other debates. This is the sort of liberalism with which Evangelicals can positively engage. Whoever occupies the seat of St Augustine, from whatever churchmanship or position in the Church, must be able to stand in the mainstream of the faith and yet also to embrace the other theological positions in a creative way. Certainly a Catholic who is open, a Liberal who is not extreme or an Evangelical who is not hard-line can fulfil that position.

In addition, Robert Runcie has clearly shown himself to be a person concerned with the Gospel and with activities and enterprises in different sections of the Church which are seeking to press forward the Kingdom of God with life and vitality. Evangelicals working in the inner city and great urban corporations saluted his determined initiative to have the *Faith in the City* report produced even if they felt it weak on theology. Similarly, the Church Urban Fund has been his initiative. When Gavin Reid went across to the United States of America in April 1987, armed with an impressive file of invitations to Dr Billy Graham, written by many Christian leaders in England, pressing him to come for Mission England, he also carried an envelope with a hand-written letter inside from the Archbishop. Dr Graham opened that one first and read a warm promise of being his loyal supporter if he would come. He was visibly moved and that assurance of welcome was decisive. In all churchmanships there was tremendous benefit from Mission England and I, like many other bishops, have confirmed many new members of the Church in churches of all shades. In England we are much in debt to Robert Runcie that Dr Billy Graham came to be amongst us.

The balance of theological persuasions in Boards, Ordination Courses and Committees is not so readily observable in the Church of England at the end of Robert Runcie's Archbishopric as many of us would wish. There are certainly areas where there has been a real attempt to bring about a balance, or where the voting capacities of synods have brought that balance about. As far as I can discern Robert Runcie has often wanted to achieve that balance but has not always seen it as vital to do so. Some of the General Synod's Boards are well mixed in theological positions and have a creative and productive dialogue resulting that can make their work acceptable throughout the Church. However, some Boards and some Ordination Courses (meant to be for Ordinands from all sorts of churches) tend to be more one way, or even entirely one way, with membership or staff of the same theological ilk. As a result, what they produce has only a limited and, indeed, inadequate usefulness to the Church as a whole. The care in setting up Boards, Committees, Courses, Commissions and sub-groups with a carefully balanced representation of churchmanship and theological perspective wherever possible is an agenda to be taken strongly in hand within the next quinquennium by the new Archbishop. It is noticeable, for instance, that no Evangelical has been in the close coterie of the top five bishops in recent years.

Appointments to bishoprics have been far fairer than Gary Bennett suggested in his Crockford's Preface. How much this is through the action of Robert Runcie or the Crown Appointments Commission is a matter of speculation. The mix is far more representative now than eight years ago, and approximately a quarter of the House of Bishops would be considered Evangelical in the full or broad sense of that term. It certainly was not so when I became a Bishop in 1982. The creativity in the House of Bishops between "catholic", "liberal", "radical" and "evangelical" is a real one, and it can exist because of the personal relationship and respect that we have for one another. We do not always enjoy the meetings but we enjoy meeting. Those who rail against the House of Bishops for its apparent collegiality have failed to understand the relationship of oneness in Christ that is in the House and its members.

The experience of pain draws people together. The brickbats, attacks and criticisms that a bishop receives are bad enough, but for an Archbishop of Canterbury these are a hundredfold more. It was when the press so viciously and erroneously attacked his marriage relationship that he felt the pain almost to breaking-point, and it was at that point that the House of Bishops responded with a collegiality of overwhelming love and support in a very special way. He himself shows great concern and care for those in the firing-line or suffering – as demonstrated by his support of Terry Waite's mission and then of Terry in his imprisonment, or with the Bishop of Bradford in the middle of the Rushdie crisis. He will be sad to lay down the ministry of worldwide contact which he has pursued so brilliantly, but he will be glad to move out of the cauldron of media attacks and misrepresentation. At least, in his retirement hobby of raising pigs he will not receive criticism from his constituents, but I wonder whether he might have names for some of them, particularly the names of some press reporters?

It would be true to say that most Evangelicals would have wished for a more prominent emphasis upon the centrality of Christ as Saviour and Lord and upon the richness of the Word of God, as well as a more explicit lead in evangelism, in Robert Runcie's Archbishopric. There have been times when some of us have been restless to see a more biblical approach in certain matters. This was true, for instance, over a service that the House of Bishops considered recently for ministry to the sick and dying. There seemed to be a total absence of the assurance that rings through the Funeral Service, and there seemed a failure to recognize the enormous comfort that comes from that assurance as in 2 Corinthians 4. Robert Runcie replied to that discussion by saying that the differences of approach showed the differences of theological background. So the service, in its use of quiet phrases and prayer, without a strong note of affirming and assuring, went through.

Evangelicals are concerned that so much has happened, particularly from the extreme liberal wing of the Church, that has denigrated revelation and some of the most valued parts of Christian doctrine. They are concerned that very few people in the Church, let alone outside it, study the Scriptures with love, thoroughness and expectancy, and feel that, to some extent, this is because of the underlying atmosphere of doubt that can so often be engendered by extreme liberalism. They long for a fresh encouragement to all members of the Church to be true Anglicans in the heritage of daily reading of Scripture, prayer and worship. Yet, although they will wish that Robert Runcie had spoken out more strongly against the damaging statements by extreme liberals and their deviations from the Church of England's position, they certainly will not accuse him of promoting such deviations but are thankful for his holding to the centre of the Faith.

Most Evangelicals will want to thank God for a great Archbishop in Robert Runcie. They appreciate, as far as one can from a distance, that he has carried an impossible weight of authority, position and sheer pressure of work. They would want to express their admiration and gratitude for that supreme dedication. Yet, most of all, they would want to give thanks for an Archbishop who has walked close to God in devotion, prayer and worship and who has, it seems, many, many times fallen onto his knees or leant back in his chair or car-seat to say from the heart, "This is an answer to prayer".

An Anglican Catholic View

ERIC KEMP
Bishop of Chichester

There can be few informed members of the Church of England, of whatever party, who are not grateful to Robert Runcie for the leadership that he has given in a time so fraught and complicated, and who do not resent the treatment that he has received at the hands of the press. Michael Ramsey had guided the Church through the traumas of the sixties and seventies with some difficulty. The five Coggan years saw the first full impact of the Synodical Government changes in their unexpected and undesigned weakening of episcopal leadership. The Anglican Communion was beginning to be in disarray after the near fiasco of the 1978 Lambeth Conference. Many of us felt that Robert Runcie was the only English bishop who could promise real guidance through an unhappy tangle. He leaves a considerable mess behind him, but it is one which would have been far worse if he had not been at Lambeth during the last ten years, and it may be questioned if anyone else could have achieved more in an impossible office and a distracted Church.

I have been asked to write about his archiepiscopate from the point of view of a leader of the Catholic Movement in the Church. I wish whatever I now say to be read against the background which I have just described, and that appreciation of the Archbishop's achievement.

Catholics welcomed Robert Runcie's appointment. They felt that he stood firmly in the Catholic tradition, and both understood and cared about the things that mattered most to them. They also believed that through his chairmanship of the Anglican-Orthodox dialogue and his many close relations with Orthodox bishops he could be relied upon to see the problems of the Church of England in relation to the hopes of Orthodox and Catholic unity. Had he not spoken in the Synod against the ordination of women on ecumenical grounds?

He went to Canterbury in the period between the two Loughborough Catholic Renewal Conferences, and there was a hope that his archiepiscopate might provide the breathing space from controversy needed to allow the positive fruits of those Conferences in mission and renewal to develop. Sadly this did not happen, but it was not wholly his fault. The false start, after the Ten Propositions, led inescapably to the fiasco of the Covenant. Scarcely was that out of the way when another movement began, first to allow the ministry in England of women ordained priests overseas, and then for the ordination of women in England.

It is difficult to explain to those who do not share the Catholic concept of ecclesiology, and of the Church of England as only a part of Western Catholic Christendom, how these proposals seem to Catholics to strike at the roots of the Church of which they believe themselves to be loyal members. One who has already left the Church of England over the ordination of women said: "The rest of Catholic Christendom told us not to do it, and we have gone against their advice." Most Catholics are still hanging on but the whole controversy has been and continues to be a blight on the mission and renewal that are there.

After a year at Lambeth Robert Runcie declared that he had been converted to the Anglican Communion. With the enthusiasm of a convert he has travelled incessantly to all parts of the Communion, but most frequently to North America. A benefit of all this was seen in the acceptance of his leadership at the 1988 Lambeth Conference. The Conference was, in many respects, a personal triumph for him. A few years earlier the visit of Pope John Paul to Canterbury, the signing of the Common Declaration and the setting up of ARCIC II, had seemed a great achievement which really forwarded Anglican-Roman Catholic relations and filled many with hope of closer union. The Archbishop's call for serious consideration of the need for a universal Primate, made in his keynote address to the Lambeth Conference, and the Conference's strong endorsement of ARCIC I, might have strengthened that had the Conference not opened the way for women bishops, necessarily a much more divisive decision in internal relations in the Communion, and in relation to wider unity, than the feeble utterances of the 1978 Conference on the ordination of women to the priesthood.

Whether the Archbishop could have done anything to stave off the disaster is doubtful, given the determination of the Americans to go ahead. In the American speeches one heard the echoes of the American Declaration of Independence, and there were some who would have welcomed an American UDI which did not compromise the rest of the Communion. What influence the Archbishop tried to exercise to prevent this is not known. The result was that unity with Rome and Orthodoxy, as far as the Anglican Communion as a whole is concerned, has been set back for generations. The subsequent visit of the Archbishop to Rome, important and positive as some of its features were, underlined that.

The sad episode of the Crockford's Preface and death of Gareth Bennett exposed to the general public a situation of which Catholics in the Church of England were only too well aware. While many of us regretted the terms in which he wrote of the Archbishop, we could only agree with his diagnosis of the condition of the Church of England. It is, however, a situation for which Catholics have very largely themselves and their fathers to blame by reason of their failure since the war to be an effective missionary force. By 1939 the Catholic Movement had very largely captured the Church of England as far as externals went, and indeed in theological leadership. Sadly this was not equalled by pastoral and evangelistic zeal, and gradually those who wanted a living faith turned elsewhere.

Things are changing. In my own diocese I see a substantial number of young Catholic clergy who are bringing a new as well as an older look to the parochial ministry, who are drawing people to their churches and who are able to work very happily in association with their Evangelical brethren. I believe this to be happening elsewhere also, and there is promise of a deeper unity among ourselves than we have seen for a long time. I pray that fulfilment of this promise will not be killed by a wrong decision by the Synod in 1992. By then, however, Robert Runcie will have left the centre of the stage and it will be for another either to steer the ship through the exciting voyage of the Decade of Evangelism or to do what he can to salvage something from the shipwreck.

Where Catholics have been in whole-hearted support of Robert Runcie has been in his social concern and teaching. This has been a leading element in the Catholic Movement from early days. Dr Pusey and others at both the theological and pastoral levels, lay leaders such as Lord Halifax, and the Lowders, Dollings, Mackonochies and many others in the slum parishes showed Catholic concern for the poor. Later this concern became rather too diluted by somewhat dubious sociology, though the books of Demant, Scott Holland, Reckitt and others are still powerful reading. A social concern has never ceased to be part of what the Church Union stands for, and recent publications by its committee for social concern are helping in an understanding of the principles which should undergird the work of the Church Urban Fund, and should also help to ensure that what Robert Runcie set on foot in that does not remain simply ambulance work but leads to a positive reconstruction of society.

Catholics are grateful to the Archbishop for his courage in speaking plainly to government and nation on such occasions as the Falklands War and in relation to social problems of our time. They are well aware of the many hurts done to him by the Press and have been anxious to support him by their sympathy, prayers and when possible, words. They have been anxious to listen to him themselves, knowing that although on occasion they might be disappointed in what he said there would be more times when they received hope, encouragement and instruction.

They have been aware that in devotion he is one with them and shares their deepest concerns.

He has been archbishop at a more difficult time than any of his predecessors in this century. I should not be surprised if the verdict of history ranked him equal to any of them, and higher than some.

A Listening Archbishop Speaks

DIANA McCLATCHEY
Moderator of the Movement for
the Ordination of Women 1985–88

At his enthronement in 1980 Robert Runcie spelt out the lead
which he believed a Church faithful to its Lord must give:
"a firm lead against rigid thinking, a judging temper of
mind, the disposition to oversimplify the difficult and
complex problems." Ten years later Anglican Catholics
mourn a lost leader; Evangelicals have condemned a
pragmatist; impatient reformers bemoan his inconsistency
and unwillingness to take definite action. Evaluation is the
price of high public office. Let it be by the criterion of his
own words.

As Bishop of St Albans his priority in the General Synod
seemed clear. In February 1978 he presented a report on
Anglican-Orthodox relations, as joint chairman since 1974
of the joint doctrinal discussions. A promising start appeared
to be in risk of foundering over the issue of ordained women
within the Anglican Communion. This was not an open
question for the Orthodox; if the Church of England
contemplated such a move it would register as a "different
sort of Church". He used the same argument in November
that year, when the House of Bishops sought to introduce
legislation to remove the barriers to the ordination of
women. There well might be a "prompting of the Holy
Spirit" in the question, so he urged the setting up of
tripartite talks with the Roman Catholics and the Orthodox;
and he admitted "there are some very disreputable
arguments against the ordination of women, and I
sometimes wince at the company I am compelled to keep
in voting against the ordination of women at the present
time". But vote against it he did.

In July the following year it was proposed to implement the Lambeth Conference's plea for mutual recognition and hospitality between those provinces in the Anglican Communion which already ordained women to priesthood and those which did not. Clearly the Anglican Communion did not figure high among Runcie's priorities at this stage. Again he pleaded the claims of the conversations with the Orthodox and with Rome. He poured scorn on the merits of "exposure to fresh doses of women's ministry" and bemoaned "synodical fidgeting which makes us the despair of our ecumenical partners in debate".

In 1980 the new Archbishop had other pressing ecumenical concerns nearer home. The proposal for Covenant between the Church of England and three of the Free Churches was reaching the point of final decision. Runcie had supported the earlier Anglican-Methodist scheme, and as a diocesan bishop had encouraged local ecumenical projects, but he had taken no prominent part in the Synodical process. His speech before the crucial vote was taken about the Covenant was shot through with reservations. He was unhappy about the theology implicit in the Service marking the reconciliation of ministries; he was fearful of the mechanism for joint decision making. The commitment which he urged upon others was but bleakly present in himself. In the interests of a wider ecumenism he announced his support for the scheme, but his attempts to marry a Catholic understanding of episcopacy with the Orthodox ability to contain untidy divergence pleased neither committed supporters nor opponents, and the uncommitted middle ground failed to find the clear inspirational guidance they looked for. The Covenant went down.

During the debate Runcie had stated his belief that negotiations with Rome and the Orthodox would not have been wrecked by entry into the Covenant, though he was well aware of the difficulties presented by the existence of the Free Church women ministers. Conversations with the Orthodox had now come to something of a standstill, but those with Rome were increasingly significant. After the unforgettable scenes in Canterbury Cathedral in May 1982, where Pope and Archbishop kneeling together committed themselves to the quest for healing after three hundred years of schism, hopes of finding some method by which Anglican Orders might be recognized by Rome were high. In this climate women were urged to subordinate aspirations to the priesthood to the greater good of the Church Catholic. In public and in private Runcie made his priorities clear. In no way could he promote so controversial and potentially damaging a cause, however much sympathy he may have had for the individuals concerned. Although he had always supported the non-priestly ministry of women – and had taken a deaconess with him to Lambeth as his private secretary – up to 1984 his contacts with the Women's Movement had been minimal. His basic lack of comprehension had been apparent in 1981 when at the WCC Conference on the Community of Women and Men at Sheffield he had spoken of a complementary relationship within the Church, and as an example had recommended short courses on spirituality as an appropriate contribution which women might make. The women listening had hoped for some appreciation of their equal standing within the Body of Christ, of the justice issue involved. The feminists from America and Europe had been scornful; English women had been bitterly disappointed.

The narrow defeat by the House of Clergy in 1978 of the attempt to introduce legislation led to the formation of the Movement for the Ordination of Women. Membership grew quickly, encouraged by periodic visits by ordained women from the United States, Canada, New Zealand and Hong Kong. Problems soon arose as to their standing and activities in this country. The Archbishop made it clear to individual women that he recognized and affirmed their ministry as priests; equally clearly, there was no official welcome, nor any permission to exercise their ministry in an English church. Grey areas of uncertain legality abounded. Therefore in July 1982 a motion asking for positive legislation about "women lawfully ordained abroad" was moved in the General Synod. The Archbishop gave it a qualified welcome. "I believe, very firmly, that consistency, like patriotism, is a virtue, though it is not enough, and we need to grow." His new responsibilities within the Anglican Communion, where the numbers of ordained women were growing rapidly, presented a new perspective, "I have grown to believe that the coherence of our Communion is very important . . . I would certainly like to see some movement now."

The draft for "general approval" of this legislation was presented in November 1983 and passed by comfortable majorities in all three Houses. Had the two Archbishops then accepted legal advice that the Measure did not warrant "Articles 7 and 8 designation" (requiring majorities of two-thirds in each House) it would almost certainly have been given final approval the following year. But because a principle of Catholic order was involved which overrode the claims of the law, the Measure was referred to the dioceses, following the process of revision, in July 1984. The support which Runcie gave was by now considerably more forceful: "I am even more convinced that the time has come to take some action." Clearly, the increasing numbers of women priests "overseas" were there to stay. His own international role as Archbishop, however, was in danger of becoming ambiguous. "An office which should be a focus of identity and affection in fact embodies rejection and division. . . . They are questioning the sincerity of our loyalty about respecting those parts of the Anglican Communion which do ordain women." He saw the Measure as a strictly controlled attempt to "offer hospitality to women presbyters of Churches with whom we remain in communion" and unequivocally he urged support.

However, by the time this Measure returned to the Synod with the necessary diocesan backing, majorities in all three Houses had already voted to introduce legislation on the main issue, ordaining women priests in England. The "final approval" debate in July 1986 was therefore dominated by discussion of the principle involved, as yet unresolved in England. A tiny minority of speeches was concerned with the Anglican Communion, none with the role of the

Archbishop. In a cogent and closely argued speech Runcie urged the need for the Measure, on grounds of the integrity and unity of the Communion and as a contribution to the wider ecumenical scene. He warned of the dangers of a "little England" mentality, and stressed the "freedom for diversity at all other levels" which a "common life at its basic Christian level" made possible. For the first time in the Synod he referred to the positive theological arguments for ordaining women, instancing his recent correspondence with Cardinal Willebrands. He concluded: "If we fail to pass this Resolution we shall threaten the unity of the Anglican Community, which I believe is to be cherished and worth many a lesser sacrifice." It was a clear and forceful lead − and an indication of his current priority; but the emotive accusations of a "back door" approach to the ordination of women had had their effect. Like the Covenant, this Measure was defeated despite a lead from the Archbishop.

That November it became abundantly clear that Runcie was not convinced that the time had come for change in the Church of England. He continued to drive down the middle of the road, admitting that he had become convinced that the arguments for the ordination of women now "tip the balance favourably", but urging the ecumenical advantages of "reticence". "We have a duty not to be seen acting in an abrasive and unfraternal disregard of very large Catholic bodies with whom we share the very fundamentals of the faith." There were dangers to the internal unity of the Church of England. He urged Synod to refrain from embarking on legislation, recommending a policy of gradualism. He instanced the support he had given to the concept of hospitality in the previous debate and advised the English to watch carefully developments overseas. The Church of England should concentrate on the inclusion of women in the diaconate, for which he had already evinced support. For those who believed that the inclusion of women in full ministry was already overdue, it was a deeply disappointing speech. The fact that Runcie was clearly unhappy about his own position added to the sense of frustration. Perhaps the Synod as a whole sensed this. By comfortable majorities, largest of all in the House of Bishops (41–6), the Synod accepted the risk and voted for legislation to be prepared authorizing the ordination of women priests in England. Once again it had declined to follow the Archbishop's lead.

With hindsight it is clear that the assurances which Runcie sought, the proven acceptability of women priests elsewhere and the satisfactory admission of women to the diaconate, were the intellectual conditions which he set himself before he would allow his head to follow his instinctive desire to include women in the presbyterate.

Earlier that year Florence Li Tim Oi celebrated forty years of ministry. The Movement for the Ordination of Women, with the active co-operation of the Dean and Chapter of Westminster, organized a Eucharist presided over by Bishop Gilbert Baker, who in 1971 had ordained the first English woman to priesthood in the diocese of Hong Kong. A few women priests from overseas joined hundreds of deaconesses and a number of bishops and clergy in a packed church. They heard the Dean read out a warm letter from the Archbishop. Indeed, during the next few difficult years individual priests from overseas who met him never doubted his personal acceptance and affirmation of their orders. Personal conviction and inclination, however, were by no means in harmony with his public *persona*.

This became very clear in the spring of 1986. MOW had taken the initiative in planning a Service of Thanksgiving in Canterbury Cathedral for the many diverse ministries, lay and ordained, which women were exercising all over the Anglican Communion. It was a theme close to Runcie's heart. He wrote, "I welcome the service. . . . I hope very much that I can be celebrant at such a gathering. It would be a great help to me as I see it in my Anglican Communion responsibilities." However, fears that the event would be used – or interpreted – as pressure on the Church of England led him to listen to cautious advisers. Eventually he withdrew. It was an occasion of high ecumenical romance, spirit-laden with a sense of joy and prophecy.

Every major women's organization in England was represented in Canterbury Cathedral, and women from twenty-six countries in the Anglican Community and beyond. As the Bishop of Dover wrote to the diocese, ''It was an act of total sincerity and deep joy. . . . There was nothing approaching a protest or a demonstration, no hint of a propaganda exercise, but a sense of thankfulness deeper than words, expressed with a profound joy and often with tears . . . It expressed to me with a vivid new awareness that these women with their great gifts were not pressing, like the suffragettes of old, for a just recognition of their rights, but seeking to respond to a sense of vocation, not less keenly felt than that of any male ordinand, in an obedience which has often been costly and painful.''

Now, as on many other occasions, Runcie used the pastoral, one-to-one, approach. A telephone call at 11 o'clock that evening brought his congratulations and thanks to the organizers of the Canterbury event. But the women who had come from overseas were not convinced. A group of a dozen, each representing a different province, had the day before met the Archbishop in Lambeth. Each had spoken of the ministry of women in her own country, varying enormously in culture and tradition. Each had made her own plea. As he listened, his face had expressed very clearly the tension of his conflicting emotions. Understanding this, American women sent him flowers.

In July that year Professor McClean presented to the General Synod a report of proposals for provision for dissenting bishops, dioceses and parishes, including separate jurisdictions, with and without women priests. The response of the Archbishop was now clear. He would have no part in legislating for schism. He urged the Synod to reject the report, promising that the House of Bishops would bring forward their own proposals. With manifest relief the Synod complied.

Shocked perhaps at the lengths to which opponents were threatening to go, Runcie reiterated his doubts. ''No one can predict the day when the Church of England will proceed to the ordination of women." He quoted the judgement of Solomon on the disputed baby, and the sacrifice which the real mother was ready to make. "Perhaps both sides in this debate need to ask themselves whether their claims will end in the division of the Church of England." He was not a happy man. Nor were many of his hearers.

When in February 1987 the report of the House of Bishops was presented it was clear that the Archbishop was still not convinced of the desirability of legislation. He emphasized the lengthy process ahead, lightening the tension in Synod with his characteristic wit: "It is a little early to be taking the tarpaulin off the lifeboats, or even signalling to other shipping to stand by to take on board some of the passengers." But he was wholly serious when he emphasized the unanimous decision of the bishops that if change were to come it would not be at the cost of separate jurisdictions in the Church. "I for one do not intend to preside over the abolition of diocesan episcopacy and the parochial system as the Church of England has known it from the time of my predecessor, Archbishop Theodore of Tarsus." He counted himself now as one who was convinced of the arguments in favour of ordination. But he remained "doubtful as to timing, for ecumenical reasons or because of a concern for the unity of the Church of England". He needed more evidence of consensus in the Church of England. This, he now appreciated, could only be tested by legislation. But the argument which would eventually prove determinative was beginning to appear: "those in favour will see the ordination of women as developing and completing the wholeness of the threefold ministry for mission in today's world." The principle which had consistently underlain his handling of marriage and divorce – traditional Catholic teaching interpreted with inspired pragmatism, the compassionate common sense which he had admired in the Orthodox – was coming to bear in this other sphere of Catholic practice.

But he was by no means ready yet. The draft legislation was introduced in July 1988, at the same session at which he presented the promised report of the House of Bishops on the theological issues involved. This was a tortuously balanced document detailing the arguments for and against, with no corporate attempt at evaluation. His own speech, however, recorded for the first time his intellectual conversion. He now developed the "incarnational approach to the whole question of Christ's high priesthood and our salvation" which he had used in correspondence with Cardinal Willebrands earlier. "I have come to sympathize with those who believe that in at least some societies an all-male priesthood may now increasingly obscure the fact that Christ's humanity is inclusive of women." His extensive visits throughout the Anglican Communion had enabled him to listen to arguments quite foreign to him seven years before. He admitted the force of the argument that "the absence of an inclusive ministry made it harder for the Church to be a sign of the unity of the Kingdom", and then made the statement that so many had waited years to hear from him. "I have come to the judgement that the ordination of women would actually be an enlargement of the Catholic priesthood, an opening up of priesthood, rather than its overturning." From this hard-won theological premise he saw the way through the ecumenical dilemma to which he had witnessed so loyally. "If we judge that a priestly ministry, inclusive of women, would witness to unity in a broken world, ought not this vision of unity to be the one that we offer our partners in ecumenical dialogue?"

The following day he dashed the hopes of all who were rejoicing at the prospect, at last, of a firm archiepiscopal lead. The draft legislation had reawakened all his fears. Could the Church of England really survive this imminent prospect of no-go dioceses, of parishes forced to come to terms with controversial decisions? "I am no happier that this legislation is likely to achieve a development which will signal a greater unity in mission and service to our people" – this, of course, remained the consistent criterion. "The proposals before us do seem to me to be a kind of legislative schism, and I must ask Synod to consider the cost of such advance without greater consensus." He voted against giving the proposals general approval. Again, a majority in each House rejected his lead, but the numbers were noticeably reduced, particularly in the House of Bishops. Those as yet uncommitted, those convinced intellectually, but reluctant to risk the step, grasped at the Archbishop's objections. Despite the different outcome of the vote it was the story of the Covenant all over again.

Sixteen months later, in November 1989, the Synod spent two days debating a revised form of the legislation. Over four hundred amendments had been considered, and the main objection of the bishops to permanent no-go dioceses had been met. And Runcie's speech in urging the Synod to send the legislation to the dioceses revealed the confidence of a man who had rediscovered his sense of direction. He chided both sides in their use of apocalyptic language. "I remain of the conviction that the ordination of women to the priesthood ought to be construed as an enlargement and extension of the historic Christian ministry . . . development rather than revolution." He was still fearful, he yearned for greater consensus, a simpler way forward; but his very doubts led him to turn to the dioceses, so vitally affected by the proposals. He was confident that "here as so often, God will surprise us by the way he guides the Church which is faithful to the Gospel call with courage and a sense of real purpose for the future." He described the two days of debate as "the most taxing . . . in terms of attention, detail and emotional investment that I have know in nineteen years as a bishop here." Back in 1984 he told the Synod: "Slow progress has one merit – it allows time for the Holy Spirit to prepare the hearts and minds for change." He knew what this meant, and five years later he knew the toll this activity exacted.

Other related problems challenged him to avoid the over-simplified solution. The election in the autumn of 1988 of Barbara Harris as Suffragan Bishop of Massachusetts demanded that explicit response must now be made to the theoretical questions of "communion" and "recognition". In November he attempted to spell out to the Synod the canonical position of the Church of England. With the experience of the Lambeth Conference behind him, he knew the reality of "communion", both inevitably incomplete and provenly present. But to define the "recognition" or "acceptance" of Holy Orders he relied heavily on a legalistic judgement. It was not convincing. Manifestly he had accepted the orders of individual women priests; nor did he accept a theological distinction between priest and bishop, as he had made clear in November 1984. Common sense suggested that although English law continued to bar the exercise of a woman's priesthood in the Church of England, the principle of recognition had been defined and affirmed as long ago as the Lambeth Conference of 1978. In 1984 the Archbishop had ignored his lawyers for the sake of a principle. Perhaps in 1988 sensitivities were too inflamed and the stakes too high. The Church of England was not officially represented at Bishop Barbara's consecration in Boston in February 1989. Nor was it at Dunedin in New Zealand in June 1990, and what was said in a private interview at Lambeth with the first woman diocesan bishop remains (rightly) unrecorded.

In 1989 Runcie reminded the Synod: "It cannot be irrelevant to evangelism that so many unbelievers think that the place we give to women in the Church is frankly absurd." But he has insisted on listening to both sides in this controversy. And throughout his Primacy he has listened. He has listened, often painfully and at length, to the Black Anglicans in England, and through them to the pain, disillusion and bitterness of a much larger constituency outside the Church; with the consequence that despite the quashing of the Commission they had hoped for and the perceived rebuff in a synodical vote in 1988, they have never ceased to doubt that he personally understood their feelings and was anxious to integrate them with honour in a Church which had treated them with such scant love or imagination. He has listened to the leaders of the Orthodox, understanding them and gaining their confidence. He has listened to Free Church men and women, to Germans and Lutherans and has kept their insights before the frequently purblind ecumenical vision of the General Synod. He has listened with realistic attention to Pope John Paul and his representatives, and has communicated what he has learned. He has listened to the men and women he has met in every corner of the Anglican Communion, letting their actions as well as their words speak to him.

He has listened, and he has often spoken forcefully. When he deemed it necessary he has criticized government attitudes. Thus, in a debate in February 1988: "Broadcasting, at least in our distinguished tradition, exists not to sell but to serve its viewers and listeners: and it resists the tyranny of numbers masquerading as consumer sovereignty. These are marks of respect for human dignity which our faith compels us to defend." On the issues of disarmament and nuclear defence in the early eighties, he again resisted the temptation to opt for the oversimplified solutions to complex problems. His contributions to the theological debates 1968–87 enabled him to share a vision of a Church in which there was room for pilgrims at very different stages of their journey. "We grow in freedom", he argued. "There is statement and definition, certainty, but they are distinguished all along by a spirit of humility and reverence in the face of the inexpressible and undefinable, and a recognition that there are perhaps the deepest truths about God which cannot be packed into the capsule of ideas."

Throughout his period at Lambeth, in his handling of the many issues related to marriage, divorce and remarriage, he has consistently spoken and voted for a traditional church discipline which could find room for the compassion of Christ to individuals; one that, like the Orthodox model, could combine strictness of principle with mercy that was frequently untidy. Runcie is *not* a legalist. He may not have helped the homosexual community in November 1987 by defining the condition as a "handicap" but he has never condemned. Nor has he doubted, in the whole realm of sexual morality, that "Christians have no monopoly of loving and true relationships".

In February 1989 he spoke of the need, not only for mature people who take on priesthood later in life, but for young priests who would grow to maturity as they exercised their office. The same is undoubtedly true of archbishops. Certainly as he struggled with the ''women problems'' which dominated the eighties in the Church of England we have seen this process of response, slow change and development. Where will it all end?

First among Equals

DAVID SAY

Bishop of Rochester 1961–88

Bishop George Bell, in his monumental life of Archbishop Randall Davidson, said that there are two kinds of leadership. ''There are those who are leaders of a cause on the success of which they stake everything they have. Such leaders will drive forward as fast as they can and will cry aloud to their followers to make haste after them. But there is another kind of leader who, having a charge entrusted to him and a body of people at whose head he is placed, rather seeks to act as the interpreter of the best mind that is in them and to give it expression. . . . He runs the risk of misrepresentation, and is unlikely to win great popular applause. But he is not on that account to be dismissed as an unsuitable kind of leader in dangerous and unsettled times.''

Half a century later the leadership of the Church of England given by Robert Runcie has not been that of the leader of a cause. Rather he has sought to bring out the best in those with whom he works, to listen to what they have to say, and to reach a consensus of opinion wherever possible. He has been relaxed and cheerful in style and, because he has refused to be hustled into quick judgements and precise answers, he has understandably been misrepresented by those who sometimes seem to be more keen to create news than to report it.

Runcie became Primate at a time when the House of Bishops was beginning to flex its muscles in General Synod, after ten years of seeming to bend over backwards to allow the clergy and laity to co-operate in church government in the way that the Hodson Report *Government by Synod* proclaimed that ''theology justified and history demonstrated". Runcie was the first Archbishop to come to office with experience, as a diocesan, of being a "bishop-in-Synod". This undoubtedly influenced the style of his leadership of the bishops, as it did the manner in which he led the General Synod. He had accepted government by Synod from the start and had no interest in perpetuating prelacy.

The House of Bishops, like much else in the Church of England, has been on a moving staircase in recent years. Archbishop Geoffrey Fisher gave a higher priority to the private "Bishops' Meetings" where for many years the Church at large thought the power lay. This was far from the truth, as one quickly found on becoming a diocesan bishop! Fisher regarded a Bishops' Meeting as a meeting of housemasters with the headmaster – who talked for a large part of the time! With the coming of synodical government, Bishops' Meetings gradually became less formal, more pastoral in outlook, and regularly included suffragan bishops as well as diocesans. At the same time the House of Bishops in the General Synod began to have more demanding agenda and to be of increasing importance. This coincided with Runcie's arrival in the chair, and his style of leadership – patient, listening to all sides, not expressing his own view too quickly – understandably gave the bishops a new sense of confidence and resulted in the House taking a more active corporate role in the Synod. After one session at York, Clifford Longley commented in *The Times* that "what had emerged enhanced was the collective leadership and authority of the bishops". This was the occasion when Bishop David Jenkins of Durham found his niche, as what Longley called "a lovable old eccentric, not a heretic trying to destroy Christianity".

In General Synod Runcie spoke fairly frequently when he was not in the chair. He had the remarkable capacity of putting a personal imprimatur on what he said and of conveying a buoyancy about it that was very good for morale. He did not always win the day, but on occasion he undoubtedly influenced votes in all three Houses. He also had the capacity to reappraise his position, as for instance

over the ordination of women priests. Many saw this as a
strength rather than a weakness, but in the climate of the
1980s it attracted an easy denigration. There were those who
felt he spoke too often but others welcomed an Archbishop
who assumed the role of "Leader of the House", especially
as it was obvious that all his speeches were well researched
and carefully prepared.

At the same time as he was evolving a new style of
leadership among the English bishops, Runcie was also
working hard at being *primus inter pares* among his fellow
bishops of the worldwide Anglican Communion. His
relentless round of overseas travel meant that, when the
bishops met at Canterbury in 1988, he was no stranger to
them and they responded to him as their host with warmth
and enthusiasm. For both Robert and Lindy Runcie the 1988
Lambeth Conference was a triumph which even the English
press were obliged to acknowledge. Less than two years
earlier the House of Bishops had been so enraged by the
scurrilous and baseless attacks on them both in two papers
that it had taken the unusual step of publicly dissociating
itself from the sentiments expressed and of passing a
unanimous vote of confidence in the Archbishop's
leadership, and pledging its love and support to him and
his wife in the face of the personal distress these attacks had
caused them.

Robert Runcie was not only the first Archbishop to
understand the world of television, with its appetite for
instant news and immediate comment, but he was also the
first to have to augment the staff at Lambeth Palace so that
public relations could be handled adequately. A gatekeeper
at the Palace once said that in the 1980s they had as many
calls on a Sunday as they used to have on a weekday in the
1970s.

When he arrived at Lambeth, with the domestic chaplain
who had served him at St Albans, it was not easy for the
new Archbishop to adjust to a larger staff and to learn to
delegate to different colleagues matters affecting the
Anglican Communion, national and public affairs, or the
diocese of Canterbury. The appointment of Bishop Ross

Hook in 1980, followed by Bishop Ronald Gordon in 1984, to head up the Lambeth staff and to provide an immediate episcopal contact at Lambeth for the diocesan bishops, was an important development which also facilitated relationships across the river with Whitehall, Church House and the Church Commissioners at Millbank.

The Archbishop's Secretary for Public Affairs had always included among his responsibilities relations with Parliament and with Government departments. Runcie was anxious that the bishops should play a full part in the House of Lords, and he was not content that they were sent briefs for speeches, although this procedure had been greatly improved by Michael Kinchin-Smith and later John Lyttle. He was concerned that the bishops should give a higher priority to being in the House and about the place. This proved to be an uphill struggle as a new generation of bishops, preoccupied in their dioceses, seemed not to have the same enthusiasm for the task as many of their predecessors. Runcie feared that if bishops had only a specialized responsibility they would lose sight of the general responsibility of being a Lord Spiritual. He was anxious for a "rounded" presence of the bishops in the House of Lords, and the Temporal Peers were the first to encourage him in this.

Sadly, his own heavy programme at home and abroad did not allow him to be in the Lords as often as he would have wished. However, he and the Archbishop of York, as well as several bishops, were present when the Chief Rabbi was introduced as a Life Peer. Runcie made a number of notable speeches on such matters as the British Nationality Bill and the Falklands War and the peers always listened to him eagerly. He clearly enjoyed being in such stimulating lay company and it is much to be hoped that, when he leaves Lambeth, he will have time to sit regularly as a Life Peer.

The international, national and local arenas in which an Archbishop of Canterbury has to move simultaneously have long necessitated some delegation of responsibility, and under the pressure of recent times this has become even more urgent. None of the Archbishops who have held office since 1945 have been ready to abdicate completely from any part of their responsibilities. Robert Runcie has always insisted on the necessity for him to be grounded in a diocese, and as first among the Primates to be regularly in orbit round the world visiting other provinces. He is, however, the first Archbishop to devolve a large measure of responsibility for the diocese of Canterbury to the Bishop of Dover, and to leave the chairmanship of the Church Commissioners to a diocesan bishop for most of the time. His sharing of some responsibilities with the Primate of York has been noticeable, and he has called upon the services of a wide variety of people as advisers and as script writers.

The number of dioceses, colleges, schools, religious communities and voluntary organizations who feel that they have a claim upon an Archbishop's time are legion, and perhaps Runcie has been more generous in making time for some of them than his other commitments really permitted. But he has made a real attempt to devolve some of his inherited tasks to others, and he has prepared the way for his successors to make even more radical changes.

Canterbury diocese will always want an Archbishop to feel at home in Canterbury, but it may also look for a bishop with diocesan rank to provide leadership for its parishes. Now that the Anglican Communion has regular meetings of the Primates as well as of the Consultative Council, a future Archbishop of Canterbury may be able to plan his travels over a longer period. If the House of Bishops becomes more of a collegiate body than it is, it could well develop a sharing of leadership which eventually might ease the pressure on the Primate. If any of these developments come to pass, credit will be due in large measure to Robert Runcie, one hundred and second Archbishop, for having pioneered the way.

A View from the USA

EDMOND LEE BROWNING
Presiding Bishop of the Episcopal Church in the USA

Though we have a theological understanding of vocation, our sense of that is always sharpened when we see evidence of one who has been called to a certain place at a certain time and has been such a good fit that the hand of God is made plain. Such is certainly the case with Robert Runcie as Archbishop of Canterbury.

We are living in a time of great tension between where we are and where we are meant to be going, between the already and the not yet. Perhaps we mortal folk always experience that sense of "in-betweenness" here in this earthly place, which is only a temporary home for us. However, I suspect that as we approach the millennium, as changes we would not have thought possible just a short time ago take place in our society and in our churches, the tension is greater than before experienced. Having the spirit, and wit, and skill to lead a church through the tension of becoming is a very special gift, and it is possessed in abundance by Robert Runcie.

I was interested to read that he said in an interview not long ago that it would have been far easier for him to come out for or against whatever came along. This was not to be his ministry. His ministry was one of enabling the various factions to work things through to better effect than through his direct intervention. I well understand the difficulties of this, as we have our share of controversies in the Episcopal Church in the United States. Our own situation has helped me to know deeply that not choosing sides so that a situation can work through with some grace is the harder course. No wonder the image of "fence straddling" is an uncomfortable one! Not only is the position difficult, it is not well understood and can be mistaken for lack of conviction or of firmness or, perhaps worse, of trying to please everyone. But those who try to take the middle way, and not only allow for diversity but value it, know there are times you risk pleasing no one. Nevertheless, you must stay steady on that course and seek the will of God.

What the Archbishop has been able to do with great skill, and no small cost to himself I am sure, is to keep people talking around difficult issues. He has held them together, not simply to "keep peace", which is frequently impossible and not always desirable anyway, but because he values them and their views. He does not belittle the apparently misguided (though I am sure he must strain not to unleash his considerable wit on a hapless soul from time to time), and he has not rallied people to him at the expense of the continuing dialogue.

Following the Lambeth Conference in 1988, the Archbishop appointed the Commission on Communion and Women in the Episcopate, chaired by Archbishop Eames of Armagh. The charge he gave to the group laid the groundwork for the spirit of respect and courtesy that has, in large measure, prevailed in the Communion to this day, in spite of the differences of opinion during this time of reception. The comprehensiveness of belief of those appointed, the tone that he set for the Commission, the clarity with which he defined their task, from the beginning made adherents to all positions hope that the Anglican Communion would grow in grace from this tension rather than wither from ill spirits. I am quite sure that the former has occurred, certainly thanks to the fine efforts of that body, but also owing to its foundations as laid by Canterbury.

I think that the grace with which His Grace handled the controversy around the election and consecration of the Rt Rev. Barbara Harris as the first woman bishop in the Anglican Communion is an example of both clear-headedness and compassion. His response to Barbara Harris and her election was marvellously affirming. It was a time of great joy for the great majority in the Episcopal Church in the USA, and he affirmed that and joined in celebrating.

At the same time, he took care not to marginalize those who could not support this election and consecration. His actions made it obvious that he was well aware of his position as the spiritual leader for people who were not in agreement about something of great consequence to them, and to our Communion. Lesser persons might have allowed a spirit of partisanship to spoil the event and disfigure the memory for one group or another. Regardless of our views on this issue, we were all blessed that his large spirit was able to encompass all.

I am reminded of the words of the great Anglican apologist Richard Hooker. Our true nature, he said, is as selves who are "sociable parts united into one body". We are bound "each to serve unto [the] other's good, and all to prefer the good of the whole before whatsoever their own particular." I do believe that the Archbishop of Canterbury has lived in an understanding of this "good of the whole". This understanding has not only been invaluable in times of controversy. It has been foundational to the way he has managed to hold and weave together the diverse body of men and women, from the world around, who name themselves as Anglicans. The respect and affection in which the bishops of the Communion hold the Archbishop, quite splendid to see at the Lambeth Conference, gives some witness to his ability to unite the sociable parts into one body.

In the spring of 1989, the Primates of the Anglican Communion gathered in Cyprus. During their time together they issued guidelines for a decade of evangelism. One of the guidelines was this: Discover and use distinctive Anglican gifts. "Our heritage of liturgical and sacramental worship, our apostolic continuity, and our 'reasonable tolerance' ", said the Primates, "are all evangelistic tools and distinctive gifts to the larger Christian community. Effective evangelists are true to themselves." Those of us who have had the opportunity to work and serve in Christ's Church with Robert Runcie might say that he himself is characterized by "reasonable tolerance". This particular gift, as given to the Communion in his ministry among us, has enabled him to keep the church from getting stuck in the swamps of discord and unable to do the mission to which we have been called. He has not forgotten, and has helped the churches in our Communion to remember, that it is the *mission* that is important, and not simply how we organize ourselves to go about it. That is a simple truth but simple truths are sometimes easily forgotten.

There is no question in my mind that Robert Runcie's gifts are grounded in his theology, rather than in political skills or sociological understandings (though he is not without these). Because of this grounding, his actions are of a piece; they "hang together", as we Americans say. Further, his actions and his words are in agreement. They come from a deep place that does not get stirred and befuddled by the winds of popular opinion. In short, though he is open to change and to new understandings, he is not pulled from a clear course because it may be disapproved of, or unpopular. I think that in future years, as we look back at and reflect on these times of controversy, the importance of this theological steadiness in the Archbishop will become even more plain.

There is hardly a better ally during times of tenseness and controversy than a ready wit. One can hardly spend time in the company of Robert Runcie without being aware of his marvellous good humour. This can not only take the tenseness out of a difficult time, it can make a heavy task a great deal lighter. Those who know the Archbishop no doubt have their own remembrances of his bringing a certain playful zest to a particular moment. I will end these reflections with one of my personal favourites. During a plenary session at the Primates' meeting in Cyprus, we had before us for our line-by-line approval a rather long statement. The Archbishop led us through this expeditiously and with his usual good humour. When we, as the Primates of the Anglican Communion, had expressed our "concern" just one time too many, he chided us by noting: "I read in the press the other day that Anglican bishops are so devoted to their various 'concerns' that they always have three in the morning before breakfast!"

When we think back on the ministry of this wise Archbishop, I do believe we will remember not only his theological groundedness, his ''reasonable tolerance'', but his wonderful humour. Most particularly we will remember and give thanks to God for Robert's love and caring for each and all of us who are the Anglican Communion.

A View from South Africa

DESMOND TUTU
Archbishop of Cape Town

At the closure of the 1988 Lambeth Conference the Primates of the Anglican Communion gathered round Robert Runcie. One of us read out a short tribute to him and then we all broke out into very warm applause. The entire conference joined us in giving him a long standing ovation. This was not just conventional stuff; it all came from the heart because Robert Runcie has endeared himself to us in the Anglican Communion outside the British Isles. We have been puzzled that he has appeared to be so unpopular in some of the British press. In the rest of the Communion he is held in very high regard and affection. The almost unanimous view was that Lambeth 1988 turned out unexpectedly to be a huge success and a personal triumph for Robert Runcie. In preparing for this essay I wrote to my brother Primates (awful word, especially when you are from Africa!) and in the responses words such as sensitivity, concern, caring, warmth, etc., kept being used. Let me write about how I have experienced him.

Once I was travelling overseas as the General Secretary of the South African Council of Churches, when one or other of my utterances aroused the ire of the South African government. Mr P.W. Botha threatened to deal with me effectively on my return, including withdrawing my passport which, according to him, I had abused so ungratefully. I was in England on that same trip when Terry Waite called to say the Archbishop would like to see me at Lambeth Palace. In a high profile meeting the Archbishop gave me a postage stamp commemorating his joint visit with the Pope to Ghana, requesting me to hand it over to the Holy Father at the audience that Lambeth Palace had arranged for me. The Archbishop was hoping that the evidence that we had fairly powerful friends might serve to restrain the South African authorities. As it happened, Mr Botha ignored my influential friends and went ahead to confiscate my passport. But the whole episode demonstrated just how caring Robert could be, and at the time I was not even a diocesan bishop. His view was that anyone who touched an Anglican bishop touched the Anglican Communion, and that I can tell you was wonderfully reassuring in the dark days of government harassment which many of us experienced in the Third World part of the Anglican Communion. What I will not forget is that Robert saw me on that occasion when he had just had a painful session with his dentist – indeed he was still decorously spitting blood.

Soon thereafter the South African government appointed the Eloff Commission to investigate the SACC, hoping that enough damaging evidence would emerge which would justify government punitive action and which would persuade the SACC member churches and its partners overseas to distance themselves from such a tainted body. Never was anyone hoisted more thoroughly with his own petard. As General Secretary I picked up the telephone in Johannesburg and called our friends overseas, and during Holy Week in 1983 some of the most impressive and high powered church delegations testified before that Commission. The Archbishop of Canterbury responded by appointing a four-person international delegation, including Terry Waite, to represent the Anglican Communion.

When one of our bishops had his house petrol-bombed and was to appear in court, the Archbishop sent Terry Waite to express his solidarity, support and concern. On other occasions it was the Bishop of Lichfield who came twice as the Archbishop's emissary to alert the South African government that we did have prominent friends and that we belonged to a worldwide community of some importance.

In the period 1983–89, the Archbishop sent emissaries no less than five times to South Africa to express his support of our church in its struggle. When I was awarded the Nobel

Peace Prize in 1984 Archbishop Robert Runcie was there at Heathrow Airport to greet us on our way from the USA to South Africa before we went to Oslo. He invited us to stay at the Old Palace in Canterbury and I preached in the cathedral. He insisted that I walk next to him in procession into a packed cathedral, and I was not still even a diocesan at the time. He arranged for me to have lunch at Lambeth Palace with Oliver Tambo, the President of the then banned African National Congress, at a time when both the British and South African governments frowned on meetings with so-called terrorists. There was no fence sitting here for Robert. The climax to this expression of pastoral concern and caring happened when the Archbishop attended my enthronement as Archbishop of Cape Town. It was considered an occasion of some significance to the Communion because many of the Provinces were represented by their Archbishops.

One of the letters I referred to earlier describes just how the Archbishop showed his sensitivity to the Communion by sending Terry Waite to the Province of the Southern Cone in South America at the height of the Falklands War, to say he cared. And of course in the celebrated sermon in St Paul's Cathedral to celebrate the British victory, it appears there were those who were annoyed that the Archbishop did not preach a chauvinistic sermon but talked about reconciliation. In the rest of the Communion we have been thrilled to have a spiritual leader who knew that the Church cannot be neutral, but must take sides with the poor and marginalized against the powerful and affluent – as he has done in the case of the miners' strike and in holding forth about the underclass in Britain, and about the casualties of policies that seem so callous and uncaring, almost making out that the poor are to blame for the plight in which they find themselves. We have been thrilled to know that he could stand up for attributes such as compassion, gentleness, caring and sharing. He has taught boldly that human beings count, with an intrinsic worth that has little to do with achievement but is God's gift to all. All must thus be treated with reverence since they are created in the image of God.

Robert has held together this disparate and untidy thing, our lovable Communion, because he is a warm person who makes people feel wanted and important. Robert laughs not just with his teeth, but with his whole person. He has a remarkable intellect but he has never intimidated us who believe that human beings are not just cerebral creatures. Some in the West are very clever and know it, and often do not suffer fools gladly and show that arrogance which makes us lesser mortals wilt. Robert has not surrendered his intellectual integrity but has carried it all so graciously and taken our points of view seriously. One of the Archbishop's letters says he allowed for regional presentations at the Lambeth Conference because geographical groupings felt they had issues they wanted aired – and those regional presentations were significant high points in the Conference.

Because the Archbishop of Canterbury has been so caring of the Communion, the rest of us have tried to emulate him. And so four Archbishops (of Canada, the West Indies, of South Africa, and the Presiding Bishop of the United States of America) carried out a pastoral visit to Nicaragua and Panama in 1988. And others of us have visited our sisters and brothers in Palestine and elsewhere to express solidarity, caring and concern.

When he and Lindy have been badly mauled, the rest of the Communion has I know sent flowers and messages of support and love. Perhaps the lasting legacy of his period as Archbishop will be the fact that we have held together despite so much that has conspired to split us apart (not least the issue of the ordination of women to the priesthood and the episcopate). In this we have been greatly helped by his warmth and friendliness and caring. He and Lindy surprised people in a Latin American country when they got out of their car and helped to push it out of the mud. Maybe they have pushed the Anglican Communion out of the stuffiness of English establishment and made it the possession of all of us. Thank you, God, for Robert – and thank you, Robert and Lindy! We love you.

A View from Central Africa

WALTER PAUL KHOTSO MAKHULU
Archbishop of the Province of Central Africa

When I think of Robert Runcie my mind goes back to our first encounter at the Primates' Meeting in Washington in 1981 – a meeting clearly under the influence of eloquent, experienced and in some cases strong-willed personalities. By contrast, there were other participants whose mother tongue was not English and whose manner was diffident and even at times compliant. In the midst of this company stood a tall but almost fragile-looking figure, gentle and softly-spoken, seeking to promote dialogue between these leaders of the Anglican Communion. He listened intently to those who were struggling to communicate in a second or third language, and encouraged everyone to play a full part in the meeting.

There have been successive Primates' Meetings in Kenya, Canada and Cyprus, and over the years the composition of the membership and character of the meetings has gradually changed. The Archbishop of Canterbury has welded together the participants, from diverse backgrounds and with different outlooks, into a cohesive force within the Anglican Communion. There can be no doubt that he has earned the respect and enjoyed the affection of his brother Primates, partly because he has sincerely regarded himself as the "first amongst equals", and has reciprocated their respect and affection.

Moving from the Primates' Meetings to the Anglican Church as it finds itself in the world at large, our Communion consists of disparate elements and is not without its problems and disagreements. For example, when dissension arose at a high level within the Church in the Sudan, strenuous efforts were made by the wider

Communion to mediate between the warring factions, with the active encouragement of Dr Runcie. In today's world Church-State relations can be a point of friction. Recently the Church of the Province of Kenya has seen some of its bishops come under fire, accused of fomenting trouble because of their opposition to a one-party state. In response to this situation letters of support were dispatched to the Primate, Archbishop Manasses Kuria, and Bishop Henry Okullu by the Archbishop of Canterbury and a small working party of Primates. Inevitably, the Church has also been involved in human rights issues. When the Primates were meeting in Limuru, Archbishop Brown of West Africa was unable to travel, because his passport had been withdrawn. The Primates, under the leadership of Dr Runcie, called for the restoration of his travel documents.

However, Dr Runcie's caring and compassion has gone beyond the limits of the Anglican Church. When Pope Shenouda III of the Coptic Orthodox Church fell foul of President Sadat and was banished to a monastery in the desert, the Archbishop of Canterbury asked me to visit Pope Shenouda on behalf of the Anglican Communion, together with Canon Christopher Hill, and to convey to him the love, care and prayers of the Anglican Church.

Although very English in character, Dr Runcie has been by no means insular in outlook. He has been a tireless traveller and quick to appreciate the qualities of a wide variety of peoples and cultures. The Archbishop has been conscientious in getting to know the wider Church through carefully prepared journeys. These have been demanding, but a source of great pride and joy to the hosts. When the Archbishop of Canterbury came to my diocese in Botswana there was tremendous happiness among our people, irrespective of church allegiance. His coming was seen as bestowing an honour upon our nation.

In this connection I must mention two small but significant incidents which occurred during the Archbishop's visit to the Province of Central Africa. Soon after his arrival he was offered a gift on behalf of the province. It was presented in the traditional Malawian manner. That is to say, the donor went down on one knee and held the gift up high over her head towards the tall figure towering above her. Without hesitation the Archbishop dropped on to one knee beside her to accept the gift, displaying great sensitivity and a touching humility.

That acute sensitivity to the feelings of others is a hallmark of the man. It was evident later the same evening when Robert Runcie met Father Wellington Mabuto from the diocese of Grahamstown. Father Mabuto's son had been a refugee from South Africa for many years, living in Botswana, but had recently been killed in a road accident. The bereaved father came to Botswana and made a courtesy call at Bishop's House, only to find a reception for the Archbishop of Canterbury in progress. On being informed, Robert Runcie diverted his attention from the party guests in order to give a listening ear to the bereaved priest – a sympathetic gesture immensely appreciated and strictly in tune with the local culture.

The Archbishop's journeys have also, on occasion, made dialogue possible between the Church and the State. In one instance the Archbishop's visit, in an unprecedented way, facilitated access to the Head of State for the local Church. Dr Runcie travelled to Ethiopia to encourage the giving of aid for famine relief, meeting with the Government of the country, the Organization for African Unity, Inter-Governmental Agencies, the Ethiopian Orthodox Church and other Christian denominations there.

These travels have not been confined to the Archbishop and his entourage, but have also involved the Anglican Consultative Council which meets from time to time in different parts of the world, enabling its members to relate to the local church wherever they meet. This not only strengthens the bonds of affection between Anglicans in different parts of the world, but deepens our fellowship in Christ. So, also, we become more aware of our common Anglican heritage and of belonging to the same Communion.

The Church of England has for a long time been referred to by Anglicans throughout the world as ''the mother church'', and over the years Christians from the former British colonies have looked up to England. However, these ''daughter churches'' are now growing rapidly, both in size and in maturity. Today, when the Church of England looks into the mirror and sees itself in relation to the Anglican Church throughout the world, it should realize that it belongs to something much greater than itself alone. This means that the agenda for the Anglican Communion can no longer be heavily weighted with the preoccupations of the developed world. Through the diverse cultural expression of worship, etc., we can perceive a mutuality in the faith of which we had previously been unaware. Moreover it remains to be seen how rigidly we stick to Western norms of procedure when we gather together for deliberations.

Undoubtedly, Robert Runcie has been the right man in the right place at the right time, leading his Church in a period of transition and diversity. We must thank God that the occupant of the seat of St Augustine of Canterbury over the past ten years or so has been a man of vision, able to adapt to the changing role required of him by today's Church in today's world. The Lambeth Conference of 1988 didn't just happen. It was the culmination of much careful thought and prayer, detailed discussion and practical planning on the part of the Anglican Consultative Council, the Primates' Meetings and various Commissions. The Lambeth Fathers were helped in their deliberations by experts of all kinds, but above all by the inspired leadership of Dr Runcie; and they showed their appreciation of this by giving him a standing ovation at the end of the Conference. This was not just a matter of form, but a heartfelt expression of genuine gratitude.

If we were to believe the reports in the British press just before the Lambeth Conference, we should have feared that Anglicanism was about to fall apart; but in the event the prophets of doom were confounded. In spite of severe differences over important issues, an overriding desire to stay together gained momentum. When inviting the bishops to the Lambeth Conference the Archbishop of Canterbury had asked them "to bring their dioceses with them". This meant they were to carry with them the mind of their dioceses, or in other words the concerns of the worldwide Church. The representation of so many diverse dioceses by the bishops and the participatory manner in which the conference was conducted further demonstrated that the voice of the churches in the younger nations can no longer be restrained. As for the future, something has started which cannot be stopped. The Anglicans of the Third World are caught up in the process of self-discovery which must continue into the future so that we can express our faith in diverse but authentic ways, along with our brothers and sisters elsewhere.

A View from Australia

JOHN DENTON
General Secretary of the General Synod

The character of Robert Runcie's travels throughout the Anglican Communion may be conveyed if I collect reports of a few incidents during his time in one country. His first visit to Australia began in Brisbane. It happened that the Premier of Queensland, Sir John Bjelke-Petersen, was in the midst of an industrial dispute with the electrical power unions in the course of which all tradesmen on strike were dismissed. Badgered for comment by the media, the Archbishop said that in all the free societies he knew the right to strike was recognized. This upset the Premier, and the Archbishop joined a select band of persons who received the Premier's advice to leave Queensland! This encounter ensured the Archbishop's welcome across the country. He was dubbed "a good bloke" in every pub and lounge-room in the land.

Shortly before his first journey to Australia the Archbishop was obliged to accept a major public engagement in London, which meant the cancellation of the last ten days of his long-planned Australian itinerary. Visits to Aboriginal communities of the north and west were to suffer. But the Archbishop promised to return as soon as possible, and this return visit was made in 1988, the year of the Australian bicentenary. It turned out that he has family connections in Australia, quite a clan in fact, and while in the Diocese of Newcastle he spent three hours enjoying himself over lunch with his extended family gathered at Toronto, on Lake Macquarie. On a day of recreation the Cairns Harbour Authority provided a motor cruiser to take the Archbishop and his party forty miles to the Great Barrier Reef. He very patiently attempted to catch a fish on the Reef. Eventually he handed the line to his Chaplain while he went for lunch. Almost immediately the Chaplain caught a magnificent nine-pound schnapper! The Archbishop quipped that he must have let down the line on the other side of the boat. An imaginative event in Perth was a Rock Festival attended by a thousand young people. There he unwound with a highly entertaining and impromptu speech for thirty minutes in a most informal style. Then, as an encore, he seated himself at the drums and demonstrated his musical talents by playing with the band. He spent three days in the Diocese of North West Australia. It was February, the hottest time of the year in the hottest part of a hot country. After visiting the vast North West Shelf natural gas plant, he went to a genuine Aussie barbecue, meeting a hundred parishioners for a meal by the sea on a pitch-dark and steamy night. He met and talked with everyone there, including a small boy who taught him to say ''Australia'' with the right accent.

The main day of that visit to the North West was spent consecrating four new churches in remote mining towns of the Pilbara region. The day began before dawn. Then he and his party flew by jet to each of the four towns which were hundreds of miles apart. At the end of the day hundreds of people throughout that huge area felt that they had not only seen the Archbishop of Canterbury but had personally met him and spoken with him. His great gift of enthusiasm, personal friendship and charm stood up right to the end. He travelled up the north-west coast to the Northern Territory, where he visited Groote Eylandt in the Gulf of Carpentaria. He had expressed a desire to meet with Aboriginal people. Bishop Clyde Wood writes that his clearest memory of his visit is that he was one of the last to eat at a large open-air barbecue meal. The reason was that he had been adopted by a boy aged about six years who led him off by the hand to play with a ball and a piece of stick. He then appeared to be perfectly happy being shown the sights by the small boy.

Max Horton of Alice Springs had met the Archbishop at the Anglican Consultative Council. The Archbishop, while making his way to his seat at the Wimbledon Tennis

Championships, spotted Max and stopped to greet him by name. On another occasion Max had been briefed to lead the intercessions at the Lambeth Conference Service in St Paul's Cathedral and was one of some six hundred people processing. As he passed, the Archbishop recognized him and said, "Max, don't make the intercessions too long". In Alice Springs the Archbishop was taken to St Mary's Child and Welfare Service, where Peter Hoy notes "that the Archbishop happily talked to disabled children who were totally unable to respond to him. He simply looked into their faces, held their hands and was content to be with them. It was difficult to entice him away or to direct his attention to other issues."

Peter Hoy adds: "What seemed to me to be unusual was that a group of people of great diversity, white and black, young and old, should comment so unanimously on the impact this man had on them. All felt that they had been speaking to a person of marvellous simplicity; one who lived each moment honestly. It was also most notable that Aboriginal people, young and old, warmed to him immediately and spoke to him readily – Aboriginal people are often quite shy and reticent with strangers." In the words of Bishop Clyde Wood: "He offers to all an experience of being a special person to him and to God. It is a gift that crosses all barriers of race and language."

Gathering Local Churches

SAMUEL VAN CULIN
Secretary General of the Anglican Consultative Council

It has been written of Robert Runcie that he is the most widely travelled Archbishop to have occupied the See of Canterbury. There is no doubt that he has travelled extensively throughout the world in his ten years as Archbishop and that his travels have been notable occasions. International travel has been demanding and at times exhausting for him, but it has on many occasions refreshed him. It has always provided an opportunity for his unique gifts of friendship and attentive listening to be offered in the ministry of building up those Bonds of Affection which have been essential to the maturing of the Anglican Communion. He has visited twenty-two of the twenty-eight Churches of the Anglican Communion – missing only Papua New Guinea, Melanesia, Tanzania, the Sudan, the Indian Ocean and the Philippines. Some of his visits to churches have been very brief indeed – and really undertaken for quite special reasons – such as his visit to Ghana in the Province of West Africa, in 1980. He was there only for a few days and then his purpose was his first meeting with Pope John Paul II. This in itself, of course, was an historic occasion and one that gained universal attention.

In other visits he covered every diocese in the Province, visited Heads of State, spent time individually with bishops and leaders of the Church and spoke to large congregations and crowds on a variety of occasions. This was the character of his visit to the eight dioceses of the Anglican Province of the West Indies in 1984 when he visited Belize, the Bahamas, Turks and Caicos Islands, Jamaica, Antigua, Barbados, St Vincent and St Lucia, Grenada, Trinidad and Guyana. Similar visits were undertaken to Australia in 1985 and 1988, Canada in 1985, the Church of North India in 1986, the Nippon Sei Kokai in Japan in 1987 for their centenary celebrations, and to the Church of Central Africa in 1989. In this last full year of his primacy, 1990, he has visited the Church of Pakistan, the Church of Bangladesh, the Church in Brazil, and the six dioceses of the Province of the Southern Cone – Argentina, Chile, Paraguay, Peru and Uruguay. I remember discussing his visit with one of the diocesan bishops in whose diocese he had visited, who described it as one of the highlights of his time as a Bishop. The Archbishop's presence gave a unique visibility to the local church, demonstrated a comprehensive concern for the whole of society, and reassured the local church that it was not isolated from the wider Anglican household.

As his years of travel unfolded, I realized increasingly that Robert Runcie's conversation was laced with stories of people he had met and experiences he had had. With ease he spoke of discussions with Vietnamese refugees in California, Heads of State in Africa, parish clergy in Japan, and university students in Argentina to mention only a few. He still delights in telling the story of his visit to the Church in Nigeria when thousands of balloons were distributed to the crowds with the inscription written on them "Blow up the Archbishop of Canterbury".

He has travelled overseas on four different occasions to preside at the meeting of Anglican Primates – in Washington, DC, USA, in April 1981, in October 1983 in Limuru, Kenya, in 1986 in Toronto, Canada, and in May 1989 in Cyprus. The accumulated experience and shared friendship developed in these gatherings of the Primates with Robert Runcie have helped them to exercise their office more effectively for the unity of the Church. They have, as a result, discovered a new depth of collegiality among themselves.

· In his ten years as President of the Anglican Consultative Council (ACC), he has travelled to Nigeria for the sixth meeting of the ACC in July 1984 and to Singapore for its seventh meeting in April 1987. He opened the eighth ACC meeting in Cardiff in July 1990, and was showered with loving tributes at the conclusion of the meeting, as he approached retirement. He has also attended every meeting of the Standing Committee of the ACC in those ten years. As a result he has helped to integrate the ACC more effectively into the total life of the Communion. One evidence of this is the fact that the work of the ACC, both in Nigeria and Singapore, helped effectively to prepare for the Lambeth Conference of 1988.

There are two phrases that come to my mind as I think about Robert Runcie's extensive travels on behalf of the Communion. One such phrase was in his opening address to the General Convention of the Episcopal Church in the USA in 1985 when he said, "It is the responsibility of the Archbishop of Canterbury to gather the Communion, not to rule it". It has been my observation over the years of our association that he has spent himself in travel in order to fulfil this responsibility inherent in his office. His presence in various parts of the world, time and time again, has provided the opportunity for the Church to "gather" in prayer, worship, reflection, consultation and commitment. This model of a "gathering" Primacy has been a powerful one. It is the authority of love and pastoral care in him that has drawn response and persuaded others to draw together in spite of differences and conflicts.

The other phrase was one that I first heard him share with a group of clergy in the diocese of Easton, Maryland, USA, when he quoted, "Nothing is real unless it is local". He was referring at the time to ecumenical considerations – the ecumenical Church is not real until it is local. Time and again in our association I have seen this commitment to "the local reality" vividly alive in his thinking, planning, activity, and personal relationships. His travels provided him with the opportunity to meet the Church throughout the world as a "local church" – not as an abstraction. His capacity for careful listening, kindly enquiry and conversation with particular persons in their own situation has brought reinforcement and hope to the local church. I am sure that one of the major reasons why he was so effective in leading the Lambeth Conference 1988 is because so many of the bishops and others present there had welcomed him in their "local church" and had confidence that he appreciated their situation. They listened to him with a willing mind and a consenting heart because they could say of him "He has been where I am".

Authority for Anglicans

MARK SANTER
Bishop of Birmingham and Co-Chairman of
the Anglican-Roman Catholic International Commission

By temperament and training Robert Runcie is not a theologian. His natural strengths lie elsewhere. Nevertheless the pressures and responsibilities of office have led him to articulate ideas of some theological importance about the relationships between unity and diversity within the bonds of communion, and about the nature and exercise of authority in the Church. He has also addressed himself to the ecumenical implications of these questions. The particular interest of Robert Runcie's approach to these issues is that it comes from someone whose office has given him a special responsibility for the maintenance and fostering of communion between diverse (even diverging) Christians.

The central act of the Anglican Reformation in the sixteenth century was the repudiation of a central authority focused in the Papacy, and the assertion of the right of a particular or national church to govern itself. Canonical means were retained for the maintenance of unity within the national church and its component dioceses. But no such structures were retained for dealing with relations between national churches. In the nineteenth century, in the wake of Empire and of American Independence, the Anglican Communion came into being as a communion or federation of churches united in faith and episcopal order and a shared liturgical inheritance, but still acknowledging no overriding authority. The principle of national or provincial sovereignty remained inviolate. This structure has been reinforced by the parallel development of the British Commonwealth of Nations. At the centre of Communion and Commonwealth alike there is a figure who is a personal focus of loyalty and who exercises considerable moral authority while possessed of no coercive power.

For as long as the patterns of political and ecclesiastical life exported from the British Isles remained more or less unquestioned and intact, no serious problems arose. But the weakening of inherited cultural and social bonds, combined with insistence on unqualified local autonomy, has produced sharp tensions in the Anglican Communion. The manner in which decisions have been taken to ordain women as priests and bishops in some provinces has resulted in a situation in which the sacramental bond of a universally acknowledged ministry is no longer intact. This represents a grave weakening of communion in one of its essential aspects.

It is important to recognize the nature of the problem. In speaking to the Lambeth Conference of 1988, Archbishop Runcie put it like this: "The problem that confronts us as Anglicans arises not from conflict over the ordination of women as such, but from the relation of independent provinces with each other. Although we have machinery for dealing with problems within a diocese and within a province, we have few for those that exist within the Communion as a whole" (The Unity We Seek). He pointed out a further dimension of this fundamental issue: "Another reason for looking critically at the notion of the absolute independence of provinces arises from our ecumenical dialogues with worldwide communions. These require decision and action at more than provincial level." He could also have instanced questions of liturgical divergence. If it is central to the notion of communion that we are able to recognize one another's sacramental acts, how are we to respond if one national church develops rites or practices which are regarded as gravely defective or erroneous by another?

Archbishop Runcie has maintained that Christians of diverse views cannot, if they are loyal to the New Testament, simply settle for mere co-existence. Whilst the Church of the Apostles certainly contained striking diversity, it also

believed in One Lord, One Faith, One Baptism, and in the
visible unity of One Church (*ibid.*, p.13). The crucial
questions therefore for Anglicans, if their communion with
each other is to be some kind of foretaste or realization of
God's will for the whole of his people, are:

  – How are unity and diversity to be secured together?
  – What are the limits to legitimate diversity?
  – How is conflict to be handled and if possible resolved?

Much Anglican talk about "dispersed authority" has been
altogether glib. In this context Archbishop Runcie has
spoken about the development of visible signs of unity in
the Anglican Communion:

  – The Lambeth Conference
  – The regular Primates' Meetings
  – The Anglican Consultative Council
  – The office of the Archbishop of Canterbury

Without undervaluing those organs in which lay and clerical
representatives have a place, he clearly sees great value in
meetings in which those who hold pastoral responsibility
for the churches are brought together. He is also, through
his own experience, aware of the responsibilities and
opportunities of the primatial office. He has stressed the
provisional character of Anglicanism and its institutions:
"We have no intention of developing an alternative Papacy.
We would rather continue to deal with the structures of the
existing Petrine ministry, and hopefully help in its
continuing development and reform as a ministry of unity
for all Christians" (*ibid.*, p.7). This is important. More than
once he has spoken of the significance of the Assisi meeting
in 1987 when Christian and other religious leaders met
together to pray for peace: "Whether we like it or not, there
is only one church and one bishop who could have
effectively convoked such an ecumenical gathering" (*ibid.*,
p.17). He has seen that meeting as a kind of sign of the role
that Papacy could play in a renewed Christendom.
Addressing the Pope himself in Rome on 30th September
1989, he spoke first of his own archiepiscopal office as a

response, within the Anglican Communion, for "a personal focus of unity". He continued:

> But for the universal Church I renew the plea I made at the Lambeth Conference: could not all Christians come to reconsider the kind of Primacy the Bishop of Rome exercised within the Early Church, a "presiding in love" for the sake of the unity of the churches in the diversity of their mission? In Assisi, without compromise on faith, we saw that the Bishop of Rome could gather the Christian churches together. We could pray together, speak together and act together for the peace and well-being of humankind, and the stewardship of our precious earth. At that initiative of prayer for world peace I felt I was in the presence of the God who said "Behold I am doing a new thing".

Critics will say that this is too rosy a view; that there is no Papacy available, however reformed, which will not claim and exercise coercive power. Others will say that, in a Church marked by the effects of human sin, it is unrealistic to suppose that unity can be maintained without the recognition of an authority with power to intervene and demand compliance. Such criticisms should not divert us from the insight which Robert Runcie has given us: that, precisely for the preservation of diversity in unity, the Churches of Christ require not only at a local level, but also universally, a personal focus of loyalty and unity; and that in the office of Bishop of Rome there is someone already present who is able to "gather the Christian Churches together". Ecumenical history will remember him as the Archbishop who helped Anglicans to face some of the questions which cannot be avoided if we are serious not only about Anglican unity but about the unity of all Christian people.

Anglican Theology Emerges

KEITH RAYNER
Archbishop of Adelaide

The directions which theology takes are not a matter of
chance. They emerge as a result of dialogue between an
inherited theological tradition and the new questions which
confront that tradition. Take the circumcision controversy
of the New Testament. The earliest Christian tradition
assumed that candidates for baptism would first have been
admitted into the covenant by circumcision. But
unexpectedly Gentiles were converted. This raised questions
for the received tradition, and the dialogue which those
questions provoked resulted in a new theological
understanding and a major development in the Church's
tradition.

Sometimes it was experiences like this which raised new
questions; sometimes they came from deeper reflection on
the scriptures. But often the questions come from secular
sources and the movement of world history. It may be that
theology has to be rewritten in terms of a new prevailing
philosophical framework, such as mediaeval scholasticism
or twentieth-century existentialism. Or new scientific
discoveries like those of Galileo or Darwin or modern
geneticists may raise new questions. Or it may be changes
in the pattern of social life or the adjustment required when
a theological system shaped in one culture finds itself set
in a different culture. Theology constantly faces new
questions, and if it is to speak to real life it must engage in
dialogue with those questions. In a rapidly changing world
like ours the questions will come thick and fast.

The character of the Anglican Church makes this dialogue
particularly intense. There are some churches which simply
ignore the questions posed by contemporary life and retreat

into their tradition. Eventually they face an explosion, but in the meantime they avoid the questions and proceed serenely on their way. There are other churches which sit lightly to scripture and the Christian tradition, so that they readily embrace new ideas without seriously testing their consonance with the received faith. But the Anglican Church straddles that divide. It stands firmly on the biblical revelation as it comes to us through the great tradition of the Church. But it also takes seriously the fruits of human discovery and thought, and argues that there can be no ultimate dichotomy between faith and reason. For Anglicans the dialogue between the received tradition and the new questions cannot be evaded.

The Anglican ethos is not one of authoritarian control over the questioning or dissenting voice. There is freedom to explore and to follow conscience. The degree of autonomy possessed by the member churches of the Anglican Communion also permits the questions raised by local culture to be faced without the constraints which highly centralized authority is inclined to impose. Yet at the same time there is the compelling recognition that every new idea must come under the scrutiny of the Bible and the tradition.

To lead the Anglican Communion in an environment of rapid change, as an Archbishop of Canterbury must do today, is a particularly challenging responsibility. Robert Runcie would not claim to be a profound or original theologian, but he is theologically alert and articulate. His theological stance has been criticized from opposite directions: he is either too liberal in encouraging the theological debate to take in new questions; or he is too conservative, not giving a radical lead. The contradictoriness of the criticisms suggests that neither is just. Robert Runcie's strength is that he knows that theology must be related to life, and he is alive to the questions which need to be faced. Yet he is also rooted in the received tradition and recognizes that the dialogue between the tradition and the new questions must be both searching and prolonged.

One key issue in recent years has been the identity of Anglicanism. For centuries the Church of England, intertwined as it was with the life of the nation as an established church, could take its identity for granted. Even in the colonies when the British Empire reigned supreme the question of identity scarcely arose. Only the American Episcopal Church was an anomaly. But in the post-colonial era Anglicans in Ghana, or the Philippines, or even multicultural Australia, cannot authentically belong to an *English* church. Even in a modern secular England the identity of the Church of England can hardly be taken for granted. So the question of what it means to be an Anglican demands an answer, even if such a question might seem heresy to the pillars of English Establishment.

Closely related is the question of authority in the Church. It naturally arises in a social climate which questions all authority; it is underlined by biblical criticism which questions the authority of the Bible; and it inevitably comes into focus in dialogue with other Christian traditions and other religious faiths. This raises quite practical questions: if there is authority in the Anglican Church, how is it exercised and by whom? What are the roles of bishops and synods, of the ordained ministry and laity? And how does a communion of autonomous churches speak with a common voice?

The topic which has raised most heat in recent theological debate is of course the ordination of women. One reason is that it brings into focus divergent understandings of authority. Does the ordination of women challenge the authority of scripture by overturning biblical teaching? Is it contrary to the relationship between the sexes which God has ordained? Does one part of the Church have the authority to change a Catholic tradition of two thousand years? The controversy has probably been fiercer in the Anglican Church than in any other, and the unity of the Anglican Communion has been sorely tested. This is precisely because of the Anglican determination both to face the new questions and to be faithful to the tradition. There is no doubt that the place of women in society has radically and permanently changed in the Western world, and the same will eventually be true everywhere. So the question will not go away. But it cannot be assumed that the ordination of women implies that the Church has been wrong for two thousand years. The question is rather whether the theological principles of those two thousand years lead to a different answer when the context is radically changed.

In many parts of the Anglican Communion, however, the relationship of Christianity to non-European cultures and to other faiths is a more pressing matter. Anglicans outside Europe are no longer prepared to take for granted that the academic theology grounded in the intellectual and cultural traditions of western Europe must be the norm for people with entirely different cultural roots. In this context the exploration of the positive strengths of theological pluralism – which has long been characteristic of Anglicanism but has often been viewed negatively – is receiving particular emphasis in contemporary Anglican theology.

Theological controversies are often fierce in today's Anglican Church. That is not new in the history of the Church. Nor is it simply negative. It is out of the wrestling of the tradition with the new questions of a changing world that the Holy Spirit leads the Church to a fuller hold on the truth. We shall be more open to his leading if we argue with charity and hold together in unity.

Anglican Evangelism Emerges

BISHOP MICHAEL NAZIR-ALI
General Secretary, Church Missionary Society;
Co-ordinator of Studies, Lambeth Conference 1988

Before coming to Lambeth in 1988 the bishops of the American Episcopal Church had attended their own General Convention, where the Commission on Evangelism brought forward a resolution calling for a Decade of Evangelism. This was approved without much debate. Alden Hathaway, Bishop of Pittsburgh and Convenor of the Commission, was somewhat disappointed at such an outcome. He had hoped for some discussion on the nature of evangelism and on models for evangelism which may be appropriate in today's world. In the event there was no such discussion and he commented ruefully that evangelism is, like motherhood and apple pie, difficult to be against! Some thought that was the end of the matter. An innocuous-sounding resolution had been passed and would now be consigned to oblivion.

Evangelism, however, was in the air. Already in 1987, the Pope had called for a decade of evangelization to win a billion new Christians by the end of the century "as a present for Jesus on his 2000th birthday". Christians of many denominations who were involved in Charismatic Renewal were also committed. So at the Lambeth Conference the Planning Committee provided a whole evening for a plenary session on *Evangelization and Culture* with bishops from Africa, Asia and Europe reflecting on how the sharing of Christian faith may be related to the values, idiom and thought-forms of particular cultures. In the Section on Mission and Ministry, meanwhile, a consensus was emerging that there needed to be a significant shift in the Anglican Communion from an emphasis on pastoral models of the Church to a mission orientation. Such awareness is becoming characteristic of church leaders throughout the world, but particularly in Asia, Africa and Latin America.

At the Lambeth Conference in Canterbury, two currents of Anglican life and thought came together in a creative and transforming way. On the one hand, there were bishops from rapidly growing churches and from situations where Christians were widely scattered. In such contexts, the traditional pastoral models of Anglicanism were proving wholly inadequate to the task. The Church was growing among people who had a nomadic style of life, for example. Sedentary models for evangelizing and discipling such people were proving to be ineffective. Dynamically new strategies were needed. Bishop Gitari, in his address, spoke of clergy and evangelists in his diocese who had been equipped to be travelling evangelists and pastors with the nomadic people of Northern Kenya. The rapid growth of the Church in Singapore, by contrast, has taken place in a growing modern city. At least part of the secret of this growth is the willingness of congregations to divide and divide again, so that more and more *local* expressions of the Church become possible. Typically, a congregation begins in a flat in a sprawling housing estate, grows to "school-hall size" and then to a size where it needs to use a cinema or a theatre for corporate worship. When it reaches a set figure, however, it starts to divide into smaller units again.

Bishops from those Northern Provinces where the Church is experiencing a numerical decline were also conscious that the parochial structures of a past age, which assumed that the whole population was "Christian", may be inadequate for contemporary situations which demand missionary responses. How, for example, may new churches be planted in England? The Church of England neatly divides the whole country into parishes. In theory there is a church for everyone. In practice, many in the new housing estates, among ethnic minorities in the inner cities and among those belonging to alternative sub-cultures have little access to the Church and the Church has little access to them. How can the principle of *locality*, enshrined in fundamental Anglican documents, be allowed expression in church growth, so that local churches are grounded in the local culture? Different answers are given to this question. In some cases it is thought appropriate for the parish church to "plant" another congregation in a specific area of the parish. In other cases, people from outside the parish may be invited to "plant" a church in a particular part of the parish. In yet other cases, diocesan authorities may permit extra-parochial communities to engage in mission and evangelism within defined areas. "Basic communities" centred in people's homes, and movements such as Cursillo and Anglican Renewal also become foci for evangelism. It is no accident that the conference's resolution on the Decade of Evangelism (No. 43) was followed by a resolution on missionary structures.

The emerging consensus on evangelism was well articulated by Bishop Dinis Sengulane of Lebombo, Mozambique. "We would like the Lambeth Conference to call on all Anglicans to evangelize", he said. "The consequence of evangelism will be the increase of the number of people with whom we have spoken about Jesus Christ, and an increase in the number of places where Jesus Christ has been proclaimed. The very name evangel means good news. All good news has to be shared with others." From the very beginning there was, however, disagreement about terminology. Some wanted evangelism, others evangelization.

Some believed that "evangelization" was not simply calling men and women to faith in Christ but also imbuing local communities, nations and the world with Gospel-values. This aspect of the matter was emphasized by Bishop David Jenkins of Durham. There is some support in the New Testament for the view that the presence and preaching of the Gospel should bring about a real change in those who are exposed to it. Such a change should not be merely "spiritual" but must affect the whole of life. Interestingly enough, the bishops from Africa tended to agree with such a holistic approach to evangelism, with the proviso that Christian involvement in community development and indeed political activism should not be at the expense of "faith-sharing".

Others were concerned that evangelization should be seen as the process which begins with Christian presence in the community, goes on to "faith-sharing" and the discipling of new Christians, and continues in the teaching and sacramental ministry of the Church. It makes sense, therefore, to speak not only of the "evangelization of the baptized" but even of the evangelists (1 Corinthians 9:23). It is possible to hold to such a "process" view and yet to believe that there are moments of "crisis" in such a process when people are profoundly challenged by the Gospel. Their response determines the future course of their lives.

Those who insisted on the use of "evangelism", however, were apprehensive that abandoning it would mean losing the cutting edge of proclamation and that "evangelization" would come to be synonymous with mission in general. For them evangelism is, as the Chief Secretary of the Church Army has put it, "helping people come to a living relationship with Jesus Christ and to live as his disciples day by day".

Whatever terminology is used, it is worth recalling that Lambeth '88 based its call on the recognition that God is a sending God. He has sent his Son into the world for the sake of the world and he now sends his Church to continue the work of his Son in calling people to repentance (i.e. coming to a new attitude to God, the world and one's self). The Church does this by proclaiming the imminence of God's Kingdom which is both a judgement on the past and a fulfilment of all that is authentic in human aspirations. It is both profoundly disturbing to human societies and human thought, and comforting to those who put their trust in God and live in fellowship with him. Those who live in expectation of the Kingdom mediate the demands and promises of the Kingdom by word and act to those around them.

Plans for the Decade of Evangelism are now well under way in many Provinces of the Anglican Communion. People are being encouraged to pray for the decade in the context of the liturgy as well as in other ways. There are bold initiatives such as the Nigerian decision to appoint eight missionary bishops in the most unreached parts of the country, and the decision by the dioceses of Sabah and Singapore to hold a Congress on Evangelism. There are stories of a personal conversion to evangelism such as that told by Bishop Alf Holland of Newcastle in Australia. This has resulted in new priorities for a diocese in the Catholic tradition. In a quieter way, perhaps, many dioceses are conducting parish audits with a view to relating all that the parishes do to the sharing of faith. Some parishes are encouraging home-based hospitality or "fellowship" groups which have outreach as their primary aim.

Nor is the decade a purely Anglican affair. Many other families of churches and even Councils of Churches have become involved. Interdenominational agencies such as the Bible Society are preparing to offer support in terms of literature, audio-visuals and other aids. A tremendous amount of energy has been released and is being channelled into constructive and creative work for the decade. Most of all, "evangelism" or "evangelization" are terms which have gained common currency in the Anglican Communion, making many to think of their obligation as Christians in this area of the Church's mission.

At the beginning of the Lambeth 1988 process Robert Runcie had called the bishops of the Anglican Communion to consider carefully how the Church is to go about making new Christians and nurturing them. It seems as if his call is being heeded not only by the bishops but by the whole Communion.

4
THAT ALL
MAY BE ONE

Ecumenical Progress

MARY TANNER
Theological Secretary,
Board for Mission and Unity, Church of England

"All round" and "all level" ecumenism was the way Robert Runcie described Anglican commitment at the Lambeth Conference in 1988. Although he came to office well known for his own commitment to Anglican-Orthodox and Anglican-Roman Catholic relations he has proved himself loyally supportive of "all round" and "all level" ecumenism. Not surprisingly there have been disappointments as well as triumphs during his archbishopric – for the more progress made and the more ground cleared, the more exposed become the remaining obstacles to unity. Throughout Robert Runcie has remained true to a vision of the visible unity of the Body of Christ; he had never been tempted to settle for mere co-existence or a federal model of unity. He has been insistent that amidst the variety of tasks *en route*, the hard search for agreement in faith must never be abandoned.

Nowhere was this clearer than in the position he took over the scheme for Covenanting which came before the English Churches in the early eighties. His speeches in the General Synod showed him committed to our Methodist, Moravian and United Reformed Church partners. Yet, at the same time, he was troubled by the unclarities of this particular scheme. He did not shrink from expressing his reservations on the subject of the incorporation of ministries; not incorporation into the Church of England, but into the ministry of the universal Church. His heart sank at the extra bureaucracy he feared the scheme would bring. Yet, troubled by the hasty process and the unclarities of the scheme, he nevertheless cast his vote in favour hoping, perhaps too optimistically, that the scheme would be improved in the months ahead. His speeches on the Covenant, like those later on the ordination of women, show his characteristically costly wrestling with the complex issues, weighing them, and coming to hardwon conclusions. His conviction that there can be no ecumenism on the cheap has marked his leadership for ten years. He has not been afraid to accept criticism for the stand he has taken in order to uphold a vision of the One, Holy, Catholic and Apostolic Church.

The national scheme came to nothing, leaving behind it much despondency. But eight years later new hopes are being set on firmer foundations. Robert Runcie has played a significant part in supporting the development of local ecumenism in Local Ecumenical Projects and local covenants, the introduction of ecumenical canons in the Church of England and the achievements of the theological dialogues. As President of the British Council of Churches he has played a part in the demise of that institution and the birth of the new ecumenical instruments. It is a tribute to him that he is to be one of the presidents of Churches Together in England and the Council of Churches for Britain and Ireland, not automatically because of the office he holds, but as a man the other churches recognize as having played a major role in the ecumenical journey in this country. He has commended the exercise of episcopal oversight without any of the trappings of prelacy.

Pictures often say more than words. The photograph from the Vancouver Assembly of the World Council of Churches, showing the Archbishop presiding at the celebration of the Lima liturgy flanked by a Lutheran woman pastor form Denmark, a Reformed from Indonesia, a Methodist from Benin, a Baptist from Hungary, a Moravian from Jamaica and a minister of the United Church of Canada, symbolizes his commitment to all-round ecumenism. That liturgy marked an important ecumenical moment. The standing together (though not concelebrating) with other ministers, as well as the presence of Orthodox and Roman Catholics who did not receive the bread and wine, was a powerful sign both of how far we have come and how far we have yet to go. Robert Runcie was the only person at that moment in history who could have expressed where we are and where we are going. His acceptance of this role showed him in line with the great Anglican ecumenical leaders of the past.

It is within his commitment to the search for the visible unity of all Christians that his special relations with the Orthodox and Roman Catholic Churches need to be seen. To have had as Archbishop of Canterbury a former Co-chairman of the Anglican-Orthodox dialogue has been of immense benefit at a time when Orthodox confidence in Anglicans was shaken by the decision of some provinces to ordain women. Indeed it was uncertain after Lambeth 1978 whether the talks would be resumed. But, following a series of visits to Orthodox Patriarchates by him when Bishop of St Albans, the dialogue continued. The affection the Orthodox have for our Archbishop has done much to ensure that our Anglican understanding of the mystery of the Church and of spirituality has been enriched by our Orthodox partners.

The lovely photograph of the Archbishop and the Pope kneeling together in Canterbury Cathedral captures so well the Archbishop's convictions about unity with Rome. It symbolizes too his own search grounded in prayer, in which we open ourselves to receive the gift of unity the Lord offers his people. In Anglican relationships with our Roman Catholic partners Robert Runcie has been able to match Rome's seriousness over the search for doctrinal integrity. His contributions in the debates in the General Synod on the work of the Anglican-Roman Catholic International Commission, and his letters to the Pope and Cardinal Willebrands on the ordination of women, show a theological rigour coupled with a desire for unity with Rome. The gentle way he commends the benefits of a universal primacy, "an ARCIC primacy rather than a papal monarchy", "a brother among brothers", has helped many to acknowledge the potential of such an office, as has the grace-filled way he has exercised his own primacy within the Anglican

Communion. The esteem and affection in which Robert Runcie is held by so many Roman Catholics has helped to ensure that, in spite of differences over the ministry and authority, the dialogue continues. It would be sad if the official Roman Catholic response to ARCIC I is not received by him personally before he relinquishes office.

Robert Runcie's time as Archbishop began with disappointment over the Covenant. It is fitting that it ends with a firm success. It was due solely to his initiative during visits to East and West Germany during the Lutheran Celebrations in 1986 that official conversations were set up with Lutheran, Reformed and United Christians in the tow Germanies. The *Meissen Declaration* committing our churches to move into closer fellowship symbolized in eucharistic fellowship, lived out in twinnings and exchanges, is grounded in agreement about the goal of visible unity and in the large degree of agreement in faith that already exists. One of the final acts of the Archbishop will be to preside at a Eucharist to celebrate this new agreement. The Meissen way shows that it is possible to make progress when opportunities are seen and grasped by the leaders of the churches. Robert Runcie's part in setting up official conversations with the Nordic and Baltic Churches and with the Moravians ensures that this part of the ecumenical movement in Europe will go on into the next decade.

It was his keynote speech at the Lambeth Conference on the *Nature of the Unity We Seek* that expressed most clearly his ecumenical commitment. It describes the vision of unity he has sought to pursue. It holds together the search for Anglican identity and unity with the search for the unity of all Christian people; it sets this in the context of the unity of the human community and the vision of the Kingdom. It was rightly acclaimed by the bishops at Lambeth and affirmed in the responses of the ecumenical guests; it is a classic statement for the last decade of this century. It shows beyond doubt his commitment to "all round" and "all level" ecumenism and the imperative of unity for the mission of the Church.

It did more than that. Throughout it was punctuated by

stories of people he had met, friendships formed, insights received from and through others. For Robert Runcie ecumenism is not dry academic table talk but finds expression in affectionate personal relations and in the offering and receiving of hospitality. In a decade when our dialogues have emphasized the communion of the Church, grounded in the relational life of the persons of the Holy Trinity, and of the priority of the personal over the institutional, Robert Runcie has demonstrated this in his own living of the ecumenical journey with warmth, friendship and humour. He is to be numbered among the outstanding ecumenists of our time.

I especially owe him gratitude for the support, encouragement and friendship he has given me in my own search. I am proud to have had a Lambeth doctorate conferred on me by Robert Runcie, an ecumenical Archbishop.

Ecumenical Pilgrims

PETER CORNWELL

One sad autumn John Henry Newman preached out at Littlemore his famous sermon "The Parting of Friends". When, about to make a similar move into the Roman Catholic Church, I preached my farewell sermon as Vicar of the University Church of St Mary the Virgin in Oxford, it was in springtime and I took as my theme " The Re-union of Friends". In retrospect was that unrealistic and euphoric?

Robert and I have been friends since the early sixties. I owe to him not only the opportunity to teach at Cuddesdon but also to meet through Lindy my wife Hilary. Since it has been alleged that the Runcies would only offer tea in bone china cups in the sitting room, I have to say that our courtship took place over mugs of tea in the Cuddesdon Vicarage kitchen. The college was then a rather traditional Tractarian place and, amongst the many things I learned from Robert, was the way in which such a solid tradition could live and develop through facing the difficult conflicts of the sixties. Roots were never to be severed but to live was to change, and to be perfect was to have changed often. After Cuddesdon our geographical paths were to part. We moved away to parishes in the North East.

But then came the more serious parting of the ways. To me it seemed that the tradition of faith which I valued, that living, developing Catholicism, was to be secured in communion with Rome. Sharing this conviction with Robert was one of the most painful experiences of my life. By that time he had become Archbishop of Canterbury, and my passage to Rome would inevitably seem to be a vote of no confidence in his leadership. To a hardboiled archbishop such a falling away would be a mere pinprick, lightly dismissed as a midlife crisis, but Robert was neither hardboiled nor over-secure on the throne of Augustine. We had a difficult lunch together at Lambeth, during which the Archbishop in him used sharp and telling arguments while the hearts of friends bled. It is no use imagining that tears have been banished from such transitions. There may not be a nineteenth-century breakdown of a relationship – the clean cut, no further meeting, none but the most stilted letters – but there is a peculiar pain in working to maintain the friendship in spite of the objective separation. And the separation is objective. Robert and I may be in partial communion but we cannot now share together in the eucharist of our common Lord. That is monstrous – a revelation of the monstrousness of Christian division. When you are separated at the Lord's table from family and friends, then it is that you wake up to the real scandal of division.

Robert, a convinced ecumenist, has always been quite sure that the Anglican experience still has something to say to the rest of Christendom. It may be on a world scale a minority vote, but its vision of holding together commitment to the Evangelical Gospel with the freedom to explore that Gospel honestly and faithfully within the context of Catholic order and sacramentalism is one to which he firmly adheres. This witness must not be diluted. Yet the firmness of this commitment has gone along with complete realism about the Anglican Communion. He has too much humour and realism to be haunted by the ghost of the British Empire. He is a man of universality who sees that the great issues of the day which concern the environment, peace, justice and the reconstruction of Europe require a Christian vision that thinks bigger even than the collected experiences of a Lambeth Conference. So he has always been a consistent apostle of an Anglicanism which looks beyond itself, that sees itself as incomplete, always orientated towards a wider unity.

Robert has acquired an acute understanding of the complexities of holding together the burgeoning cultural variety of worldwide Christianity, for he has lived through the pain of the Anglican Communion's unity being strained to breaking point. Ever more clearly he sees the need to see proper local autonomy qualified by an equally proper universal authority. Under his leadership the Anglican Communion has been challenged to take seriously bands of authority and unity capable of preserving universal communion. Whether the Communion has yet paid attention to this point, an outsider begs leave to doubt, but it is the fate of Archbishops to be called on to give "a firm lead" and then have that lead ignored. This in itself highlights the ambiguities of the Canterbury office. You keep having to wear different hats. Are you speaking for yourself, giving a prophetic lead, or are you trying to represent the consensus of the House of Bishops of the Church of England, or are you, in addressing the Pope, speaking for the whole Anglican Communion? Robert has consistently refused to be edged into the pretence of being a second Pope. He has always been clear that that particular job is already filled. The task of the non-Roman world is to begin to see the need of this Petrine element and to see it embodied not in some theory but in the actual ministry of the Bishop of Rome. There have been moments when he has glimpsed the face of a universal primate who would be acceptable to the disciples of the Reformation, and has not been afraid to say so. Standing in the dinner queue, or boarding a coach together at Assisi with John Paul II, were such moments. It has to be said that his task would have been made easier if Rome has reciprocated with greater vigour, shown more signs of understanding the Reformation demand for the proper autonomy of the local church and the need for Pauline critique as well as Petrine rock.

It has been bad luck that a man of consensus and unity should find himself in a role of leadership during a time of abrasion and reaffirmation of separate identity. Someone whose instinct it is to think big, to look beyond national and denominational borders, has seemed sometimes enslaved by the self-absorption of the Church of England and the agonizings of the Anglican Communion. A similar self-absorption, the post-Vatican tidying up and holding things together on the part of Rome, has slowed down the

ecumenical process. Robert's discomfort in such a situation
at least nails the lie that he is "trendy". That is the last thing
he has been. He has firmly swum against the abrasive
divisive tide of the eighties and his reward may be that the
eighties have ended with dramatic events which confirm his
every instinct for universality and openness. With the Iron
Curtain down and Europe once again a seething mass of
cultural diversity, Christianity can no longer afford the
luxury of brooding over its various separate identities. There
is work to be done to which Robert's heart must warm. The
eighties are over, and one's prayer is that the new occupant
of the throne of Augustine will not be found fighting the
battles of the last decade. My guess is that in a few years'
time not only Anglicans, but Roman Catholics as well, will
cry out for the broad vision and reconciling skills of the good
old Runcie days!

But Robert himself is much more understanding about
such things. He is an historian by trade and has something
of Newman's feel for the ebb and flow of church life. He
has never been a man for the "ever upward and onward"
view of history, for he knows that periods of advance are
followed by periods of retrenchment which can look like
retreat. He thus has an understanding of the post-conciliar
era, and sees why things are as they are. I have been present
when he has let down his hair and spoken very frankly
about ecumenical matters, and I have to say that his
comments on Pope John Paul have never been other than
affectionate, and those on (what seems to most) Vatican
conservatism, other than shrewd and understanding. He
has a great admiration for practical people, for those who
oil the wheels and keep things going, who edge the
lumbering machine a few yards nearer the journey's end,
and has always spoken with appreciation of the sheer hard
work and dedication of the Curia. He is not likely to see the
difficult heart-breaking eighties as a period of loss and
drawing back, but rather as a taking of breath before the
next leap forward.

We are pilgrims together in this search for unity. So much
of Robert's vision I share that it is really quite difficult to

see where we part company. But of course we do part company, else we would not be out of communion with one another. I suppose it comes down to a difference about where we ought to be. We both treasure the same Anglican thing, at best a rebellion against dividing up and parcelling out the riches of Christ. We both long for the day when these riches are no longer held in separate boxes. It ought to be possible both to be perpetually dazzled by these riches and for the faith which receives them freely to seek understanding of them. It ought to be possible for the Catholic Church to embrace cultural variety and yet hold us together in bands of love. We are truly pilgrims together roped on the mountain by our common baptism and love for the Lord Jesus Christ. But on this mountain mists come down and we shall sometimes seem to drift apart. There will be strain on the rope. Then we have to go on believing in the objective strength of that rope which holds us together, believing that this friendship is rooted and grounded in the friendship of Christ who has called us his friends.

Robert has a gift for friendship and has used it. Some have thought that this is at best a sentimental substitute for clear thinking and solid achievement. It is not. The *communio* we seek is friendship with God and, in that mystery, friendship with one another. At the end of the day, despite pain and differences, I do not think that my sermon on "The Re-union of Friends" was euphoric or unrealistic. I have come to see it as the basic thing, the very heart of ecumenism. Christians can have all sorts of sharp and highly principled differences, and these are not to be dissolved in some limp and sweaty handshake. But we can with integrity advance and discover that through friendship there is growth, both in understanding and in faith.

When the time came for me to be ordained/reordained in the Roman Catholic Church, I wrote to another ex-Archbishop of Canterbury, Michael Ramsey. He had ordained me both priest and deacon in the Church of England in York Minster. We had remained friends since that time. What would Michael make of what was about to happen to me? A few months before his death a typically spidery letter came back, saying that while a few years ago he would have asked me what I thought I was doing having been ordained priest in the Church of Christ in York in 1960, now "everything is mysteriously different and I rejoice that you can continue your ministry in the Roman Catholic Church". Things are different, mysteriously different, since the nineteenth-century days of the "parting of friends". There is still pain and the reality of division but in that friendship we see, in John Paul II's words, that we are "pilgrims together". We accept each other's integrity. One chooses one path and one another. We are not indifferent about paths, nor insensitive to the stress and pain which our different choices cause, but we are confident that the kindly light will lead us o'er moor and fen to our common goal.

Tractarian disciples often seem to divide between those of John Keble and those of John Henry Newman. The former have utter confidence in the Catholic completeness of the Christian life which they find in the experience of their parish. Lambeth Conferences may err, bishops may be heretics, synods may falter, but here is the genuine thing. The disciples of Newman value what God has given to the Church of England, but they see it squashed and squeezed in too restricting a room. It needs greater space in which to breathe. Robert Runcie has a touch of both the Keble and the Newman in him, but perhaps he follows most closely in the footsteps of that other Tractarian, the great Dean Church, whose generosity of judgement and enduring friendship even then defied the parting of friends and bridged the gulfs of bitterness and misunderstanding. I dare to think that a friendship has not only survived but deepened through tribulations and pain. I am personally grateful for that and have a hunch that we have stumbled across something here which is quite central to ecumenism. There is nothing which can separate us from the friendship of God in Christ.

In the British Council of Churches

PHILIP MORGAN
General Secretary 1980–90

Robert Runcie was not a natural President of the British Council of Churches: it was a responsibility to be worked at. Archbishops of Canterbury were not automatically Presidents, but all the Presidents have been current Archbishops, and Robert Runcie was chosen by the Council, consisting as it did of Orthodox, Anglican, Reformed, Baptist, Methodist, Salvation Army, Society of Friends and Pentecostal church people. He found the disciplines of presiding at debates of the Council almost as irksome as did an earlier President and Archbishop, Michael Ramsey. The niceties of obtaining a seconder to a motion or asking the Council's permission to do something obvious, like giving permission to a great speaker to speak, on occasion rather escaped him; and the complex, multi-claused resolutions of the BCC came from a tradition different from his own. However, like his predecessors, not only did he commit himself by setting aside time and making himself available, but by his conduct and contribution he won the respect and affection of all.

It was a role made difficult constitutionally. Although the President was *ex officio* a member of the Executive Committee, which met six to nine times a year, he was not expected to attend its meetings. Yet at these meetings, between Assemblies, major policy decisions of the Council were taken and the various radical, revolutionary, irresponsible or prophetic actions of the Council and its departments endorsed or set in motion – the adjective is the choice of the reader! As President he was held personally responsible by the general public and the media, when it suited them, for every decision taken and all its implications and nuances. Even if he had been present for the debate which led to a particular decision such an attitude would have been unreasonable, but not to have been present nor a party to a decision and yet held responsible for it was indefensible. At a final dinner for the Executive Committee he commented on the delicate footwork required at times to distance himself from some decisions whilst wholeheartedly endorsing others.

This sensitive awareness of the implications of particular issues and decisions was a major gift to the Council. It came, no doubt, in part from his personal temperament and the attitudes resulting from that, in particular his ability to see many sides to any question, in part from his long involvement in conversation with the Orthodox Churches and more recent involvement with the Roman Catholic Church. To some it appeared to be caution carried to the point of indecision, and was certainly irritating to single-issue activists, but those who made such a judgement were mistaken. It reflected the understanding of a man brought, somewhat to his surprise, into the cockpit of church and community affairs on a national and international scale at a time of rapid and unpredictable change, in which the temptation of many a politician and churchman alike was to act now, even if neither the background to nor outcome of the action proposed had been understood. His cool assessment of the appropriateness and effectiveness of an action frequently stood the Council in good stead and made all the more effective his active endorsements.

1982 proved to be a difficult year. It provided however a springboard for three examples of the leadership given by Robert Runcie which demonstrated his ability to act decisively with resolution and courage. Three events of great significance occurred within a matter of a few weeks in the late spring and early summer. The Pope visited Britain. The first series of ARCIC reports were published. The proposal for a national covenant in England, between the Church of England, the Methodist Church, the United Reformed Church and the Moravian Church, an outcome of a long and difficult series of consultations from the Nottingham Faith and Order Conference in 1964 onwards, came to the final vote in the churches. In national life these were overshadowed by the war with Argentina over the Falkland Islands, and in church life were undergirded by a remarkable growth in local ecumenical projects and local covenants, as local congregations, from Roman Catholic, Anglican, Reformed, Methodist and Baptist traditions, sought to embody local unity within the rules of their respective churches, and by the growing convergence of understanding identified in the WCC report *Baptism, Eucharist and Ministry*. All manner of expectations were in the air, some realistic, others, to say the least, euphoric! Perhaps the Pope would recognize Anglican orders at the service in Canterbury Cathedral! More realistically (perhaps?) a national covenant would resolve all the tensions experienced by congregations in local union with their mother churches which still operated denominationally.

The papal visit proved a great success, but few specific changes in inter-church relations followed immediately from it. ARCIC I was succeeded by ARCIC II. The proposal for a national covenant foundered on the votes of the House of Clergy in the General Synod of the Church of England.

The disappointment of realistic hopes, not least for a national covenant and for closer co-operative working within the extensive framework of councils of churches between the Roman Catholic Church and the other churches, proved very painful indeed for many deeply committed to this style of ecumenism. This was particularly true for many Methodists and not a few Anglicans who twice before had attempted a closer relationship. At the next conference of workers in local ecumenical projects and local covenants at Swanwick the mood was a mixture of frustration, anger, despair and very obvious pain. The Archbishop was due to address the conference on its third day, and the organizers felt it essential to warn him of the reception he might receive. The then Bishop of Derby, Cyril Bowles, chairman of the conference and of the Consultative Committee for Ecumenical Projects in England, had had a foretaste of this in the earlier part of the conference. The mood proved to be exactly as predicted, and those present watched the Archbishop accept the anger and pain and frustration and deal with it as a pastor, making no excuses, suggesting no easy palliatives, recognizing fundamental differences of viewpoint and providing at least a glimmer of light for many who felt betrayed and deserted. He had voted for the proposals for closer relationships, whilst being sympathetically aware of the profound hesitations of many fellow Anglicans.

At the first British Conference on Faith and Order in 1964 there had been brave hopes that by Easter Day in 1980 significant advance would have been made towards organic unity. It was not to be. Anglican/Methodist reunion had proved as elusive. The papal visit had contributed some ringing ecumenical phrases, such as the Pope's question in Bellahouston Park, Glasgow: "May we not continue this pilgrimage hand in hand?" A most imaginative Pastoral Congress had been held in Liverpool by the Roman Catholic Church in 1980, and its initial report had been far ranging and excitingly encouraging, but early optimism was quickly followed by much disappointment at the lack of movement. A similar fate appeared likely for the Papal visit. Local ecumenism was burgeoning, but with the danger of becoming another tradition apart from the denominational traditions. Some new initiative was clearly needed. If given by the BCC, assurance would be needed that it would be taken up by the churches and not least by the Roman Catholic Church, without whose presence in real ecumenical commitment any new initiative would lack seriousness.

A series of delicate discussions began, at first with individual church leaders. In time a small group met, and after the nicely balanced delegation of Roman Catholic, Anglican, Church of Scotland and Free Church leaders had paid a return visit to the Pope in Rome, a pattern of possible meetings emerged. Joint invitations would be issued and a broad spectrum of church representatives invited to meet to discover if possible a new way forward. But joint invitations proved impossible. Perhaps we had not fully understood each other, or perhaps other influences cautioned against such an approach. In the event a group of church leaders was invited to meet for a day with the Episcopal Conference of the Roman Catholic Church in England and Wales, at New Hall in Essex, which not only provided a notable photograph for *The Times*, demonstrating without a doubt the elderly male domination of church leadership, but began to clear up some surprising misunderstandings. Shortly afterwards Archbishop Runcie invited a broad spectrum of church leaders, including a most significant Roman Catholic delegation, to a number of days of reflection and prayer at Canterbury.

Throughout all this period Robert Runcie trod resolutely a difficult path, using his personal influence, giving wise counsel, overcoming a variety of setbacks which endangered the whole enterprise, and, with more at risk than most involved, enabling the enterprise to go forward. The Inter Church Process, with the theme ''Not Strangers but Pilgrims'', would have had no chance of beginning without this earlier behind-the-scenes leadership.

This was essentially his style as President of the BCC – supportive, encouraging, shrewd but undoubtedly committed to the cause of unity. He was not always best served by his advisers, who misjudged the effect of laidback English humour on an international audience at the WCC conference on the community of women and men in Sheffield, and who on occasions expected over-subtle nuances of balance to be picked up by synods and conferences, and – worst mistake of all – by the media. But in the situations and on the occasions when it really mattered he spoke for all the member churches of the BCC. His sermon at the conclusion of the Falklands war marked him in the minds and hearts of church people of many traditions as their spokesman and representative. It prompted a later and not entirely humorous comment from a Free Church source, when the General Synod of the Church of England was passing through some rough waters. ''If the Anglicans don't want Bob Runcie as their Archbishop, we will be only too happy to have him as ours!''

Factors external to the BCC made this a difficult time in which to be its President. Self-conscious nationalisms of different kinds in Scotland and Wales and in troubled Ireland required an Archbishop of Canterbury seen as an Englishman (although of Scots extraction and brought up near a Liverpool held by many to be the capital of North Wales!) to speak and act with care. Robert Runcie's warm humanity and astonishingly apt humour achieved this on most occasions. After the surge of self-assurance given to the Roman Catholic Church in Britain by the papal visit, the media were trying to set up cardboard cut-outs of Archbishop and Cardinal as rivals for status – with some backing from misguided church sources. A domineering, insensitive, confrontational style of political leadership in the state went a long way to devalue the concept of leadership, whilst a significant change in moral values caused Alastair McIntyre to write in *After Virtue*: ''the barbarians are not waiting beyond the frontiers; they have been governing us for quite some time. And it is our lack of consciousness of this that constitutes part of our predicament.''

It was not a time for grand gestures and universal designs. Damaged people and fractured relations needed support and delicate nurture. New possibilities needed careful exploration, initially away from the glare of publicity. Positions necessarily taken in public needed detailed preparation and achievable objects. Robert Runcie gave such leadership. In the summer of 1990 he ends his Presidency of the BCC, as the BCC ends its own life, with a broader base of co-operation established between the churches and with the prospect of new ecumenical groupings including the Roman Catholic Church in these islands. There are many possibilities of the churches owning their work together in a way not grasped before. But few dramatic breakthroughs in church relationships can be expected in the near future. The style has changed. Organic unity is still on the agenda but its achievement is over the horizon. Gradual, often uneven, growth may be expected, with a balanced stress on local renewal and denominational commitment.

The Council's positions on the moral issues and choices in many major situations, including South Africa, Hong Kong, Eastern Europe, Northern Ireland and the complex political and socio-economic situation in the United Kingdom, are more clearly articulated, command more support and increasingly are justified by events. The world was never likely to be changed overnight, but the churches are better placed to use all their resources of insight and information to identify their role in enabling that change. The work of the last ten years has enabled these changes to take place. Robert Runcie's Presidency has played its part in all of this. Rosalind Goodfellow aptly commented in her vote of thanks to the Archbishop at the final Assembly of the British Council of Churches: ''You have sought inclusiveness but not doubted the validity of difference.'' Her tribute was warmly endorsed by the Assembly – representative on this unique occasion of its traditional member churches and of those joining the ecumenical pilgrimage through the new Council of Churches for Britain and Ireland, which will replace the BCC.

In Europe

BARNEY MILLIGAN
Anglican Chaplain in Strasbourg

Arranging an archiepiscopal visit is a complex operation. When Robert Runcie came to Strasbourg in November 1989 for a five-day visit, there were twenty-six different events – church, political, civic, social, diplomatic, academic, gastronomic, and simply for the fun of it. And it all started over a year before when the ground rules were laid down by Lambeth – only three major speeches, a time for rest every day, and no impromptu question and answer sessions. "You will find he is very tired", they said.

Well, he obviously was tired when we met him on the tarmac at the airport; but not looking older than was to be expected almost exactly ten years after he had installed me as a canon of his old cathedral of St Albans in 1979. And we had duly ensured that the programme was as – quite rightly – ordered. But the interesting thing was how the visit provided its own momentum and how Bob Runcie swam with it. Unscheduled, unforeseeable and therefore unprepared speeches – at dinner with the Judges of the Court of Human Rights, or over coffee at the university – turned out witty, wise and quotable. Questions from students at the final session at the Council of Europe got a little out of hand, and some of these spontaneous encounters between the Archbishop and the young were what many people remember best from the whole visit.

I think the good chemistry started when things went badly wrong on the first day at the European Parliament. The speech to members was to have been at 3 p.m. But as we sat in the gallery at 10 a.m., I was appalled to hear a decision that voting should be at three. So the time had to be changed

– twice. And the Archbishop had to hang around for two and a half hours before making his speech. And in an odd way – which tells you a lot about the unpompousness of Robert Runcie – this need to adapt to the wayward habits of the Parliament, providing as it did a chance to meet over successive cups of coffee a variety of members and others, created an extraordinarily positive mood to which the Archbishop seemed to respond and which, indeed, he helped to create. The visit thus took off. To assess where it stands in relation to the Runcie story, however, I must stop telling stories and place it in a wider context.

It was significant that the Archbishop chose to pay a visit to Brussels early in his time at Lambeth. His speech there was vintage Runcie, peppered with historical allusions and personal memories, but also full of European commitment. "Christians can make decisive contributions to the new Europe", he said. This was in 1981, at a time when the Community was in the doldrums: I have been told that he provided a fillip to certain jaded eurocrats. Certainly his references to the whole continent of Europe and the Iron Curtain – "not a totally insurmountable barrier" – expressed a hope which was being rapidly fulfilled when he came to Strasbourg eight years later. And in a speech at the Jean Monnet Institute at Lausanne he spoke on "The Common Witness of the Churches in Western Europe" on All Saints' Day 1986 (the very day when I took up my appointment at Strasbourg). He used the picture of the Church as the "sign, instrument and foretaste" of the Kingdom – a picture which features strongly in the Anglican/Reformed dialogue. This picture formed a model for the churches' witness in Europe.

Despite these earlier sorties, Robert Runcie declared, when he came to Strasbourg, that he came to listen and to learn. And this was not an idle statement. For on several occasions – notably one whole morning at the Council of Europe – he did just that. This was one of the reasons why his speeches were taken so seriously and are still remembered. *Chaleureux* is a word much used by the French to describe warmth and friendship. It is a word I have heard constantly as friends and neighbours have summed up their impressions of the many-faceted visit.

But perhaps most striking was the effect the visit had on the Archbishop himself. Not only did he leave Strasbourg looking much less tired than when he arrived. (Was it the walk in the Vosges on the only day of snow during the whole of last winter?) He also appeared to have been caught by the crucial importance of Europe at this time – a conviction reflected in his visit to the church leaders' gathering from east and west the following April at Geneva; and in his speeches at the July session of General Synod in York when Europe was high on the agenda.

In China

BISHOP K. H. TING
President of the China Christian Council

My friendship with Robert Runcie has not only been rewarding on a personal level, but has also opened my eyes to see what unique roles an Archbishop of Canterbury can play in society as well as in church, in politics as well as in religion.

After some twenty years' lack of communication between churches in China and elsewhere, my first surprise was his suggestion, brought to me by Terry Waite in 1980, that he and I should get together, either in Nanjing, my town, or Hong Kong where he would soon be visiting. I was delighted but not without foreboding because, so soon after the catastrophic blows of the Cultural Revolution on the Church, we were just starting anew and hardly in a good shape to receive such a distinguished visitor. So I suggested Hong Kong. But the Archbishop himself chose to come up north to Nanjing. We were moved by this act of humility. It made him the first Archbishop of Canterbury ever to come to China.

The bishops of the Chung Hua Sheng Kung Hui (the Holy Catholic Church of China, i.e., the Chinese Anglican Church) decided unanimously long ago to join the other non-Roman Catholic Churches in the Three-Self Movement and later in forming the China Christian Council which many understand as the (future, united) Church of China in the process of coming into full being. Would it not be awkward, I thought, if the Archbishop's reaction to such a post-denominational existence should turn out to be negative?

But two things prior to his visit happened. (1) His long-distance call to me from Hong Kong with all its personal, chatty conversation, including remarks about his experience in raising pigs, immediately put me at ease. At that moment I knew his visit was going to be an altogether warm and happy one. (2) His reference, in a sermon in Hong Kong shortly before his coming, to the English Reformation as also a sort of three-self movement moved and elated me as well as all my colleagues who learned of it.

The Archbishop endeared himself to all the Chinese who met him. The first post-Cultural Revolution class of students at the Theological College in Nanjing wanted to do "something in English" to welcome him, and came as near to it as singing the Londonderry Air. It moved the guests visibly. One student raised the question, probably not without some mischievousness, as to how an Archbishop of Canterbury was produced. The answer was at the same time to the point, instructive, humorous and winsome, ending with an invitation to visit England and see for himself, and this he did.

The Archbishop and his staff came up to Nanjing only for forty hours, during which he gave two well-reported press conferences. In less than two days he did more than many in all their lives to make Christianity known and respected in a country in which Christians were (and are) fewer than one per cent of the population. He affirmed the value of Christian faith within any social system, and what the China Christian Council and the Three-Self Movement stood for. Chinese Christians were overjoyed.

One casual event which actually was of importance to my subsequent relation with world Anglicanism as shown, for instance, in my attending a Primates' Meeting in Canada and the last Lambeth Conference, happened when he and I were visiting together Dr Sun Yat-sen's mausoleum. Upon hearing me referring to myself as an Anglican bishop, a TV reporter from England questioned me: "Shouldn't you say you *were* an Anglican bishop? Aren't you now an ex-Anglican and an ex-bishop?" At that point, the Archbishop answered that I was right in using the present tense, and that I was "an Anglican bishop plus, not an Anglican bishop minus". That affirmation overcame in me any remaining sense of distance. I was really happy over the encouragement and help his visit brought to the Church and to me myself, at a time when we were just emerging from the hardship and isolation imposed by the ultra-leftism of the so-called Cultural Revolution.

The Archbishop's second visit to China was in 1983 at the joint invitation of the Chinese People's Friendship Society and the China Christian Council, and as the leader of the British Council of Churches delegation. During that visit we had ample time to discuss the opportunities and difficulties we were faced with, and the theological issues that were preventing the consummation of the post-denominational unity. To maintain a historic episcopate in China, non-diocesan and non-administrative, with an authority solely spiritual, pastoral, ethical and theological, was a Chinese thought and decision, but his encouragement and advice, and those of Bishop Woolcombe who was in the delegation, were more important than they knew. Prior to the consecration of these bishops – who are not of the Anglican order but bishops of the Church of God – the Archbishop wrote me at great length, giving his blessing to our experiment, stressing the role of bishop as focus of unity, and affirming the advisability of not tying ourselves to one particular theology of episcopacy. The depth of his understanding of our situation is shown by his saying, "My personal delight is also mixed with a sense of humility that the Chinese Church should be taking into itself something very dear to Anglicans when we were a very small part of the total Christian spectrum in the past."

On that occasion, in a visit with the President of the People's Republic of China Li Xian-nian, he raised the question whether, in the campaign going on at that time, religion was to be regarded as a form of "spiritual pollution", which evoked the answer: "Certainly not, otherwise we would not have invited you to come to pollute us." That became the front-page headline in newspapers the next day and brought peace and happiness to many religious people.

Besides the inspiration the Chinese Christians received,

a most important result of the Archbishop's two visits to China was to enable the leaders and the masses of the Chinese people to see in this high representative of the Church a human being who could fit into the Chinese cultural and church milieu so naturally. This ability to fit into the Chinese situation enhances tremendously a favourable image of the Church as a universal fact. This universality has in itself an evangelistic appeal, and is at the same time the very vision we Chinese Christians now need to catch, in addition to all the worthy efforts since 1949 to find a Chinese national Christian selfhood.

Canterbury and Rome

CHRISTOPHER HILL
Canon of St Paul's

As Robert Runcie's Secretary for Ecumenical Affairs from 1982, and as an ecumenical bureaucrat at Lambeth Palace from the final year of Michael Ramsey until 1989, I have had a privileged vantage point from which to view the ecumenical scene. I make no claim to objectivity; I have been too closely associated with Robert Runcie's ecumenical strategy and tactics to pretend detachment; I have too much affection and respect for him to attempt impartial assessment. I heard of his nomination to Canterbury in Venice, at the Anglican-Roman Catholic International Commission in September 1979. A Lambeth colleague had telephoned me just in advance of the public announcement. Within that body the news was joyfully acclaimed; here was someone who would be both committed and realistic. Even before his move from St Albans to Lambeth, he was anxious to talk to his ecumenical staff about "foreign policy". He expected Lambeth to be proactive, but consideration had first to be given to the overall ecumenical goal, even before particular relationships, however important, such as Canterbury and Rome.

Robert Runcie was more aware than previous Archbishops of public perception and image. His experience on the Advisory Council for Religious Broadcasting had taught him much. He was conscious that at least within the Church he was known to be pro-Orthodox – he was co-chairman of the Anglican conversations with the Orthodox until his move to Lambeth. Moreover, there were family connections with the Roman Catholic Church and long-standing wartime experience with Dutch Catholic friends, including Professor Jozef van Beeck SJ, now Cody Professor of Theology, Loyola

University, Chicago. He knew he was perceived by some as committed to an Orthodox-Romeward ecumenism. He was very clear that an Archbishop of Canterbury must present all the facets of Anglican ecumenism, so from the beginning he was faced with the problem of encouraging Anglican-Roman Catholic relations without succumbing to the exclusive media obsession with Rome.

So far as the Free Churches were concerned, this was not a major problem; from the beginning he was to emphasize how much he owed theologically to Free Church scholarship. He often cited giants such as C.H. Dodd and Gordon Rupp, and in St Albans he had encouraged pioneer work in local ecumenical projects. Continental Protestantism was, however, largely a blank in his experience – with the important exception of a period as an exchange student in Bonn immediately after the war. Fortunately, history presented him with the ideal excuse to rectify this omission: the five hundredth anniversary of the birth of Martin Luther, in 1983. Major ecumenical visits to the two Germanies and to Berlin East and West gave him a significant platform to call for closer relations between the Church of England and the German Churches. This needs to be said here in view of the Paisley accusation, "Runcie the Romanizer".

Nevertheless, a major issue at the beginning of this archiepiscopate concerned the papal visit to England. Explorations had already been made with the Vatican about the desirability of the Pope and the Archbishop meeting away from either Canterbury or Rome. Rome welcomed the proposal, and their first meeting was *en passant* in West Africa in 1980, where they were both making pastoral visits at the invitation of their respective churches. I well remember telephoning Cardinal Hume with confirmation that they were to meet in Accra. The line was bad. He replied with some amazement, "In a car?" But away from the burden of history in Accra, they were able to meet, talk and pray together in a more intimate way than would have been possible at headquarters. At Accra, Robert Runcie extended his own ecumenical invitation for the Pope to visit

Canterbury Cathedral – but with the knowledge of the English Roman Catholic authorities. When they next met in Canterbury in 1982 – against the background of the Falklands War – Pope John Paul II came very much as Robert Runcie had invited him, an ecumenical pilgrim. He was not on home ground. Together, Pope, Archbishop of Canterbury and Free Church Moderator renewed the baptismal vows of an ecumenical congregation in the "cradle of English Christianity". The occasion was rightly described by the overused word historic. The way back had been blocked.

It is also typical of Robert Runcie that he was anxious to escape from a narrow ecclesiastical agenda. He spoke to Pope John Paul of his hopes that Christian leaders might come together to discuss and pray for peace, that only the Bishop of Rome could convoke such a gathering and that if the Pope would do so, he would strongly support such an initiative. Here he was recognizing and indeed encouraging a kind of *de facto* universal primacy. The Assisi Day of Prayer for World Peace in 1986 was in part a response to a Canterbury initiative.

As far as the work of ARCIC was concerned, Robert Runcie relied more on his historical intuition than on systematic theology. He did not understand how anybody could fail to recognize the historic fact of the Roman Primacy, but he also recognized the historical context of Rome and its debt to centralized Roman law. Moreover, he knew how suspicious the Orthodox were of Rome, and he shared their anxieties about a jurisdictional primacy. But his cautions about the present expression of Roman Primacy were tempered by what he saw as Archbishop of Canterbury of the worldwide Church. The vigour, size and commitment of the Roman Catholic Church in the developing world impressed him. He often encouraged Anglicans to be true to Anglican history by being a Church with a local face, but privately he saw that this was often being achieved more successfully by the Roman Catholic Church. He admired the Roman Catholic religious orders and saw real value in the Papal diplomatic corps, especially in the face of local tyranny in, for example, Uganda. In Iran Terry Waite was supported by the Papal Nuncio.

In the face of inter-Anglican tensions he began to see – and to speak cautiously of – the need for some authority on a wider than Provincial level, at least as far as matters vital for unity were concerned. At the same time he disclaimed any idea of a Canterbury Papacy. He spoke rather of a renewed Roman Primacy in terms of the Patristic description of Rome as a primacy of charity. Critics said that such a primacy – an "ARCIC Primacy" – needed teeth to make it work; they would then point to the existing teeth of Rome and ask whether that was what Anglicans really wanted. But it was not Robert Runcie's way to come with detailed proposals. He preferred to sow ideas, to allude to principles, to illustrate from history; he was always critical of "ecuspeak" or "ecumenese" and other jargon.

His greatness in Anglican-Roman Catholic relations was to persevere at a time of ecumenical regression. Many of his sympathies lay with the liberal Roman Catholic theologians and lay people who considered themselves marginalized by the present Papacy. But he was always sympathetic to those who exercised authority. Seeing – and knowing himself – the immense problems of holding together a worldwide communion, he did not wish to criticize publicly other church leaders; he knew how difficult radicals and conservatives can be and he understood the problem of trying to be a shepherd to both. His historic instinct allowed him to see beyond the ebb and flow of the debate between traditional and renewed interpretations of Catholicism. He felt able to say in Rome in 1989 that he looked forward to a unity which would include some expression of the Roman Primacy. He has put the matter on the agenda – whatever the colour of the Papacy of the day – together with the wider question of which it is part: how the Universal Church judges developments of faith and order in the modern age when Scripture, Tradition and Reason are no longer (if they ever were) self-evident. Newman's question – if not Newman's answer – has been at the heart of the twentieth-century ecumenical and theological quest. Robert Runcie saw that the role of the Bishop of Rome as a focus of communion and authority cannot be divorced from this wider issue. Convinced that Anglicans had something to bring to this debate from their own experience, he spoke with the Pope of the ecumenical journey as not only being about the removal of obstacles, but also about the sharing of gifts. He felt that Anglicans and Roman Catholics in separation had not evolved satisfactory institutional structures for the exercise of authority in the Church. He was less complacent about Synodical Government than some Anglicans, but neither was he enamoured of a male prelatical autocracy.

He did not despise diplomacy. In letters and in direct conversation with high Roman authorities, including the Pope himself, he tried to be honest about the complex developments taking place within the Anglican Communion in relation to the ordination of women − not all of which were congenial to his taste. Nor did he ever disguise the fact that theologically he thought the "ayes" had it. At the same time he realized just how difficult a psychological and institutional barrier this issue, and the fact of the ordination of women, had become for Rome. During his conversations with Pope John Paul in Rome in 1989 it was agreed that the real focus of the problem was in the area of authority. This was not a diplomatic avoidance of the issue; it was a theological clarification arrived at because of their deliberate avoidance of what Robert Runcie has called "megaphone diplomacy". Since the Lambeth Conference of 1988, authority has become much more clearly seen to be the real issue. Roman Catholic observers of the Lambeth Conference were delighted by its strong affirmation of the Final Report of ARCIC I. But they were disturbed by the way in which the Lambeth Fathers avoided the actual issue of women in the episcopate by simply reiterating the apparently infallible Anglican dogma of provincial autonomy, without noticing that this was inconsistent with what they had said about ARCIC. The point being made by otherwise sympathetic observers was not that Anglicans should not ordain women, but that communion and independence are not as easily compatible as the Lambeth Fathers appeared to think.

In consequence there was a great depression in Rome about Anglican-Roman Catholic relations. This in turn complicated the already complex process of an official Roman Catholic response to the Final Report of ARCIC I. It says much of Robert Runcie's diplomatic skills, his sympathetic understanding of how other people view Anglicans, and his genuine warmth of personality that the visit to Rome of 1989 largely dispersed the Curial pessimism. The problems remain, but the Archbishop of Canterbury's determination to confront them and to persevere in the search for unity impressed Rome, as did his determination to recognize publicly the ecumenical role of the Pope – at some personal cost when controversy came. More tangibly, the Pope himself came to see how damaging was the delay in the production of an official Roman Catholic response to ARCIC I. There had been a stalemate between the Council for Unity and the Congregation for the Faith – two Vatican departments with rather different ecumenical perspectives. John Paul II agreed that this must be overcome.

When the time comes for mature reflection on Robert Runcie's archiepiscopate and when the story of the restoration of communion between Canterbury and Rome is eventually written up – and when the story of the ordination of women in relation to Canterbury and Rome reaches its conclusion – I believe his role will be seen to be very significant. The heady days of Vatican II and ecumenical initiatives were over when he came to the throne of St Augustine. Ecumenism at an institutional level was faltering all round. Obstacles arose on either side in relation to authority in the Church. When the seas are rough and the course uncertain, a steady, strong and determined hand on the tiller is called for. That is what Robert Runcie gave to Anglican-Roman Catholic relations. He leaves Canterbury with the affection, trust and sympathetic understanding of the Roman Catholic Church. Pope John Paul II said to him as they parted in 1989: ''our affective collegiality will become effective collegiality: nothing effective without the affective first.'' When one ponders this spontaneous remark by an admittedly cautious Supreme Pontiff, it speaks volumes about the character of the Archbishop of Canterbury to whom it was addressed.

Canterbury and the Orthodox

A. M. ALLCHIN
Director of the St Theosevia Centre
for Christian Spirituality, Oxford

It has often been remarked that Michael Ramsey knew more of the theology of the Greek Fathers than any other Archbishop of Canterbury since Theodore of Tarsus. But as Owen Chadwick points out in his biography, it was not until his years at Canterbury that he began to have much direct contact with the Orthodox Churches. His earlier impressions were gained either from books or from contacts with Orthodox scholars in the West, men like Father Georges Florovsky and Dr Nicholas Zernov, or from his part in the activities of the Fellowship of St Alban and St Sergius.

The case of Robert Runcie is very different. While he would not claim the same deep engagement with the patristic theology of Eastern Christendom, already before he became Archbishop he had had more first-hand acquaintance with the Orthodox Churches than any Archbishop of Canterbury since the seventh century. Partly on account of his long-standing interest in Greece and the Near East, he had travelled widely in the Eastern Mediterranean. Then particular circumstances had given him special contacts in Romania. Finally, from 1974 to 1979, as Anglican Co-Chairman of the Anglican-Orthodox Joint Doctrinal Discussions, he made a decisive contribution to the development of Anglican-Orthodox relations at the official international level. It is a remarkable fact that during the last twenty-five years the Church of England has had two Archbishops of Canterbury, both of whom in different ways have had a deep concern for, and knowledge of, the Eastern Orthodox Churches.

I shall speak here mostly about Robert Runcie's contacts

with Romania, because it was with them that I had most to do. On the Russian side, the Archbishop himself has published a vivid account of his impressions of the visit he made in 1988, in his book *The Search for Unity*. But I shall begin by speaking about the work of AOJDD and the part in it played by the then Bishop of St Albans. The beginning of the work of the commission was slow. Set up in the mid-1960s, it was not until 1973 that the first full meeting took place in Oxford. Up until that time, the chairman on the Anglican side had been Bishop Harry Carpenter of Oxford. After 1973, Robert Runcie took over.

It was at once clear that the commission was too large to work efficiently as a single body. It was decided to split into three smaller groups for the next two years, and then to come together again in plenary session in 1976. The sub-commission of which Robert Runcie was chairman met in Romania in 1974 and in St Albans in 1975. In 1976, our second full gathering took place in Moscow. This meeting represented the high point in the early work of the commission. We made an agreed statement covering a number of significant topics, including the question of the *filioque* clause. We were meeting in a Moscow still fully Communist and strongly anti-religious, and we felt that we had been able to think and speak together as Christians of East and West in a way which had had no precedent in earlier Anglican-Orthodox discussions. Never before had such a representative gathering of the two Communions made such a common declaration.

1976 was a high point. In the autumn of that year, the General Convention of the Episcopal Church of the USA decided to proceed to the ordination of women, and at once the first fully canonical ordination of women priests followed. The effects of this action on the conversations were very serious. The meeting of the commission in Cambridge in 1977 was overshadowed by this issue, and it was decided to hold a special meeting at Athens in 1978 wholly devoted to it. That meeting could not be an easy one. The Orthodox spelt out their objections to the move carefully and firmly; the Anglicans stated briefly the three major viewpoints on the matter held within the Anglican Communion. We were meeting in Athens in July. It was exceptionally hot, even by Greek standards. It was a small comfort to discover that one of our African delegates could be totally overcome by a heat so different from that to which he was accustomed! However, while we ended in disagreement, we did not end in mutual hostility. Much of this was due to the care and skill of our two co-chairmen. Robert Runcie proved himself even more effective in the difficulties in Athens in 1978 than he had done in the achievements in Moscow in 1976.

At the end of the meeting, however, it was unclear what the future of the commission would be, or whether it had a future. This uncertainty became more marked when it became evident that the Lambeth Conference in August that year, while listening politely to the protests of the Orthodox members of the commission, delivered by the Orthodox co-chairman, Archbishop Athenagoras of Thyateira, did not intend to counsel the American and Canadian Churches to draw back from the steps which they had taken. What was the future of AOJDD? Should the talks be broken off altogether? Should they be, as Archbishop Athenagoras suggested, reduced to the level of friendly discussions between academics (mostly laymen on the Orthodox side) which did not engage the Churches fully as Churches? Or should they continue?

The fact that in the end the third option was taken is due to a very large extent to the actions of one man, Robert Runcie. At the end of 1978 and early in 1979 he made, on behalf of the Archbishop of Canterbury, a number of visits to the Near East and Eastern Europe, making contact with the leaders of the Orthodox Churches and finding out from them that the churches which they represented, while naturally disappointed by what seemed to them to be the appearance of a major new obstacle on the way towards unity, did not wish either to break off or to reduce the work of the international commission. Hence it was possible after a pause in 1979 for its work to resume, work which culminated in the publication of a second agreed statement, at Dublin in 1984. By that time the commission had acquired a new Anglican Co-Chairman, Bishop Henry Hill of Kingston, Ontario, since on his appointment to Canterbury Robert Runcie had of course retired from that position.

The Archbishop continued to follow this work with close interest. It was a special joy to him that during the visit of the Ecumenical Patriarch Demetrios I to England at the beginning of December 1988, the delegation from Constantinople, which had just concluded a series of visits to all the Orthodox Churches, reaffirmed with great emphasis the intention of the Orthodox to maintain the dialogue as a fully representative action of the churches, aiming, whatever the difficulties, at an eventual full communion of faith and life in the body of the One Church. The way was set for the work of AOJDD II, which began in the summer of 1989.

So far, I have spoken of the influence of Archbishop Runcie on Anglican-Orthodox relations through a period of some considerable difficulty. This influence was due not only to his gifts of diplomacy, but also to his understanding of human character in all its diversity, and to his willingness to take endless trouble to bring good out of what looked at times an unpromising situation. I want now to turn to a very different level of activity and say a little about Robert Runcie's contacts with a particular diocese.

In the years when he was Principal of Cuddesdon, a priest of the Romanian Orthodox Church, Father Lucian Gafton, came to study at the college. Through him, the Runcie family came into contact with Romania and its Church. Father Lucian was the son of a bishop, for though in the Orthodox Church a bishop cannot be a married man, there is no canonical bar to a widower being consecrated to the episcopate. It so happens that the great and courageous man who led the Romanian Church through the years after the Second World War, Patriarch Justinian, was himself a widower. He evidently liked to appoint men to be bishops who had had the experience of pastoral ministry in the married priesthood.

The father of Lucian Gafton was Bishop Josef, diocesan of Rimnic and Arges, in the foothills of the Carpathians. He was a man tall in stature, with a long and impressive beard, a commanding voice and manner, a great sense of humour and a great delight in the diversity of his fellow human beings. When, more than twenty years ago, I first visited the Bishop at Rimnicul Vilcea, I was greeted with shouts and laughter. The Bishop had no English, I scarcely had any Romanian, but I understood through the timidity of the interpreter that the Bishop's greetings were, "Oh, they've made a mistake! I wanted to meet the theologian called Allchin. You're far too young. You'll have to go home and fetch me your father." After this unexpected beginning, the Bishop took me into his study and began to enquire about the situation in Great Britain, showing himself better informed about affairs in our country than one might have expected from a bishop of a country diocese in an Iron Curtain country.

I returned to visit Rimnic on a number of occasions in the following years, and I was always regaled with stories of the visits of another and more distinguished Anglican cleric, who came not alone but with his wife and family, and who came not on official business but in order to have a few days' holiday in this remarkably beautiful part of a remarkably beautiful country. As before, the conversation had to be carried on through an interpreter, whose English was more fluent in the matter of the *filioque* clause, than in the description of the sometimes complicated holiday exploits of James and Rebecca and their parents. It was not always quite clear in detail what had happened. But one thing was abundantly clear, the delight of Bishop Josef at having a married bishop staying in his house. It was a joy which he had never expected to know. One particular anecdote was also clear, at least in its conclusion, which was delivered in triumphant Latin: *Episcopus dixit; domina contradixit.*

I only once coincided with Robert Runcie at Rimnic. It was the meeting of the sub-commission in 1974. It was a memorable meeting for many reasons, not least on account of a lengthy and closely argued debate between two of the Orthodox delegates, to which the Anglicans listened with fascination. It turned on the question as to whether

Orthodoxy is inherently monochrome or diversified. Bishop Josef had evidently heard about this discussion (it lasted a day or two) from some of the other Orthodox members of the group. He invited us one day to have coffee with him in his garden. As we enjoyed sitting in the shade, he began to preach us a little sermon. "I am a gardener. I have 138 trees in my garden. I know that's the right number. I counted them all. And I know that each tree is different. That's how God made them. I can't tell you how many leaves there are on the trees in my garden, but I can tell you that every leaf is different. That's how God made them."

But for me, the most memorable impression of that visit was the vision of the affectionate relationship which had grown up between an elderly bishop of Eastern Europe and a youngish bishop of the West.It was hard not to feel that both men had gained something very important to them from this friendship. When later, during the years when I was a Canon of Canterbury, I had occasion to admire the remarkable combination of dignity and spontaneity, of formality and informality which marked the Archbishop on major occasions, and particularly when I saw the way in which he was not afraid at times to express a quality which the Romanians value highly, but which the English are often afraid of, *caldura*, warmth, I couldn't help remembering those days spent in the hospitable household of Bishop Josef. It is strange to reflect that in the late twentieth century, through the ministry of Archbishops such as Michael Ramsey and Robert Runcie, the example of the Orthodox Church should have made such a deep but unobtrusive contribution to the practice of *episcope* at the heart of the Anglican Communion.

Robert Runcie's visits to Romania were not all family holidays. He got to know the Orthodox Church in that land very well in a variety of ways. There has been, I suppose, no other Archbishop of Canterbury who has spent Holy Week in retreat as the guest of a large convent of Orthodox nuns, and has followed the unfolding of the central mystery of Christ's Death and Resurrection through the beauty and simplicity of Romanian monastic chant. But like all other countries, Romania is not all harmony and beauty. The history of the Romanian Church and people has often been in the past, and still is today, a complex and tragic one. If the Archbishop has been able, as he has, to come through periods of intense and unwarranted hostility and criticism with apparent calm, I have sometimes wondered whether it is his contacts with the Orthodox which have given him this sense of inner tranquillity, have helped him to see things in a wider perspective, not only in the light of the perturbations of today, but also in the light of the eternal Kingdom which we enter when we come into the world of worship.

Canterbury in the Third Millennium

DAVID L. EDWARDS
Provost of Southwark

Although futurology must be largely guesswork, thinking about what may lie ahead is not an entirely unprofitable exercise if it makes one ask: what are the tendencies in the present which one may reasonably guess to be important in the long term? So a few ideas about the future of the Church of England and the Anglican Communion may be useful if they help towards a preliminary assessment of the nondictatorial leadership of Robert Runcie.

To predict that his Primacy will be regarded as "transitional" is simply to state what is obvious about all periods in history, but I have in mind a number of points which may be more interesting. The appointment of Dr George Carey as his successor means that the Runcie style, fashioned in youth by Oxbridge and the Guards, will be modified by a personality equally golden-hearted but without so much polished silver. Yet Runcie's essential achievement will, I believe, be maintained, holding Anglicanism together by "bonds of affection". It is an achievement which shows how vitally important personality remains, but in leadership personality operates only within a pattern set by an institution and the pattern of Anglicanism is diversity. Probably in Archbishop Carey's time the arrival of women in the Anglican priesthood will be generally accepted despite some dissent, and the controversy over it will be regarded as a symptom of the fact that Anglicans, like the Christians in the New Testament, are free to disagree about inessentials. In the years to come there will be many other symptoms − but this Anglican diversity will not be regarded as a disease. If the Christian Church lasts until the end of the story of the human race on this planet, it may have two thousand million years ahead of it, and the interpretation of a Gospel entrusted to it in Jerusalem under Pontius Pilate will not be trouble free. New answers to new questions will have to emerge out of honest thought and utterly sincere prayer to the ultimate mystery. They will not always be the answers we knew as Catholic, Orthodox, Protestant or Pentecostal Christians, or as mere Anglicans in the 1980s. It is therefore promising that Dr Carey, like the hero of this book, is a scholar who listens to questions and does not approach every religious problem with an open mouth. It is also promising that, being a pastor, he sees that social problems matter. In Britain the tensions between "Runcie's Church" and "Thatcherism" will be over; the leading actors will leave the stage, to be succeeded (I expect) by others who will represent Christian Democracy or Social Democracy within the economic and political unity of Europe. In other countries others will seek to relate the Market and Justice. But the task of discerning the signs of the coming Kingdom of God in the world of a particular generation will not end. And it is good that Dr Carey is an Evangelical, called to lead Anglicanism during the "decade of evangelism" (or is it "evangelization"?) which the Pope (and I hasten to add, many others) suggested as the right preparation for AD 2000. Christians have a Gospel to proclaim because they have heard some answers as well as many questions. But it will remain a task for Christian leadership (official, spiritual or intellectual) to discern which are the answers of the Gospel and which are the questions that must remain open. As I write (in July 1990) much of the British press is hailing Dr Carey's appointment as an end to "the long Runcie years of well-intentioned muddle and fudge" (Derek Wilson in the *Sunday Times*) – much, he has said, to the embarrassment of the Archbishop Designate. It is also reported that Dr Runcie, at a meeting of the Anglican Consultative Council, has expressed a hope that that body, or on doctrinal questions the Primates' Meeting, might be given more authority, so that the Anglican Communion might speak as one. At the General Synod of the Church of England this summer he revealed a dream that the argumentative synod might find it sufficient to meet only twice a year, presumably leaving more to the House of Bishops without clergy or laity. So obviously in the short run the pendulum is swinging towards greater simplicity through firmer authority. But a refusal to give a simple answer is not always a sin against the Holy Spirit. Reality may be complicated. The answers which we like because they are simple may not always perfectly match truth and love.

Having collected and pondered the essays in this book, I should like now to develop these points briefly as I try to peer into the more distant future.

It seems extremely unlikely that the official ecclesiastical arrangements for England, which so far have been altered only marginally since the days of Henry VIII, Elizabeth I and Charles II, will be thought permanently appropriate in a country where pluralism will reign, and it is even more unlikely that multitudes of Christians in other continents will to the end of time be content to belong to an international denomination called "Anglican" – a word which suggests at least an element of Englishness in the definition of their spiritual identity. As the years go by it will presumably not be easy to recall the period in the Church of England's life when new worship had to be presented as an "alternative" to the Prayer Book of 1662; when a Prime Minister (Callaghan) could insist on being allowed to choose between the Church's nominees for diocesan bishoprics including Canterbury, on the ground that the senior bishops were automatically members of the House of Lords; when the House of Commons could give or withhold approval of the Church of England's rules for its own life; and when profound disagreements between Christians of Catholic or Evangelical, conservative or radical, conviction could be contained within a mutual acceptance of this traditional constitution for the National Church, with the Sovereign as "Supreme Governor". (Indeed, I expect the future to be amazed that there was so little worry about these anachronisms in the Church of England in Robert Runcie's time.) The years when the Archbishop of

Canterbury and the Bishop of London had actual jurisdiction over Anglicans "overseas" will seem even more remote over the horizon, like the sailing ships which carried the early Anglican chaplains and missionaries. Influence without power will be possible, from Canterbury for Anglicans as from Constantinople for the Orthodox, but it seems unlikely that the influence of English theology or spirituality will be decisive in the developing religious life of the Americas, Africa, Asia, Australasia and the Pacific Islands, in what Michael Ramsey loved to call "the great Christian centuries to come". In the 1990s Anglicanism has a contribution to offer in Brazil, say, or Japan, for reasons clearly stated in this book; but the growth of a reformed Catholicism embodied in churches authentically Latin American, say, or Japanese, will sooner or later be seen as the fulfilment of Anglicanism and more important than religious links with England. There will always be an England unless it is desertified by carbon dioxide or becomes an extension of the Arctic Circle, but for the foreseeable future its economic and political destiny appears to be in membership (however reluctant) of the union of the states of Europe, and the era when it left Europe in order to rule a quarter of the human race will seem one with the imperial history of Egypt, Assyria and Babylon. English will be spoken more and more widely as a second tongue (constituting England's greatest asset), but a smaller and smaller proportion of humanity will think it natural to address the Creator in the language which Shakespeare spoke and even fewer will want to brood over the theology of English churchmen. My guess, therefore, is that because Robert Runcie is right to call Anglicanism "provisional", Canterbury will diminish in ecclesiastical importance during the third Christian millennium, much as Westminster will diminish in political importance. And I am glad about it. Bishop Stephen Bayne, the first "executive officer" of the Anglican Communion, said it and it is true: "the vocation of Anglicanism is ultimately to disappear".

However, it does not follow that the insights which Anglicanism has developed during and since the English Reformation will all be obliterated. The cultural bathwater of Englishness in a bygone age and much else that makes Anglicanism an ''ism'' will be thrown away, but the baby is what really matters, and if the baby dies there will be a resurrection.

The rejection of Papal jurisdiction by the Church of England in the sixteenth century, at the behest of Crown and Parliament, was an incident in the drama of the assertion of national identities against the centralization of religious power in Christendom. Through its parishes and chaplaincies the Church of England was designed to be the Church of the English people, although continuing Roman Catholic loyalties, developing Protestant convictions and eventually modern secularization meant that there were always to be dissenters from its comprehensive fold. It was to be exported into the world along with commerce, empire and cricket. But one great paradox observable in history has been that awareness of the original Englishness of Anglicanism has eventually led to the acknowledgment that other peoples, (beginning with the Boston tea party) were entitled to their own self-government in the realm of the spirit as well as in politics. So the Anglican Communion, originating as a distinct body in one nation's declaration of religious independence, has come to be a loosely united family in which each local culture has been valued, the work of God has been seen in that culture and the Christian Gospel has been addressed to it. One climax of this international and multicultural development has come during the Runcie years: the agreement of Anglicans to disagree about whether women may validly be ordained as priests and bishops. In some cultures such a development now seems inevitable; in others, ridiculous. What is truly ridiculous is blaming the women for causing the problem. Also strange (I feel) is the suggestion that, having arisen in order to cope with English nationalism in the sixteenth century despite thunders from the Vatican, Anglicanism has had no right to reorder itself in response to the Women's Movement in our day.

It seems reasonable to expect the Roman Catholic Church and the Eastern Orthodox (and non-Chalcedonian)

Churches to become less regimented as they become increasingly numerous and outspoken in countries far from Rome and Constantinople, and also far from the traditions which are enshrined in those two cities. It is surely significant that in recent theological discussion arising out of spiritual experience, although there has been no evasion of doctrinal questions, so much emphasis has been transferred to the idea of truth from the idea of infallibility, to the idea of communion from the idea of law, to the idea of diversity from the idea of enforced uniformity, to the linked ideas of freedom, integrity and creativity from the idea of unquestioning obedience, and to the idea of consultative conciliarity from the idea of monarchy. The use of local languages, the acceptance of local customs and the liberated vigour of local communities (whether of the poor or of bishops) have been symbols of this shift in Roman Catholicism. To say this is not to deny that conservative forces appealing to loyalty and backed by power are strong in large and venerable religious organizations and are given a fresh opportunity as traditionalism reacts against pluralism. Nor is it to claim that the change of emphasis in global Christianity has been inspired mainly by Anglicanism. But it may be said with confidence that the pluralism of the Anglican Communion has become a small key to carry into a future whose precise shape is hidden from us, where "Catholicism" will mean universality as it did in the beginning.

Inevitably the problem arises: which proposed changes would make for a healthy liberty, and which would destroy the faith entrusted to the Church by Christ and his apostles? Originally the Anglican solution was to stress that the Church of England and its sister churches had preserved intact the two Testaments and the two sacraments, the three creeds and the three orders of ministry, without adding anything to the Scriptures as "essential to salvation" or taking anything away from the heritage bequeathed by the Undivided Church. On this basis no new confession of faith stricter or more comprehensive than the Thirty-Nine Articles was thought to be needed, but those with a God-given authority over National Churches had the right to insist on assent to statements such as the Articles, and to arrange those details of worship and discipline which had to be agreed for the sake of the nation's peace. Richard Hooker argued for all this and Parliaments passed Acts of Uniformity trying to enforce it all. But another paradox prominent in Anglican history has been the growing acceptance of an almost incredible amount of theological diversity as Catholic and Protestant positions have developed and as scholars and scientists have pursued researches held by many to alter the face of truth. Now the Thirty-Nine Articles seem to be very dated, and a definition of doctrine replacing them has been seen to be not only unnecessary but also impossible. Despite the backlashes of conservatism in Catholic, Orthodox and Protestant quarters, the acknowledgement of the reality of many disagreements seems to be an admission which will have to be made in the centuries to come by all churches larger than small sects. Religious leadership will have to work in this more complicated setting of liberty. Already theologians and laity alike have shown their impatience with, or indifference to, attempts to enforce a rigid traditionalism, whether in the writing of books or in the marriage bed.

What, then, will be the essential message, to be handed on into the new millennium? It will not set in concrete a host of traditions regulating belief and behaviour. One has only to think of changes accepted by almost everyone since AD 1000, or since the seventeenth century when the divine right of kings was Anglican doctrine, to see that Christianity cannot be a museum. But (in a phrase which Robert Runcie has used) neither is Christianity a ''dull echo of contemporary trends in the world''. I myself regard it as both desirable and inescapable that in the future most priests will be married and many will be female; that many new forms of church life will be adopted after experiments; that pictures of the At-one-ment between God and man will be drawn from life, rather than from a sacrificial or feudal system now vanished; and that in general Christianity, advancing through the continents and the centuries, will change in inessentials as its surroundings change, in accordance with a tradition whose flexibility has hitherto been one of its greatest strengths. If (as St Paul saw) the Gospel could be translated so that it grabbed the heart and mind of the Greek world, it need not be a fossil in the post-modern world. But if Christianity is to remain entitled to be called Christianity, it will be a wrestle with the message which the Bible proclaims when taken as a whole, for that wrestle will bring it into a loving relationship with the transcendent and holy God revealed in the Hebrew and Christian Scriptures. So far from destroying the spiritual authority of the Bible, critical scholarship assists Christians to hear that message and to receive it as existential truth for themselves, the light of their lives. That has been the experience of many Anglicans, despite much mental pain amid many confusions and controversies. And that hearing of the everlasting Gospel is likely to be the experience of multitudes of Christians, whether or not they look to Canterbury within the next thousand years. Having such a baby, why should Christians mourn the bathwater?

The local churches which carry this message are unlikely to be united with each other in neighbourhood or nation, or with any global centre, if "unity" is thought to involve uniformity. Some denominations and other fellowships will merge or disappear as the disputes which once animated them are buried in the sands of time. Other bodies will change but survive because they are valued and loved by living Christians. To me it seems possible that in some places the Anglican Communion will remain for some time something recognizable as such, while in other places the examples of India and China will be followed. But unless the ecumenical movement, which has been a major gift of the Holy Spirit to the twentieth century, grinds to a halt, "unity" meaning a deep communion and a strong co-operation on the foundation of a common faith in the Christian essentials will increase, and will eventually lead most Christians to a condition now often called (without any precise definition) "visible unity". In the churches which are thus in communion with each other there will be local, regional and national synods associating clergy and laity with the hierarchy, although another certainty is that the present time-consuming Church of England pattern of synods will not be copied exactly. There will be international offices and meetings, although the present Anglican Communion could never be regarded as the ideal organization. And because no one loves a synod or a committee there will be archbishops ("Primates") to focus unity in persons. Robert Runcie, who has compared this job with conducting an orchestra, has bravely looked forward to the day when the most senior of all the archbishops, the Bishop of Rome, will preside over a worldwide communion far wider that the present Roman Catholic Church. I share the hope although I do not expect to live to see it fulfilled, but will add the belief that one day the style of a "universal pastor" in Rome will be in many respects different from the present jurisdiction (much as I admire John Paul II). It will be more like the style practised recently in Canterbury, commending the disciplines which are imposed by truth and love.

5

THE BEST
IS YET TO BE

In Retirement (1)

LORD COGGAN
Archbishop of Canterbury 1974–80

"Are you doing anything these days?" an acquaintance recently asked me, impressed no doubt by the senility of an archbishop who had retired ten years ago. "Nothing at all", I replied, looking him in the eye. "I sit and twiddle my thumbs all day long." A silly question perhaps deserved a silly answer.

One thing is certain: when Robert Runcie vacates the chair of St Augustine he will not have an idle retirement. Not for him the twiddling of thumbs. There will be pigs to care for – I am referring to the four-legged variety. There will be lectures to give on Hellenic cruises, and that will call for a renewal of friendship with Plato and Socrates *et al.*, who may feel hurt that they were slightly neglected during the Lambeth days. There will be domestic chores to be seen to – no longer will he be able to summon a fleet of maids to attend his slightest wish; and there will be the grand piano to polish till it shines like new. There will be the garden to cause to blossom and the lawn to mow. No twiddling of thumbs.

There will be the mail. Ay, there's the rub. No shoal of secretaries at his beck and call. "Dear Robert, we know you have nothing to do, now that you have donned the lean and slippered pantaloon. Will you address the Mothers' Union at Nether Wallop? Will you come and dedicate the hassocks at Upper Snoring? Will you consecrate the refrigerators in the Arctic in memory of + Archibald? We enclose an envelope (unstamped) for your esteemed reply." He will wish he had initials which allowed him the brevity of answer which Kenneth Kirk delighted in when he was Bishop of Oxford: "O.K. K.O.", but that again will be denied him.

Adjustment will be called for. To *choose* what he shall do; for his ministry, like that of any priest or bishop in the Church of God, does not end when his pension begins – and he will be the first to realize that. To *preside* over few (preferably no) committees. To *share* his wisdom, accumulated over long years even at Oxford and of course at Cambridge, as curate and chaplain, and Vice-Prin. (accent on the second syllable) and College Dean and Prin. and Preb. and Bp. and Abp. People will ring him up and come to see him and find him unhurried (is he *ever* flurried?) and ready to enter into their joys and sorrows and point them to the One who kept him steady when the pressures were at their greatest. To *read* the books he longed to read when he was in office but couldn't because people wanted him all over the far-flung Anglican Communion. To *write*, and thus enrich many who will hope for some books from his pen.

And to *reminisce*, but with a kind of forward-looking reminiscence, if that is not too strong a contradiction in terms. "For all that has been – thanks. To all that will be – yes." Memories will keep flooding in, some glad, some sad. Memories of rich friendships given and enjoyed, of journeys all over the world and ten thousand welcomes from within our own Communion and far beyond it, memories of wounds given to him and forgiven by him, memories of great national occasions and of tiny village churches where the Real Presence was a great and almost tangible reality. He will look back with thanks. And "to all that will be – yes." – for he will find retirement a rich experience and, like the wine about which he knows more than most, a time for maturing. He will find a deep and lasting satisfaction in knowing that "the best is yet to be, the last of life for which the first was made". And when, far into the third millennium (we hope), he reaches the end, he will say, as Dietrich Bonhoeffer did, "For me this is the end, but also the beginning". For that is the hope which he has shared with tens of thousands to whom he has expounded the Christian Faith, and which has been at the heart of that steadiness and courteous serenity which all his friends have so greatly admired in him.

In Retirement (2)

LORD BLANCH
Archbishop of York 1975–83

Most of the contributors to this volume have been concerned with what Robert Runcie has already done. I am asked to write about what he has yet to do – retire. Retirement is never going to be easy for a busy man, and for myself, retirement from York presented me with unexpected, if trivial, problems. I had not bought a railway ticket for twenty years. I missed having a secretary. I had to make all my own telephone calls. I missed the warm fellowship of personal and diocesan staff. And of course I was getting older. I remembered the "old man's lament":

> To my deafness I'm accustomed,
> To my dentures I'm resigned,
> I can cope with my bifocals,
> But my God I miss my mind.

I remember with a certain wry amusement the specialist's comment on a brain scan I once had: "There is no evidence of deterioration more than we would expect of a man of this age!"

For all this, I do not regret retiring when I did. It was now possible to have a few evenings at home with my wife, I have had more time for friends and family, and I have been able to expand my reading into areas previously left vacant because of the prodigious demands made on a bishop or an archbishop by synod papers and official reports. Retirement will enable an historian, as Robert is by training, to catch up on the "waste years". But above all I remain a minister of the Gospel, and, for that reason, a student of the Gospel, able to give more continuous time to the detailed study of the sacred text and to contemporary theological reading. I cannot emulate those strenuous septuagenarians who break the ice to swim on New Year's day or run in Marathons or undertake stupendous journeys in the mountains. But then, apart from an inexpert game of squash, I never was capable of these dramatic physical activities. Of course there is a sense in which any older man "misses his mind". My memory is not as retentive as it once was. I sometimes have to labour excessively to master an argument. I have to make fuller notes for the occasional sermon, and even writing the next chapter of a book can be more laborious than it once was. But the Lord is good, a very present help in time of trouble, the succour of the weary. He gives sight to the blind, strength to the feeble knees. I can "cope with my bifocals". I still have no need of dentures.

So, dear Robert, not to be up and doing does not mean to be down and out. Retirement can provide a new sense of proportion. Things which seemed so important when we were in office seem less important in retirement. Small, inconspicuous actions done for the sake of God may acquire a new significance over against the feverish activity, the grand projects, the public appearances which fill the life of a modern archbishop. The God whom we have served will prove as gracious to us in our advancing years as he was in our youth or at the peak of our physical and mental powers. The best is yet to be.

Whether Pigs Have Wings

JOHN V. TAYLOR
Bishop of Winchester 1975–85

During the ten years and more for which you have sat, metaphorically speaking, in that severely venerable seat in Canterbury, you must often have wondered, dear Bob, why the see is boiling hot. So it is a comfort to your many friends to be able now to picture you leaning, no less metaphorically, of course, over the wall of your Berkshires' pen and asking yourself instead whether pigs have wings. Contemplating their broad backs, you will be free at last to indulge in all innocence in a little of that back-scratching which you have so steadfastly disdained, even when it might have served to ease your own shoulders. They will certainly seem to you, those pigs, to be more entitled to wings than some humans of your acquaintance as they gaze back, not in obsequious gratitude but with that disconcerting mutuality between man and beast that the poet laureate, Ted Hughes, so delights to observe and describe:

> The Pig that peers up at you with blubbery nose
> And eyes red from weeping
> Wants to be you.

That you are Most Reverend and Right Honourable is beyond their ken. Whatever it is they recognize and desire in you, Bob, for all their short-sightedness, is possibly more basic than the scholar or the soldier or the leader or even the husband, something closer, perhaps, to priesthood, not as we narrowly define it, but in the sense that is synonymous with humanity. You aren't even, I believe, the person who regularly feeds them. You have no role in their eyes; you are simply you. And that – if, as it seems, they appear to enjoy your company – will be immensely reassuring during the early months of retirement. For, until it happens, no one can imagine how the removal of an all-demanding role eliminates the self. When the diary no longer dictates your every act from cock-crow till midnight, a fearful pall of uselessness dims the sunlight, and the worst moment of each day will be around breakfast-time, when Lindy asks brightly, "What are you doing this morning, darling?" Then you will be tempted to accept every absurd invitation to give a paper, appear on television, contribute to a cook-book or march for the whales. Even the family will push you back into the study to stop you repainting the bathroom. Then remember the Berkshires and bask in their undemanding recognition, weeping a little for the lost splendours, until you learn, as never before, who you are. After that, all will be well.

But, alas, not only of the pigs can it be said, if Ted Hughes is right, that "all pine for the day when they will be people". The compliment is frequently reciprocated in the human propensity for what we mistakenly take to be piggishness. You, dear Bob, who have been more than generous with your pearls, have encountered this metamorphosis on many shameful occasions. Each time the chair of St Augustine falls vacant there is a Gadarene gallop after some imaginary strong leader; it takes true strength to sit, clothed with humility, and in the right mind of responsible headship. You promised "a firm lead against rigid thinking, a judging temper of mind, the disposition to oversimplify the difficult and complex problems", and you have kept your word. You foresaw that this would be unpopular, but probably never guessed that the worst betrayals would arise in the house of your friends. I am ashamed that my anger on your behalf still smoulders balefully, whereas I have little doubt that you, who find pleasure in rootling snouts and narrowed eyes, will be able to contemplate the memory of even your most Orwellian adversaries and ask yourself with utmost optimism whether pigs do not, is spite of all, have wings.

For wrath, as St Paul knew, is a wretched sundowner, and the long summer evening which, we all pray, stretches before you now is the time for spreading your wings. If, as we believe, we have each an aptitude for heaven, here and now is the time for trying it out. Getting and spending, especially in the name of religion, we have laid waste our powers, and such time as remains might be better given to wonder, love and praise. John Donne expressed it in musical terms – "I tune the instrument here at the door" – but Thomas Traherne saw it more inclusively as a capacity for delight. If that dies in this world, he thought, we shall make nothing of the next. "Your enjoyment of the world is never right till every morning you awake in Heaven; see yourself in your Father's Palace; and look upon the skies, the earth, and the air as Celestial Joys: having such a reverend esteem of all as if you were among the Angels."

So let you and me and all who have entered this second childhood called retirement devote it to the things that we know make us take wing. Not sloth nor self-indulgence which, we have learned, leave us earth-bound. Service and discipline, certainly, for they give an edge to everything else. But also family and friendship, beauty in all its elusive mystery, humanity in its contrariness, the world and its wonders, and God above all and in all. I see your legendary pigs as a symbol of all that invites us to stand and stare. Of course they have wings – and for hire.

This book
belongs to

....

Puddle's Fan Pages

Here's what other children have to say about their favourite puppy and his second adventure!

"It was so great I couldn't stop reading it till I got to the end! I hope there are more books about Puddle as I love dogs and would like to read more of his adventures." Sofia, age 7

"The story was adventurous and it was also funny. The funniest bit was when the Professor thought that Puddle was a robot dog! If you like funny books about magical adventures you will love this book. I am going to look for a magic puddle!" Ella, age 6

"Puddle is naughty and funny and brave." Hannah, age 7

"Ruby is clever. Puddle, I love you."
Ava, age 6

"I really like the bit when they jump into
a puddle and just disappear like magic;
it's so good." Florence, age 7

"The dog was so cute, I'd love one like
that myself. The professor was funny
with his words. I would really like to read
another one of these books." Lydia, age 7

Toyshop Trouble

**Other books about
Puddle the Naughtiest Puppy:**
Magic Carpet Ride
Ballet Show Mischief
Rainforest Hide and Seek

Puddle
the naughtiest puppy

Toyshop Trouble

by Hayley Daze
illustrated by Angela Swan
cover illustrated by Paul Hardman

A catalogue record for this book is available from the British Library

Published by Ladybird Books Ltd MMX
A Penguin Company
Penguin Books Ltd., 80 Strand, London WC2R 0RL, UK
Penguin Books Australia Ltd., Camberwell, Victoria, Australia
Penguin Group (NZ) 67 Apollo Drive, Rosedale,
North Shore 0632, New Zealand

1 3 5 7 9 10 8 6 4 2
Series created by Working Partners Limited, London WC1X 9HH
Text © Working Partners Ltd MMX

Special thanks to Jane Clarke

ISBN: 978-1-40930-328-2

For Eric and Janice,
great friends and neighbours

When clouds fill the sky and rain starts to fall,
Ruby and Harry are not sad at all.
They know that when puddles appear on the ground,
A magical puppy will soon be around!

Puddle's his name, and he's the one
Who can lead you to worlds of adventure and fun!
He may be quite naughty, but he's clever too,
So come follow Puddle – he's waiting for you!

A present from Puddle:

Look out for the special code at the back of the book to
get extra-special games and loads of free stuff at Puddle's
website! Come and play at www.puddlethepuppy.com

Contents

Chapter One
Amazing Discoveries
15

Chapter Two
The Puppy and the Professor
27

Chapter Three
Top Secret Toys
39

Chapter Four
The Supertronic Starblaster
49

Chapter Five
Toy Trouble
59

Chapter Six
The Amaze-errific New Toy
69

Chapter Seven
Competition Time
81

Chapter Eight
Toy Joys
93

Chapter One
Amazing Discoveries

"Look at all these toys!" Ruby gasped. She and her cousin Harry were in Grandad's lounge, peering into an old toy chest. Ruby could see a jumble of model trains and aeroplanes, marbles and motorcars. They were the toys Grandad had played with when he was a little boy.

"What do you think that is?"

Harry asked, pushing his glasses up the bridge of his nose and pointing to a gleaming red-and-green object.

"Let's have a look," Ruby said, leaning so far into the toy chest that only her feet were sticking out. She moved aside a big wooden truck, a tank, and some small metal cars that got tangled in her long plaits. Then she grabbed the green-and-red toy and passed it to Harry.

"It's a clockwork train," Harry said, his eyes shining. At the front of the train was the engine, and there were three carriages behind it.

"It's the 2:15 from Paddington," Ruby said, "and Teddy is going to

visit Chips!" Teddy was Ruby's toy
duck-billed platypus. He had a long,
furry brown body, four big feet and
a beak like a duck's. Stitched to his
bottom was a new pink
tail Ruby's mother had
sewn on after a tug-
of-war accident.

Ruby sat Teddy on one of the carriages and Harry turned the key in the top of the train and set it on the carpet. It chugged across the room in the direction of Chips, Harry's toy robot.

"Go, Teddy!" Ruby said.

Tappety, tappety, tap. The train ran into a desk leg and ground to a halt, but the noise of drumming carried on.

Tappety, tappety, tap.

Ruby leapt up in excitement. "It's raining!" she cried, running to look at the raindrops pitter-pattering against the windows. Ruby could feel bubbles of excitement fizzing up inside her. The last time it rained,

a little puppy called Puddle had
arrived, and they had all been swept
away on a magical adventure!

The back door blew open, hitting
the kitchen worktop with a bang.
A bundle of fur zoomed into the
room like a rocket, knocked over the
clockwork train, Chips and Teddy,
and leapt into the toy box. It landed –
plumpf – on the toys inside.

"Puddle!" Ruby shouted, clapping her hands with delight.

She and Harry looked inside the toy box to see a little puppy staring back at them. His pink tongue was lolling out and his white tail wagged happily.

Harry patted Puddle on the head. "I'd forgotten what a naughty puppy he is."

"He's pretending to be a toy!" Ruby said, laughing. She scooped him up in her arms. "He's definitely as cuddly as Teddy."

"Woof! Woof!" barked Puddle, as if he agreed. Then he wriggled free, dashed across the room, through the kitchen, and into the rainy garden.

"Come on!" Ruby shouted with excitement. They rushed after him.

Outside, Puddle bounded down the garden path, splashing in the puddles. His tail was wagging so hard that a blur of raindrops sprayed out. Ruby

held out her hands to catch some of
the sparkling drops. From behind his
glasses, Harry's eyes were shining.

Puddle stopped in front of a particularly large pool of water and raced around and around it. The raindrops were making the surface ripple and shimmer. He crouched down, then jumped into the water with a splash – and disappeared right through the puddle. Just like last time.

Ruby grinned at Harry. "Are you ready for our next adventure?" she asked.

"What if the magic doesn't work today?" Harry asked. "The likelihood of another magic puddle is very low."

"We won't know until we try," Ruby said. "One, two, three – JUMP!"

And they leapt into the puddle.

Chapter Two

The Puppy and the Professor

Ruby found herself in complete darkness, surrounded by soft, fluffy objects.

"Puddle," Ruby called, "where are you?"

Puddle gave a yip.

"I've never seen a Robodog toy before," said a loud, deep voice. "He looks so amaze-errifically real!"

"What's happening?" Harry whispered from somewhere next to Ruby.

"I don't know," she said, "but we need to get out of here!"

She and Harry wriggled their way upwards through the soft objects. Light began to seep through. Ruby pushed aside a cuddly dinosaur – and realized that they were inside a huge toy box. It was even bigger than Grandad's. The toy box was inside a large room with high ceilings. Shelves lined the walls, and they were bursting with every kind of toy Ruby could imagine – teddy bears, jigsaws, electronic games and train sets. Long ladders were fixed to the shelves, and people in red aprons were climbing up them, putting more wonderful toys on display. There was a cash register at the front of the room.

"Look!" Harry pointed to a sign written in enormous sparkly letters, high up on the wall.

"Gigglesworth Toys," Ruby read. "We're inside a huge toyshop!"

"And there's Puddle," Harry said, his forehead wrinkled with worry.

The little puppy was tucked under the arm of a tall man in a white lab coat. He was carrying a box with the other arm. "Brill-ificent," the man said, looking down at Puddle. "I must find out how to make one of these."

"He thinks Puddle's a toy," Harry gasped.

"We're coming, Puddle!" Ruby called.

She and Harry scrambled out of
the enormous toy box. When Puddle
saw them, he squirmed out from the
man's arm and scampered under his
feet – tripping the man over.

Crash! The man's box went flying.
All sorts of odds and ends rolled
across the floor.

"Oh, dearie me!" the man exclaimed,
running his hands through his spiky
white hair. Then he looked at Puddle.
"You're not a Robodog, are you?"

"Puddle's real," Ruby said,
smiling. "He can be rather naughty
sometimes. We'll help you tidy up."

She knelt down, gathering the
cotton reels, ribbon, string and
shiny buttons. Beside her, Harry
was collecting nuts and bolts and
an electronic circuit board. Puddle
ran to greet Ruby and Harry. When
the man patted his head,
Puddle dropped a pot of
glue by the man's feet.

"You didn't mean to make a mess,
did you, Puddle?" said the man.
"I'm Professor Toyjoy," he added,
shaking Ruby and Harry by the hand
and Puddle by the paw.

"I'm Ruby," Ruby said, "and this
is my cousin, Harry. What are these
things?" she asked the professor as he
repacked his box.

"My fixi-mend kit," the professor replied. "I can't get the thing-gummy-bobby to work. Nothing works today!"

"Perhaps we can help fix the thing-gummy-bobby," Harry said, "if you tell us what it is."

"That's wondrously kind, but thing-gummy-bobbies have to be kept hush-hush," Professor Toyjoy told them, closing the box. "What a day!" he murmured. He looked at his watch. "I have to get to work. Time's zippety-zipping away."

Professor Toyjoy backed hastily through the swing doors at the back of the toyshop.

Ruby saw that Puddle was nosing
at something behind the toy box.
"What have you got there?" she
wondered, taking the object from
Puddle's mouth.

"It's a kind of screwdriver," said Harry. He pressed the button on its side, and the screwdriver whirred round. Red and blue lights flashed on its handle. "I've never seen one like this before. It must have fallen out of the professor's box."

Ruby hurried over to the swing doors. "We need to find him and give it back!"

Chapter Three
Top Secret Toys

Ruby, Harry and Puddle pushed through the swing doors and into a long, twisting corridor. It was empty.

"Where's the professor?" Ruby asked.

The corridor was lined with open doors. Ruby and Harry peered inside the first one and saw two women in white lab coats, sawing out jigsaw pieces.

"They're making toys for the shop," Harry whispered.

"Maybe the professor's in one of these rooms," Ruby suggested.

Through each door they saw all sorts of toys – boxed games, computer games, toys with batteries, toys with wheels. There was a whole room of aeroplanes, another of trains and one of princess dolls dressed in pink. In another room, a man was pumping up brightly coloured beach balls and stacking them in a neat pyramid.

Puddle wagged his tail and trotted inside. He batted one of the balls with his paw, making it bounce

around the room. Ruby ran over and
steadied the wobbling beach ball
pyramid.

"We're very sorry," she said to
the man. "Puddle didn't mean to be
naughty – he just wants to play."

But the man was grinning. "That's
what these beach balls are for!" He
tickled Puddle's ears.

"Have you seen Professor Toyjoy?" Harry asked.

Before the man could reply, Puddle yapped loudly and scampered back into the corridor, his paws pattering against the tiles. Ruby ran out and saw the back of a spiky white head. The professor was walking towards another set of swing doors at the end of the corridor.

"Professor Toyjoy!" Ruby called.

But the professor had already gone through. Above the doors was a sign that said: INVENTORS AT WORK. TOP SECRET.

"Do you think we're allowed to go inside?" Harry wondered.

Ruby looked down at the screwdriver in her hand. "The professor won't be able to mend anything if we don't," she said.

Puddle barked his agreement, and pushed the doors open with his nose.

The other side of the doors
reminded Ruby of a giant classroom.
It was full of men and women in lab

coats bent over their workbenches. There were wires and microchips, circuit boards, computer screens, switches and batteries scattered everywhere.

"It's a laboratory! They must all be toy inventors," Harry whispered, clearly amazed by it all. "I'd like to be an inventor."

Ruby looked around the room. "But where's Professor Toyjoy gone? I can't see . . ."

But as she spoke, from the back of the workshop there came a bright flash of light and a huge . . .

. . . *BANG!*

Chapter Four
The Supertronic Starblaster

Harry and Ruby ducked under the closest bench as a shower of sparkly silver dust rained down on the workshop. Puddle hid his eyes with his paws.

"Professor Toyjoy's exploding things again," a woman said, wiping glitter from her brow. "At least it's only glitter this time. Last week it was glue, and we were all stuck to the floor."

"Puddle, Harry! Come on!" Ruby scrambled out from under the workbench and raced to the back of the workshop.

The professor was standing in a heap of gently smoking machine parts, shaking his head.

"Dearie me," he muttered, rummaging through his fixi-mend kit. "That's the end of the Supertronic Starblaster. And I'll never fix it without my –"

"Is this what you're looking for?" Ruby asked him. She leapt over a pool of silver goo and held out the screwdriver.

"Gracious me!" the professor said, beaming at them. "Thank you!"

But then his smile faded as he looked at his watch.

"Is something the matter?" Ruby asked him. Puddle slithered about in the silver goo and pattered silvery paw prints across the floor.

"I'm just a trifle flusterous," he said, running his hands through his hair. "Mr Gigglesworth will be here soon to judge the competition."

"What competition?" Harry asked, prodding what looked like a heap of crumpled-up tinfoil that had been grilled on a barbecue. Puddle growled as it fell over.

"Mr Gigglesworth's competition," Professor Toyjoy told them. "The competition to find a new bestselling toy for Gigglesworth Toys." He sighed. "The Supertronic Starblaster was my best hope. I designed it to shoot glitteroid stars to stick on children's bedroom ceilings. But it blasted itself, and now everything is ruinacious. Ruinacious!" he repeated sadly.

Puddle rubbed round the professor's legs and Ruby patted him on the arm. "Cheer up, Professor," she said. "It can't be that bad!"

"It's worse than bad, it's horribloid!" the professor groaned.

"You see, every toy inventor has to create a toy for Mr Gigglesworth's competition. And these days, all that kids want are computer gadgets and thing-gummy-bobbies with batteries…"

"Like my robot, Chips," Harry agreed.

Professor Toyjoy nodded, then pointed to his workbench. It was covered in a red cloth that was draped over strange lumps and bumps and sprinkled with silver glitter.

"I've got some fantabulous thing-gummy-bobbies under there," the professor said, "but none of them work." The professor sat down on his chair and put his head in his hands. "I've been inventing toys for forty years," he mumbled. "I don't want to lose my job. It's the most marvel-tastic job-erino in the world!"

Puddle jumped up on the professor's lap and nudged him sympathetically with his nose.

Ruby looked at Harry. He nodded, as if he knew exactly what she was thinking. "Let's help!" she exclaimed.

Chapter Five
Toy Trouble

"Woof! Woof!" Puddle pulled off
the red cloth covering the professor's
workbench. Glitter settled like
snow as Ruby rolled up her sleeves.
Under the red cloth was a jumble of
peculiar-looking toys.

Harry picked up a toy snowman
with an upside-down head. "What
are these things?" Harry asked

Professor Toyjoy.

The professor looked up. "These watcha-ma-bits? They're all floppers," he sighed, absent-mindedly stroking Puddle's soft ears. "Toys that didn't work."

"Maybe we can help fix one of them," Ruby said eagerly. "Harry's good at fixing things, and I've got lots of ideas."

"I suppose it's worth a try," Professor Toyjoy said. Puddle leapt to the floor as the professor got to his feet and picked up a toy from his workbench. "How about this one – the Whopping Whale Everlasting Bubble Maker," the professor said,

pointing to a football-sized machine
shaped like a whale with an open
mouth.

"What's wrong with it?" Ruby
asked.

"I designed it so the everlasting bubbles can be used as balls," Professor Toyjoy said, pouring a cupful of what looked like bright green slime into the whale's mouth. "But the bubble mix is a trifle unrightful..."

They watched open-mouthed as bright green bubbles the size of tennis balls shot out of the whale's blowhole. Puddle jumped up and caught one.

Pop! Puddle yelped with surprise. His nose was splattered with green goo.

Pop! Pop! Pop! Ruby jumped out of the way as the other bubbles burst,

spattering green slime everywhere.

"Yuck!" Harry wiped the sticky green ooze off his glasses. "I'd need to look at my chemistry books to help you get that mix right. We don't have time for that right now."

Ruby pointed to something that looked like a plastic toy cat sitting on top of a clay machine.

"Perhaps we can make this toy work," she said hopefully.

"It's a Copy Cat," Professor

Toyjoy explained enthusiastically. "You put different-coloured clay in the machine, and scan your favourite toy with the scantastic scanner, then the Copy Cat computer gadget tells the machine to make an exact copy of the toy."

"Then you can have twice as much fun!" Harry said.

"That's the idea." The professor sighed. "But it isn't quite correctish yet ..." He switched on the Copy Cat and handed what looked like a TV remote control to Ruby.

"Let's try it!" Ruby said, running the scanner over the Whopping Whale Everlasting Bubble Maker.

A multicoloured clay snake oozed
out of the machine.

"Grrrr!" Puddle growled, grabbing

the snake and wrestling with it on the floor.

Ruby giggled. "These are all fabulous watcha-ma-bobbies!" she told the professor.

"But we don't have time to repair-inate them!" Professor Toyjoy groaned.

"Then we'll just have to invent something new!" Ruby said.

Ruby closed her eyes tight and screwed up her freckly face in concentration. What new toy could they invent?

Chapter Six
The Amaze-errific New Toy

"Woof! Woof! Woof!"

"Puddle!" Ruby cried. "What's the matter?" She opened her eyes and looked around for the puppy.

He was in the corner of the workshop, right next to an old toy chest. She hurried over, closely followed by Harry and Professor Toyjoy.

Puddle was scratching at the wooden box, as if he was trying to dig his way into it.

Harry shook his head. "Don't be naughty, Puddle," he said.

"I don't think he's being naughty," Ruby said. "He wants us to look inside."

Puddle wagged his tail as Ruby lifted the lid.

"Ooh!" Ruby gasped in delight.
The box was full of lovely soft toys.
"Look what Puddle's found," she
said to Harry and the professor.
"Good boy, Puddle!"

Puddle scrambled into the box.
He dived into the toys, and when
he emerged again he had one in his
mouth. It was a beautiful rainbow-
coloured parrot, with only one wing.
Ruby took it and gave it a hug. Its
feathers were silky. *What a shame it's
damaged*, she thought.

Puddle buried himself again and
passed Ruby more toys. There was
a friendly-looking furry red dragon
that was missing a tail, a plump

velvety bunny without any ears and a yellow-and-black stripy bumblebee with an unstuffed tummy and no antennae. Ruby cuddled each one as he pulled them out. They all looked brand new.

"What's at the bottom, Puddle?" she asked.

Ruby dived head first into the box. She felt around in the darkness. The bottom of the chest was littered with the missing pieces. She stood up clutching them in her arms.

"Don't bother with those old-fangled things," Professor Toyjoy said. "They're unfinished try-it-outs. When I first came to work for

Gigglesworth Toys, I designed soft toys. That's not the sort of thing Mr Gigglesworth wants now, even if they are splendiferously cuddleful."

"Splendiferously cuddleful," Ruby repeated. She thought of Teddy, her duck-billed platypus, with his pink tail, duck's beak and big feet . . .

Ruby's plaits swung as she whirled round. "I've got an idea!" she squealed. Soft toys pattered on to the floor as she climbed out of the toy box. "We can use these parts to make a new toy. If everyone else is making gadgets and computer games, a strange and wonderful cuddly toy is sure to stand out."

"An entirely new crazy cuddly creature . . ." Harry said slowly. "It might work."

"That's its name!" Ruby exclaimed

excitedly. "Crazy Cuddly Creature!"
Puddle yapped and wagged his tail.
"See, Puddle agrees!"

The professor beamed at them. "So
do I. That sounds superfantastical!"

He turned to Puddle and patted his head. "Go on, Puddle," he said. "Fetch the pieces!"

Puddle leapt back into the toy chest and rummaged enthusiastically through the try-it-out toys. He emerged with a round, purple shape and passed it to Ruby.

"This can be the toy's head," she decided.

Puddle dived back into the toy chest and reappeared with two long, fuzzy pipe cleaners.

"And these are its antennae," Harry said.

Professor Toyjoy clapped his hands. "Now, where's my screwdriver?"

Puddle pulled more pieces from
the toy chest, and Ruby and Harry
decided what part of the toy each
piece would be, holding them in place
while Professor Toyjoy fitted their

creation together.

In no time at all, the creature was nearly finished. Ruby thought it looked amaze-eriffic. It was the size of a big teddy bear, and as well as its antennae, it had bright blue buttons for eyes, bunny ears, whiskers on its nose, parrot's wings, a dragon's tail and feet, and a fat bumblebee-striped tummy. It even had a pouch on its front that held a little bear.

Ruby just couldn't help smiling when she looked at it. It was a perfect Crazy Cuddly Creature.

"Mr Gigglesworth is in the toyshop!" a loudspeaker announced, just as Professor Toyjoy finished attaching the creature's tail. "Toymakers! It's time to present your toys!"

Chapter Seven
Competition Time

Puddle's furry head poked out of the toy chest. He had a long blue ribbon in his mouth.

"Well done, Puddle," Ruby said. "That's the finishing touch." She quickly tied a colourful bow round the Crazy Cuddly Creature's neck and thrust it into Professor Toyjoy's arms. She tugged on her plaits for luck and wished as hard as she could that Mr Gigglesworth would like the Crazy Cuddly Creature as much as she did.

All around them, the other toy inventors were scurrying to grab their whizzing, bleeping creations and line up in front of their workbenches. Professor Toyjoy regarded them with dismay.

"Oh dearie me," he groaned. "Look at all those whizz-bang inventions. I can't show Mr Gigglesworth a soft toy. It doesn't do anything."

Ruby and Harry looked at each other in horror as Mr Toyjoy pushed the Crazy Cuddly Creature into the

toy chest. Only its antennae were
left sticking out. Puddle whined and
nipped at the antennae.

Before Ruby and Harry could do anything, a tall, skinny man wearing a pinstriped suit entered the workshop, holding the hand of a very bored-looking boy.

A murmur of excitement rippled through the room. Mr Gigglesworth had arrived!

The boy yawned.

"Who is he?" Ruby whispered.

"That's Mr Gigglesworth's grandson, Max," Professor Toyjoy whispered. "He gets to play with every toy that's ever made."

"He doesn't look very happy about it," Ruby said. "I'd love to play with every toy that's ever been made."

"You'd soon get bored if playing with toys was your job," Harry told her, "like Max."

"Boredomification is always a problem," Professor Toyjoy muttered. "In order for a toy to win, Max has to like it, and he's very hard to please."

I'd never get bored with toys, Ruby thought, and imagined herself floating in a toy-box boat in a sea of toys.

Mr Gigglesworth made his way through the workshop with a very serious look on his face. He stopped for a few seconds in front of each new toy, and either nodded or shook his head and frowned.

Max shuffled along behind him, yawning and shrugging his shoulders, hardly bothering to glance at each new invention.

Mr Gigglesworth stopped in front of the professor's workbench. "Professor Toyjoy, where is your new toy?" he asked.

"Oh dearie me," Professor Toyjoy sighed sadly. "None of my toys were fantastical enough to present to you today. I fear my toy-making days are over."

The workshop fell silent. The other toy inventors were staring at Professor Toyjoy.

"Woof! Woof! Woof!" Puddle grabbed the Crazy Cuddly Creature's antennae. The little puppy struggled to pull the toy out. The toy was bigger than he was, but he just about managed to drag it across the workshop floor.

"Oh, you naughty puppy – come back!" Ruby cried. She tried to catch hold of Puddle, but missed. She staggered to her feet as the puppy hurled himself at Mr Gigglesworth's grandson, Max.

Thump! Max landed on the floor with Puddle and the Crazy Cuddly Creature on top of him.

"I am so very full of sorryness, Mr Gigglesworth!" Professor Toyjoy exclaimed. "I think we had better leave now. Farebye." The professor hurriedly ushered Ruby, Harry and Puddle towards the workshop door.

"Not so fast!" Mr Gigglesworth thundered. "Come back here!"

Puddle put his tail between his legs and whimpered.

"Oh dear, Puddle," Ruby said. "You've got us in real trouble now!"

Chapter Eight
Toy Joys

"Just look what you've done to my grandson!" Mr Gigglesworth boomed.

Ruby, Harry, Puddle and Professor Toyjoy turned round slowly. Puddle stood behind Ruby's legs. Ruby was afraid of what she might see.

Max was sitting up, hugging the

Crazy Cuddly Creature, with a huge smile across his face.

Ruby's mouth dropped open. So

did Harry's and the professor's.
Puddle's ears pricked up and his tail
started to wag. He ran over to give
Max's cheek a big lick.

Mr Gigglesworth's severe face
suddenly softened and his eyes
twinkled. "I can hardly believe it!"
he gasped. "I've never seen a toy make
Max smile before. He loves it."

Mr Gigglesworth turned to the

other toy inventors.

"I hereby declare Professor Toyjoy's creation the winner of the Gigglesworth Toy Competition!" he announced. The other inventors clapped and cheered.

"It's a marvel-fabulo-terrific-acious toy!" Max declared, holding the Crazy Cuddly Creature like a toy aeroplane, and swooping it round his head.

"It can be anything I want it to be. Watch out for the skydiver!"

Mr Gigglesworth caught the

little teddy bear as it flew out of the creature's pouch. He and his grandson were both smiling from ear to ear.

"Hip, hip, hooray!" Ruby and Harry cheered as Mr Gigglesworth came over to shake the professor by the hand.

"Yip! Yip! Yip!" Puddle wagged his tail so hard that his whole body waggled.

"What a flabbergastic day!" Professor Toyjoy beamed at Ruby and Harry. "I simply can't thank you enough for your help." Puddle's tail bumped against his legs, and the professor stroked his ears. "And you, Professor Puddle," he added. "You're a proper toy inventor!"

They all laughed, and then Puddle tugged at the hem of Ruby's dress.

"Is it time to go home, Puddle?" she asked.

Puddle barked, and started running in circles round Ruby and Harry. The faces around them started to blur as Puddle ran faster and faster.

"Goodbye, Professor Toyjoy!" Ruby called. "Make lots more Crazy Cuddly Creatures. It'll be a bestseller in the toyshop!"

"Absolutifferously!" Professor Toyjoy replied, waving them goodbye. Gigglesworth Toys seemed to melt away, and Ruby closed her eyes . . .

***

When Ruby opened her eyes again, she, Harry and Puddle were sitting on a picnic blanket next to Grandad's toy box. It was laid out with plates of fruit and sandwiches and glasses of old-fashioned lemonade. Teddy and Chips were already seated.

"I'm back, Teddy!" Ruby cried, giving her duck-billed platypus a hug.

Harry switched on his robot, and its eyes flashed.

Puddle ran across the picnic blanket, licked Ruby's and Harry's faces, and ran outside. Ruby and Harry ran to the window to watch him, but the little puppy had already disappeared.

Ruby bent down to pick something up from the doormat. "It's the little teddy from the Crazy Cuddly Creature's pouch," she said, showing it to Harry.

"I can't wait for our next adventure with Puddle," Harry said.

Ruby smiled at her cousin. "Me neither. I hope it rains again soon!"

Can't wait to find out
what Puddle will do next?
Then read on! Here is
the first chapter from
Puddle's third adventure,
Ballet Show Mischief ...

Puddle
the naughtiest puppy

Ballet Show Mischief

"Ladies and gentlemen, the show
is about to begin!" Ruby shouted
from behind the plush red bedspread
hanging across Grandad's living
room. She closed her eyes for a
moment and imagined a huge theatre
filled with people, calling her name.

"Ruby! Ruby!"

She waved to her imaginary fans,

until she realized they sounded like her cousin Harry.

"Ruby! Ruby, can you hear me? What are you doing back there?" he asked.

"It's a surprise." She giggled, and peeked round the bedspread. "Ready?"

"Um, sorry, Ruby, I've got to finish this maze," Harry said, pushing his glasses back in place and burying his nose in a puzzle book.

Never mind, Ruby thought as she ducked back behind the curtain, *the show must go on*. She took a big breath and tugged on her plaits for luck. Her stomach felt as if it was being tickled by fairy wings. She pulled back her pretend curtain.

"Welcome to Ruby's Enchanted Ballet," she said, holding the edges of her wrinkly tutu and curtsying like she'd seen real dancers do. The wall behind Ruby was covered with drawings of rainbows, castles, mountains and forests. Ruby had coloured them all in herself, on separate sheets of paper, and taped them together.

She twirled around on her tiptoes with her arms high above her head. But her socks were slippery. Her legs slid in opposite directions, causing Ruby to accidentally do the splits.

"Ta da!" she sang with her arms outstretched, turning the splits into a part of her dance routine.

"So that's what you've been working on all morning," Harry said, and closed his puzzle book.

Ruby pushed the 'play' button on Grandad's CD player and soft violin music filled the air.

"Now watch me do a spinning top," she said, holding out her tutu and twirling to the music.

"Those are called pirouettes," Harry corrected her, "but I think you hold your arms out like this." He got up from his chair and spun round on his toes with his arms curved in front of him, using them to help him whirl round. "Woah! That really makes you dizzy," he said, sitting down again.

"And this is my graceful swan," Ruby said. She balanced on one foot and stuck out her arms like wings.

"The real name for that is an arabesque," Harry said.

"I like my name better," Ruby replied, still on one foot. "How come you know so much about ballet?"

"My parents love watching ballet at the theatre, and sometimes they make me go too," Harry said.

Just then the wind blew the front door open with a BANG! Ruby's

pictures were whipped from the wall.
They swirled around the living room
and finally fluttered to the floor.
A puppy dashed onto Ruby's stage
and shook himself, spraying water
everywhere.

"Puddle!" shouted Ruby, twirling
on her toes in delight.

Every time it rained, Puddle the
naughty little puppy appeared and
swept Ruby and Harry off on a
magical adventure.

"Now that's what I call an entrance,"
Harry said with a laugh.

Puddle tugged at the curtain until
it closed.

"I guess that means my show is

over," Ruby said, taking a sweeping bow.

"But our fun has only just begun!" Harry said, chasing Puddle out into the rain.

***

To find out what happens next,
get your copy of
BALLET SHOW MISCHIEF today!

Puddle
the naughtiest puppy

Magic Carpet Ride

Join Puddle, Ruby and Harry
on their first exciting adventure!

Aziz wants to win
the magic carpet
race so he can be
granted a wish
by the beautiful
princess! Can,
Ruby, Harry and
Puddle help Aziz
to win?

Find out in MAGIC CARPET RIDE …

Ballet Show Mischief

Go on a beautiful ballet adventure
with Puddle, Ruby and Harry.

The children are
whisked away to a
wonderful ballet
show, but the shy
ballerina has stage
fright. The show
must go on! Will
Puddle be able to
find a solution?

Find out in BALLET SHOW MISCHIEF...

Rainforest Hide and Seek

Have you ever wanted to see a rainforest?

Puddle uses his magic to take Ruby and Harry through a puddle and into an incredible animal adventure. Things keep going missing in the rainforest – can Puddle figure out why?

Find out in RAINFOREST HIDE AND SEEK...

Dragon Dance

Join Puddle, Ruby and Harry on their new adventure in Chinatown!

Li wants to make his Grandad proud by appearing in the Chinese festival. Can Puddle and the children help him to get Lucky the dragon to dance?

Find out in DRAGON DANCE...

Magic Mayhem

Ruby and Harry are amazed to find themselves in a medieval castle...

... when Puddle takes them on their latest adventure! They meet a magician's apprentice who is in deep trouble. He's lost his spell book. Can Puddle save the day?

Find out in MAGIC MAYHEM...

Dog Safety

Hi, it's Ruby and Harry again with Puddle! We hope you enjoyed our adventure. Now it's time to find out a little more about real dogs and what they need to be healthy and happy.

So who better to teach us all about our lovely doggy friends than **Dogs Trust** – the UK's largest dog charity? They look after lots and lots of dogs and puppies – and are working very hard to help all dogs to enjoy a happy life in a loving home.

With the help of our friends at **Dogs Trust**, we will learn all about how to stay safe around dogs – so you can enjoy being near them without any worries.

Always remember, Puddle is a magical dog, while real dogs and puppies are living animals who need a lot of care, love and attention.

Stay Safe Around Dogs:

Always follow these six top tips to stay safe around dogs:

- Ask the owner if you can touch their dog.
- Hold out your hand and let the dog sniff you.
- Speak softly to the dog so you don't scare him.
- Pat the dog gently so you don't hurt him.
- Play nicely with the dog.
- Leave dogs alone if they are resting or eating.

Congratulations – you have now learnt about how to stay safe around dogs!

See you next time, when we will be learning all about walking a dog.

Remember, "A dog is for life, not just for Christmas®" Dogs Trust has 18 Rehoming Centres around the UK and Ireland. To find out more please go to: www.dogstrust.org.uk

For more fun and games please go to: www.learnwithdogs.co.uk

 DogsTrust

Find the Puppy!

Everybody is looking for naughty Puddle. Who will be the one to find him - Ruby, Harry or Max? Follow the lines to find out.

A Muddle of Puddles!

Look closely at the pictures of Puddle.
Can you work out which two puppies
are exactly the same?

C

D

E

F

Answers on the next page

Answers to puzzles:
Find the Puppy: Harry finds Puddle
A Muddle of Puddles: B&D are the same

For more magical adventures, come and play with Puddle at

www.puddlethepuppy.com

Use this special code to get extra-special games and free stuff at puddlethepuppy.com

TEDDY